1

Zehbel:
The Clever One

MERCENARY TO THE SHAH

*To Christie + Inuk,
Hope you enjoy the writing. It
is a true story. May God Bless
you.*
        Michael A Roman AKA. Zehbel

by Michael Roman

IIAF/DCS/CEM Technical Advisor
FAA Radar NAV/COM Technician
Pakistan, Iran, USA

Acknowledgments
from Michael Roman

To my dear friends in Iran: those who remain, those who escaped with their lives, and those who did not. I have not mentioned the names and titles of those still alive -- for your protection -- but all of you are in my heart. Thank you for generously sharing your lives and your love of Iran with me and my family. We will never forget you.

Thanks to my intrepid and hard-working editor, Barbara Carson. She cheerfully kept me on course through edits, publication, revisions, reviews and marketing. Thanks, Barbara!

Thanks also to the patient staff at Book Baby and Amazon/Create Space for helping me set up my first ebook, then the print book. Both stages required many questions back and forth, and enough details to make my head spin.

My warmest thanks to a gifted artist, my daughter-in-law, Jamie Roman, who designed the startling cover to *Zehbel: The Clever One,* with my brooding face leering out of the darkness. Beautiful job, Jamie!

Heartfelt thanks to six of our dear children: Carolyn, Sharon, Shelly, Cretie, Michael and Mark, who generously shared their memories of the ten years our family spent in Iran, giving a whole new perspective to *Zehbel: The Clever One.* I was away so much during their childhoods; now they know the truth about what I went through in Iran. The book is greatly enriched by their writing and suggestions. I am so proud of my family and grateful for their help.

To our youngest child, Christel: there was one incident during our stay in Iran where 3 year old Christel was rushed to the hospital, not breathing, and came home three days later, saying "my name is Mary." We all felt she had been spoken to by an angel, and it touched us deeply as I recalled events and wrote *Zehbel: The Clever One.*

Most of all, my deepest thanks to Lucretia Gladis Roman, my dear wife, partner and friend, without whose love, this book would never have come to life.

Acknowledgements, from Lucretia Roman

To all our dear friends in Iran.

I couldn't have gone through this without you.

More than friends, you became family.

From the beginning you all played such a big part in my life.

Preface

Mike and Lucretia Roman

November 26, 1960 Allentown, Pennsylvania

By September 1976, many attempts had been
made on my life, yet miracle after miracle
allowed me to survive another day. I was sure

9

my luck would soon run out. I resigned myself to the fact that I would not make it home alive. My only fear was that my body would not find its way home to my beloved wife and children back in the States. I wanted to be laid to rest near all the people I loved. I wanted my children to know who and where I was. Most of all, I wanted them to remember me.

Iran had been my home for ten years. My life there, by any standards, was fantastic. When my wife and I first arrived in Teheran, in April 1967, things were very different. Iranians loved Americans and were proud to be associated with them. There were people in Iran who were very friendly with me. Some of them helped me more than they should have. If things had remained status quo it wouldn't have mattered. Now that life was gone. In the past five years, things had changed so dramatically. It was hard for me to believe, but my paradise had turned into hell.

How was I able to get into the position I held in the Imperial Iranian Air Force (IIAF)? The Iranians called me Most Honorable Engineer. I was not an Engineer, but, because of my thorough training at the FAA academy in Oklahoma City, I was able to do engineering work. The FAA training programs were much stricter back then. Thirty percent of the students flunked out, including some who already held engineering degrees.

I had always been considered very smart, even when I was a small child. I had grown up in a town called Hokendauqua, north of Allentown, PA. We had a good-sized family; I was the second of eight children, six boys and two girls. When I attended Whitehall Elementary, I was a goof-off. School was too easy. The important thing for me was the Boy Scouts. I joined at 13, when I was in the 7ᵗʰ grade. The scout troop was sponsored by a Methodist Church in Catasauqua. They liked me because I won all the awards and brought honor to them.

I attended Central Catholic High School (CCHS) in Allentown. CCHS was an excellent school. I was two years behind when I went off to high school, so I had to catch up fast. The nuns taught me after school. They taught me a lot of things I didn't know. I caught up, then started goofing off again.

My first summer after freshman year, I worked on staff with the Boy Scouts at Camp Trexler. That first summer, all I did was wash dishes. I worked one day, and had the next day off. Whenever I had a free day, I spent it working on my merit badges. That was how I was paid, by being able to use the camp on my days off. My second summer, I was paid $75.00 for the whole summer, for peeling spuds. They called me "the spud boy." In my third year on staff, George Babyar, the camp director (another WWII veteran from the Pacific Theatre), put me in charge of the

11

largest Scout camp, Camp Hawkeye. My new
title was Area Director. Camp Hawkeye had
five campsites. George liked me because I
could beat people up, and I organized people
well. I was a Merit Badge counselor as well. I
flunked one kid because he just wasn't good
enough. The kid's dad was a bigwig in
Western Electric, and boy did he go off the
deep end! But George, the camp director,
would not reverse my decision. So I had a lot
of influence with the Boy Scouts.

It was at Central Catholic High School that I
met my beautiful wife, Lucretia Gladis. I had
heard about her first, because her name was
so different. She was interested in science
classes. I saw her because she'd come to my
class to meet Peggy, a friend of hers. Lucretia
lived in Fullerton and walked across the 4th
Street Bridge in Allentown to attend CCHS.
Later, we met again, at my Uncle Andy's
wedding. Uncle Andy married Lucretia's
cousin. Her mom was also at the wedding.
She was a beautiful woman with light blond
hair. Lucretia's hair was dark; they looked so
different. That was when we really started up.
She was in the smart classes with me, the
college prep classes, so we got to know each
other. We had one thing in common; we were
two very devout Catholics (I had been an altar
boy for twelve years). It was puppy love, I
guess, but it was real. Women were attracted
to me, but I wasn't interested in any of them,
until I met Lucretia. They liked my golden

12

blonde hair. I guess it was attractive to women. Lucretia and I went our separate ways after high school, but we wrote to each other and I knew I had plans to keep her in my life. She was in nursing school. I entered the U.S. Army to get a background for my life's work, electronics.

I went first to basic training at Camp Gordon near Augusta, Georgia. Then I took a train to El Paso, Texas. There I started my Nike/Ajax training. Once training was completed, we were given assignments. Most of the assignments were teaching positions, so I kept going to the back of the line. I didn't want to teach. You could teach Acquisition Radar (AR), which has a range of 300 miles, or Information/Friend or Foe (IFF), or Target Tracking Radar (single beam) or Missile-tracking Radar (also single beam, but coded). You would only teach one thing and forget the rest of your training.   I didn't want that. Computers were new at the time and they were included in the Nike Ajax and Hercules systems. Computers controlled either missile. All the information would go into the computer and the computer would tell the missile where to go and who to blow up. If the missile-tracking missile wasn't tracking it, after booster separation, the missile would blow up.

Finally, they declared "the rest of you will be responsible for maintaining the systems," that students learned on every day. That meant working the night shift and sleeping during the day. So I worked all night; of course, I didn't sleep much during the day. Instead, I went to college at Texas Western University. I took three classes there, and got almost no sleep. After one semester, I wore myself out and stopped attending college.

Next, someone approached me about being in the movies. I guess they liked my blonde hair too. I played one of the main characters in a training film for the U.S. Army. That was my day job for a few months. I also took courses by mail, through the Army. I was just driven to learn new things, I guess. I got off maintaining systems and spent four months training on the Hercules Nuclear Guided Missile system. These missiles were powerful enough to annihilate an entire wing of airplanes. It was a nuclear warhead missile.

I had a motorcycle when I was in the Army. It was great fun, driving around in the desert in my spare time. One time, coming back from a town near El Paso, an elderly woman cut in front of me on a highway and caused a serious accident. If I'd hit the middle of her car, I would have splattered. Instead, I hit the trunk of her car. My boots were ripped right off my feet. (I actually took 7 years to recover from all the internal injuries.) I spent three weeks in the hospital. When I got out, I went home for a month to recover. I gave my dad $300 to buy me a '53 Dodge and I picked it up a few months later, at Christmas time. It didn't last long because the bearings were bad.

Another time, I was at the rifle range, qualifying, with the rest of my group. We were shooting at targets 100 yards away. We were on the rifle range mound. The M2 carbine was accurate at up to 300 yards. My friend was bringing me all this ammunition, so we could have it when we needed it. We had access to our rifles-- we weren't supposed to. The only place you could get extra ammunition was at the rifle range. This guy would bring me ammunition and I'd stash it on me.

One of the officers came up to me that day. I was firing with full automatic, actually shooting at targets of opportunity, in front of and below the actual paper target. I'd shoot enough holes in the target to qualify, then used the rest of the bullets on other targets. Otherwise, there would be too many holes on the paper targets. I shot semi-automatic at the paper target, then switched to full automatic to shoot other targets, anything I saw. (I was a good shot. They wanted to put me on the Army Rifle Team, because I was what they called a "high expert," shooting 99-100% accuracy. All my shots were bulls-eyes.) The officer said, "Why are you firing full-automatic? You're supposed to be firing semi-automatic."

"I think there's something wrong with the carbine," I replied innocently.

15

"Go get another one," the officer replied.

I got another carbine, zeroed it in, and continued shooting, but on semi-automatic. While he was talking to me, my friend was picking up the extra ammunition. We made off with a lot of ammunition that day. I stuffed ammunition into the blousing all around my boots so you couldn't see them, in my canteen, belt, and all over me. Our aim was to shoot coyotes and jackrabbits out in the desert. He brought me the bullets and I packed them around my waist, etc. I was shooting a target. I filled up my canteen, my boots, with bullets. I was weighed down, with about 500 rounds packed all over me. My friends surrounded me as I walked to the bus from the rifle range, so I went undetected. My rifle was hidden in the '53 Dodge.

I was a popular guy in the Army. The guys all liked me because every once in a while I'd have to beat someone up. That adds to your status. I was in a unique group. I was on the experimental project, tracking the missiles. One went into Mexico and crashed near a shit house. It was out of fuel and came down, unguided, like a bomb. It was supposed to blow up, but it didn't. There was all kinds of secret material inside that missile, so the security crew had to retrieve it. You couldn't just walk up to the site and watch the missile being dismantled; it was on Mexican land. The

Mexicans were selling tickets, like at a public event. They made money however they could.

One time, I was riding my motorcycle out in the desert and saw a Volkswagen Beetle parked out in the middle of nowhere. There were two figures, a boy and a girl, in the back seat and they were causing the car to rock back and forth. I left my motorcycle down below and was up on a mesa, hunting coyotes, just for fun. I had my 30/30 with me and a P38. I had already shot one coyote that day. I had spotted him running up over the rocky side of a hill. I was above him on a cliff. I got him. That afternoon, aside from the rocking Volkswagen, it was quiet. Suddenly, bullets started flying, coming right at me. I looked down and saw these chappinos. That was what I called them, these Mexican guys. They actually belonged to a gang called The Dragons; I had run into them before. They wore a tattoo called The Cross of El Diablo, mostly on their hand or their arm. A lot of Mexicans belonged to this gang, and there were a great many of them here in the Southwest.

I was stationed at Fort Bliss when another incident happened. These guys wanted me to go with them to a Mexican party. It was across a canal where people found dead bodies sometimes. My friends and I went with them to this party. I didn't want to go, but I didn't have anything else to do, so I went along. It was just outside El Paso, Texas. This was a heavily Mexican neighborhood and a pretty dangerous area. They knew I was tough and I could probably take care of them if there was a fight. I didn't take drugs or liquor. Two of the soldiers who came with me gave me their cigarette packs so nobody would hit them up for cigarettes. I put them in my pocket. The Dragons saw that. They surrounded me and I backed up against a wall. My hand was still in my pocket. One of the Dragons asked me for cigarettes. I told them they weren't my cigarettes, I couldn't give them away. They were closing in on me. A guy I thought looked like the Cisco Kid had been watching us, lounging by the door. He came up and smiled at me. For some reason he liked me. He talked to the Dragons in rapid Spanish and told them to leave me alone, so the tension eased. They backed off and that was that.

When I was in the desert, I could see these Dragons were up to no good, but my 30/30 was handy. I picked out the leader and shot in front of him, to spray him with rocks and sand. It makes quite an impact, when propelled by a bullet. The leader went down. His friends picked him up and they all ran away. Mentally I named him El Chappino, the choppy one. I only had 2 bullets left and there were 6 of them, so I didn't go after the rest of the Mexicans.

The young couple in the VW was still making a lot of noise, moaning and groaning. I didn't bother them as I walked down from the mesa. I was heading back to my motorcycle; they were having fun. They didn't hear the bullets, apparently.

When I came back, I saw the Warrant Officer, a nice guy with seven kids. He had been in charge of the systems we maintained. There was a scene; he was disciplined for not keeping up with the Officer's Club (because he couldn't afford it). He was no longer the Warrant Officer; they assigned that job to someone else. I had already been welcomed into the Officer's group by a Colonel, but when I saw what happened to the Warrant Officer, I changed my mind about going to Officer's Candidate School (OCS). If that was the way officers were treated, I wanted no part of it.

Three days later, I was transferred to MacGregor Guided Missile Range near White Sands Proving Ground in New Mexico. Coincidence? I wasn't sure about that. However, it turned out to be a blessing. I learned so much at MacGregor. There I was exposed to firing systems that actually fired on airplanes. It also gave me a good background in electronics and shooting down airplanes. I found out about things going on in the world around me first hand. Now, I was able to understand things that I never even thought about before. It changed my outlook on the world completely.

People came from all over the world to fire missiles at airplanes there, in the desert. They were required to test their ability to fire the missiles annually, so it was a busy place. This was the only place they could practice firing real missiles. They had to go through it, step by step, check everything out. It would take several days. They put me on Pod 25, with the Ajax/Hercules Antiaircraft Missiles. The crew there had never been able to fire the missile because it was so screwed up. I got it to fire and set a new Army record 0-X, 0-Y, 0-H, meaning it hit the target dead center.

The Army Command at Fort Bliss was calling for volunteers on an experimental site. They wanted to track each fired missile, where it was supposed to go and where it actually went. It used an old prototype P-3 missile system. This system tracked missiles that were fired from all the other sites. We modified the system so we could use Target Tracking Radar. We tracked the missile until it exploded or disappeared. If it got away, we plotted the coordinates of where we lost it, so we knew where it hit the ground. Ordinarily, you couldn't use Target Tracking Radar for this; it was too fast. A guy would be positioned on the mounting plate, right on the antenna. He would manually track the missile, find the range and azimuth until it reached the right altitude. From that point it could be tracked by an operator in aided mode using Target Tracking Radar. If they lost tracking, the missiles were supposed to blow themselves up. Warheads that didn't blow up were scattered all over the desert. Army Command was pleased with my work. They offered me a job to stay there, but I felt it was time to leave the Army and move on.

I took a job with UNIVAC. Their training school was located in Ilion, New York. I went to school there for 2 months. Unfortunately, the company had some problems and let everyone go. I was unable to complete my studies due to their financial difficulties.

Lucretia and I had planned to get married after I left the Army. The date for our wedding was coming up, so I wanted to get back to Allentown. We married on November 26, 1960. I took a job with Western Electric, making devices that aged vacuum tubes for the underwater telephone lines between the U.S. and Europe. This was stupid work; I didn't plan to stay there long. I wanted a position with the Federal Aviation Administration (FAA) and got one five months later, in April 1961.

At that time, the FAA Academy taught electronics at a very high engineering level. It was actually post graduate engineering studies. We received Engineering credits for successfully passing some very difficult courses. Everything was math-oriented. Without a good math background and skill in

21

using a slide rule, it would have been impossible to pass these courses. I attended all the major schools there and collected tons of books for referral. These books would later be worth their weight in gold, when I was in Iran. As a result of that training, I was able to design electronic devices and also modify things to suit needs. In remote locations in a third world country, you were lost if you did not have that ability. My exceptional skills were badly needed in the Imperial Iranian Air Force (IIAF). That was why I had such a positive impact on so many people and events in Iran. I was good at what I did, and they needed my help.

You might ask, "How could you cope with the constant danger described in *Zehbel: The Clever One?*"

When I was growing up, one was respected if they could fight and shoot. Honor and integrity were very important. A man had to keep his word and stand up for what was right. My years with the Boy Scouts, and U.S. Army training in killing and survival skills made me into a very tough guy with a lot of confidence. Unfortunately, too often, I would go looking for trouble.

I didn't realize until many years later, when I got the offer of a position in Vietnam and Lucretia was beating me up -- I liked danger. I liked the adrenalin rush, the excitement, being on the move.

In fact, I could run rings around the average person. Working a regular job was boring. I needed constant challenges. All these experiences made me into the person that I am. It turned out to be an excellent preparation for our new life in Iran.

A book of verse beneath the bough

A jug of wine, a loaf of bread and thou

Beside me singing in the wilderness

Oh, wilderness were paradise enow!

--Omar Khayyam,

11th century Persian writer

Table of Contents

24

Chapter 1

Pakistan:

The Adventure Begins

Nacie and Mike

Karachi Airport, Pakistan, 1967

In the mid-sixties, my wife, Lucretia, and I were living in Charleston West Virginia, raising our four young daughters. We had been in a constant mode of moving since we married. She was a nurse and I was an ex-soldier. My new job with the Federal Aviation Administration (FAA) was nothing but learning and constant motion. When I arrived in Charleston, I was told that I was to be a Relief Technician. I was expected to know almost every single job in the FAA, so that if someone else went to school, got sick or took a vacation, I would fill in for them, wherever they were and whatever they did. West Virginia was our fifth move from 1961 to January 1965, not to mention intermittent four-month assignments at the FAA Academy in Oklahoma City. The whole family went with me when I attended FAA training. I got engineering credits for college by taking these courses.

My coverage territory was the state of West Virginia, parts of Kentucky and Ohio. There were four career paths in the FAA: RADAR, NAV AIDS (Navigational Aids), Communications, and at larger airports, ILS (Instrument Landing Systems). I was certified in all of them.

Most of the time, I was away from home or did a lot of traveling each day. My wife grew tired of constantly packing and relocating. Our daughters didn't enjoy our frequent moves either, because they would have to leave familiar surroundings and make new friends. I had to do something; my current job was just too hard on the family.

An assignment came up in Yugoslavia. I asked for it but didn't get it. Then I was offered a promotion – if I accepted an assignment to Pakistan. Of course, I took it. I was sure that it had to do me some good. Actually, Pakistan was the last place I wanted to be, but I needed a promotion and in 1966, at the age of 26, that wasn't easy. It was considered a very undesirable tour of duty but it had to be done. Besides, the pay was good, and we needed the money.

My flight schedule called for an overnight stop-over in Rome, a few days in Athens, two days in Beirut and then to Karachi. Beirut was my briefing place and the headquarters for FAA Flight Check. Unfortunately, when I got to Athens I couldn't go any further -- all the airline pilots in the world went on strike. What a beautiful place to be stuck!

The FAA man in Athens was supposed to brief me on the new equipment that I was to install in Pakistan but he thought that I was there to brief him on the same thing. We spent a lot of time sailing the Aegean Sea, on a thirty-foot sailboat, waiting for the strike to end. On one occasion, we went to the Island of Aegina, just an hour away by ferryboat. Right there in Aegina Bay was a ship with the words "US Army" painted on it. It was a very big ship, so I decided to check it out. I dove off the sailboat and swam over for a closer look.

When I got to the ship, I called out, "request permission to come aboard." "Who are you with?" was their response. "The FAA, Office of International Aviation Affairs," I replied. "Come aboard," they called back, cheerfully. It was a boatload of generals, both American and Greek, and they were having a party. Scotch was the drink of choice for officers. I drank a lot and started diving off the ship. I could never float in the ocean or in fresh water because my bones were so dense. But in the Aegean Sea, I could. It must have been the higher saline content. I can't tell you how it felt to be able to float with your face up. I could close my eyes and just think of the nicest things. It was so soothing to be there in the beautiful aquamarine, warm water -- like heaven!

I began getting drowsy from the Scotch and the diving activities, so I dove in the water to try to wake up. Instead, I fell asleep in the water! It was so warm and comfortable. Then, I don't know how much later, I was awakened by a Greek "Mermaid." She insisted that I stay awake and swim back to the ship. So, I swam back to the ship, stayed a while and thanked everyone for such a wonderful time. Then I dove into the sea and swam back to the sailboat.

The sailboat belonged to a friend of mine. I was eager to learn how to sail and he invited me to sail with him as often as I liked. I learned quickly and spent as much time as I could on that craft. One time, his family was on board with us. I wanted to go fast so I did, until my friend who owned the boat came almost crawling back to me and stopped the boat. His family was scared to death because I was going so fast. Life was so tough at that time; people were tense.

The airline strike ended, so my Greek vacation was finally over. I left for Lebanon to talk to the FAA Flight Check people in Beirut. Knowing I was new to international travel, they advised me what to do to stay healthy. Beirut was a beautiful city, the Paris of the Middle East, as it was called. That was a nice few days also. Now I was on the last leg of the journey to Pakistan.

I boarded the plane in Beirut, Lebanon and met a pleasant family of four. We talked all the way to Karachi. They were just beginning a long tour in Pakistan. Karachi couldn't be too bad I thought, if these two young children were going to live there for two years. The landing at Karachi airport was very smooth. Pan Am was on time. After disembarking, I immediately felt the high humidity. August in Karachi was very hot and there was a strange smell in the air. What the smell was, I had no idea.

An Embassy car picked me up at the arrival area and we sped off to the Intercontinental Hotel. It was a chain owned by Pan Am, and they had hotels all over the world. While checking in, I asked myself what impelled me to come here. I'd be by myself for a long time. The tour was six months and I couldn't imagine myself in Pakistan for that long a time.

Almost immediately, I found out the hotel rate was beyond my daily allowance. That was not good. A nice thing did happen. They gave me a room on an upper floor. The awful smell that was all over the city was gone in the upper rooms. Plus, the room had a balcony. This was a taste of luxury and it made up for the rest of the negatives, at least for a while.

People at the Embassy briefed me the next day and everything was put in order, including the doctor and his advice. After that, my next stop was the Civil Aviation people of Pakistan. Everyone's name seemed to be Khan. You had to remember them by the initials in front of their name; S.A., M.G.H., etc.

Victor was the Civil Aviation manager who dealt with things that had to do with Civil Aviation facilities at the airport. He was a very nice person and we became good friends. The Head Engineer's name was Nacie. He was my escort and coordinator.

I mentioned to Victor about the wild dogs I'd seen running around the airport, and right on the runways. "It's a serious hazard for aircraft," I cautioned him. The very next day when I got to the airport, I saw a long line of men with shotguns. They were walking a straight line across the airport and runways. BANG, BANG!! No more dogs. There were a lot of them.

My assignment was to install a new type of Distance Measuring Equipment (DME) at the Karachi airport. It enables the pilot to see exactly how far away from the airport runway he is. The work began immediately. Parts had been shipped over from the States. The vacuum tubes, new technology, were very tiny; some were half an inch, or less. This is micro-technology. Then I had to rewrite the manuals. The original manuals were so full of errors they were unusable.

My second night at the hotel, I became very ill. I was so sick and weak that I couldn't reach the phone to call the doctor. I thought I was dying. Then I passed out, but fortunately I woke up the next morning. I never found out what was wrong with me.

The people at the Embassy moved me to a Staff House leased from Agha Khan. It was a very beautiful house. There were four other people in the house besides myself, three of them women. Some of the Marine Embassy Guard would come to visit the young ladies who were their girlfriends. They were there every weekend. Each couple would pair off and go to their rooms. The whole second floor was mine. Although I was alone, I loved it.

One evening I went to the Non Commissioned Officer's (NCO) Club to see a movie with a Marine and his girlfriend. It was the first anniversary of the war with India. Some Pakistanis didn't like us because of the U.S. stance on that war. After the movie was over we went out to get a ride home. A car with five Pakistani men in it screeched to a halt as we were waiting for a cab. They all came at us. The young Embassy Secretary started screaming. The Marine was clutching her. It was apparent that he wasn't going to help me.

That left only me and five of them. It was a good thing I liked to fight. My brother Dick had given me a pearl-handled knife as a going away present. It was a strange knife. It was very thin and about six inches long. When unfolded, the long narrow six inch blade looked very formidable. I couldn't see fighting all of them at once and I didn't know what weapons they had. The knife was in my hand immediately and I got into the stance that I learned in combat training in the Army. It must have scared them because they looked at each other, ran back to the car and took off. I mentioned the incident to a new friend, the head of the Marine Guard. He was pissed.

My friend, Nacie, told me to eat my food as hot as I could stand it, to eat peppers, and drink straight whiskey. He explained that would keep me from getting sick all the time. Of course I followed his advice. When lunch time came, I didn't eat. Pakistanis have a habit of chewing on a substance that they pass around after a meal. It is red in color and served on a leaf. It's called Betel Nut. After eating it, their mouths become bright red. I asked Nacie what it was and why they chewed on it. He told me that it eases the pain associated with the teeth and it made them feel good. I'm sure it did!

One day, one of the young engineers insisted that I go with him to lunch. When we got there, I noticed all of the flies. A young boy was stationed nearby. He waved a giant fan back and forth, like you would hold in your hand, to scatter all of the flies. That was the last time I went out to lunch. The flies made it so unpleasant. Nacie wanted to make amends, so he and a group of his fellow Engineers took me to dinner the next night. I ordered Chicken Tika. It was bright red. The wine was good and I drank a lot of it. When the bill came, I was sort of shocked so I grabbed the waiter's tie and pulled him down next to my face.

The man started screaming and my friends begged me to let him go. They apologized to the man ten times over. He was glaring at me. I had screwed up. We left very quickly. It's tough to be young, away from home and full of piss and vinegar.

Growing up in Hokendauqua, I had always been a tough kid, and a good fighter. In my neighborhood, it was important to be able to fight. Things were different then, back in the 1940s. Fighting was considered a normal activity. There were fights almost every day at my grade school. That was how we resolved things with each other. A young man was respected if he could fight and shoot. One's reputation depended on it. You could never be a "yellow belly;" that would be a terrible disgrace to your family. Teachers did not stop the fights; I think it was entertainment for them.

We had big BB gun battles in the woods. As we grew older, we graduated to 22s, then shotguns, high power rifles and pistols. Guns and their use were very important to any young man back then. The movies of the times provided guidelines that we followed. I was the second child in a family of eight children. My parents expected us to work hard in school and mind our manners. We did, more or less.

The Boy Scouts were a rough outfit then. I attained the rank of Eagle Scout with Silver Palm and was a ranking member of the Order of the Arrow. Initiation into that Order was a real challenge, but along with it came respect. The camp, where I spent four summers on staff, was a wilderness, a primitive, male environment. Our Scout leaders were World War II veterans; they taught us to be tough and strong. We boys all listened to their stories of the war and wanted to be like them. Their training and good advice would come in handy, in my new assignment at Karachi Airport.

Every day I worked long and hard to finish up ahead of schedule. I wanted to get out of Pakistan and back to my young family as quickly as possible. I worked for fourteen days straight and then I made a mistake. It took two days to correct that mistake. After that, I worked only six days a week but I worked all day long.

The sedentary work made me want to do exercise. The best thing that I could think of was to run in the street near the mansion. I put on a pair of short pants and a short sleeve shirt and went outside to run. As I was running, I noticed the women looking at me then covering their face and turning away with their hands over their faces. After I passed them, they would then look at me again. I knew that I was doing something wrong.

When I asked the cook in the mansion about it, he told me that women were not allowed to look at a scantily clad man. That ended my exercise. I tried playing tennis but no one was available to play. There was a beautiful tennis count on the land attached to the mansion but nobody used it. It was surrounded by banana trees. Actually, it was very beautiful. When it's there all the time, you don't appreciate it.

Karachi was a different place. I found out what the smell was. People there burned dried manure paddies so the whole city smelled from it. One day I was relaxing and took a private tour of Karachi in a horse drawn carriage. There was a small mountain of manure on a parcel of land and a woman clothed in a long black gown was making circular paddies about a foot in diameter. The holes that were cut in her solid black veil to see through also had squares sewn into them so that her eyes were very difficult to see. The sleeves on her arms were rolled up. The smell was horrendous. I felt so sorry for her. 'What a way to make a living,' I thought.

On the same ride, I saw a tall building being constructed. There was an endless line of men walking up to the top of a multi- story building where the work was being done and then walking back down. They were carrying bricks and mortar and could be seen through the unfinished openings of the building. This procession went on all day long.

Delavar Khan was my driver. He picked me up at the Staff House early in the morning, then drove to the airport. Early morning in Karachi was quite an experience. There were dead animals in the streets. Donkeys, camels, mules, oxen and horses lay dead in the street. Some of them were skinned, and meat had been cut from their carcasses. At some locations, dead human bodies had been placed beside walkways. On my way back from the airport, all these carcasses were gone. At the airport, on the first day of my arrival, I saw a large dead mule that had been moved to the side of the road. It was still there, months later, when I left Pakistan. Wild dogs fed on it and took up residence by the carcass.

There was a large poor area where many people lived. They were refugees from India who were fortunate enough to make it out of India and into Pakistan alive. Nacie told me that there was a tremendous slaughter on both sides. This particular area had thousands of people living in it. They made shelters out of anything that they could find. I'll never forget seeing so many people living in such a filthy place. There was a peddler pushing a cart in that area. He was selling rock candy. They seemed to eat a lot of it. Not a nice place.

Delavar took me to the Bazaar when I asked him where I could buy some of the beautiful things that I had seen, made of brass, wood, ivory etc., to send home. As we arrived at the Bazaar, Delavar nearly ran over something with the car. I saw "It:" something very low to the ground which shot across the road right in front of us. We got out of the car to see what it was. I was shocked when I saw "It." There on a board with roller skate wheels was a very small man with no legs. In his hands, he held small bricks with leather wrapped around the bottoms. That's what he used to propel the board and keep him from falling. It would be hard to sit with no legs. Delavar scolded the man for doing such a dumb thing and then we went shopping. Interesting!!

One time I had a day off, a rare occurrence. The Marine Embassy Guard invited me to go crabbing with them out on Karachi Bay. Of course, I just couldn't say no. Actually I wanted to get away from the routine. On our way to the boat, we passed what might have been a village. The activity centered round a well.

I saw a very young boy there who was looking at me. He was standing by the well with the women. He looked at me with a strange, empty expression. I got the impression he was close to death. For a moment, I felt sick. We stopped and I gave him all the food and drink that I had with me. He took it but it didn't change the look on his face. The Marines told me that there was a lot of that in Karachi. I never got over it. Today, I can see his face and it still hurts. The guards and I got a lot of crabs but it didn't matter. All I could think of was that little boy.

Work continued on the DME installation. Things were going great. It was time to put up the antenna and the support that held it. The mounting fixture was beautiful. It was hand-crafted. The craftsman who made it shaped a mold and melted aluminum from a junked aircraft that was on the airport for the casting material. Then it was polished and set up. It looked like a piece of fine sculpture.

I had ordered a crane to lift everything up and put it in place on the roof of the VOR (Very-High Omni-Directional Range navigational aids) Building. To my surprise thirty-two men with ladders showed up instead. "What is this?" I asked. "The men need work," Nacie answered back. "But they could get hurt," I replied. " 'Let's get started' was my order," said Nacie. And so we did. All went well until a very young man fell off the roof. He was in such pain. "Let's get him to a hospital," I said to Nacie. "No we can't do that," he replied. "Well what are we going to do?" I asked. "Nothing," replied Nacie. "He knew the dangers so he must take care of himself." "How will he get home? He can't walk," I replied. "That's his problem," Nacie said.

I asked Delavar if we could take the young man to his village. So we did. When we got there the whole village gathered round to see the vehicle. The young man stirred up incredible fortitude and strength to get out of the car. I helped him. He then shook my hand and wouldn't let go. He wanted the whole village to see him shaking the hand of the American. They were all smiling and so was he. He looked so proud, and he was. I felt so sick and so sorry for him. I gave him money which he refused but I forced it into his hand. To him it was a lot of money. He took it and said thank you. Once again, I felt sick. I realized they wouldn't give him the medical treatment he needed.

The Marine Guard at the embassy and I became close friends. Some of the Embassy people became interested in what I was doing

41

and that came in handy later on. Well, the Marines had a promotion party one night. They had a big conference room that could easily double as a ball room. Party night was something else. Lots of people were there and it got wild. Champagne was the only drink served. Seven bottles turned out to be my share of the wine. Fortunately, my residence was close to the Marine house. I remember all of the very large drapes came down during the festivities. What a wild party!

On the way home, wild dogs started chasing me. That didn't work, for I turned, started growling, and chased after them. The dogs ran into a hole in a big wall and that was that. I had to work the next day, which was now. It was 5:30 AM. Delavar arrived on time and we went to the airport. I asked the people if they wanted a day off. Naturally, that made them all very happy. Back we went to the mansion where I slept all day long.

My work was coming to an end, so I spent time training the Pakistanis on the brand-new distance measuring equipment and waiting for a Flight Check. The Pakistani Civil Aviation Agency (CAA) would not pay for the Flight Check, so I dilly-dallied around watching the big lizards that were all over the airport. When I first arrived at the airport, I wondered what was in these big holes I saw scattered around the area. I thought that groundhogs occupied the holes but they turned out to be lizards. They were indeed big. One of the engineers

42

from East Pakistan told me that if a person eats the lizards he will have great sexual powers. Who knows?

Finally, I was able to obtain clearance to leave Pakistan. A complication arose: my friends at the Embassy told me the FAA wanted me to go to Iran. There was a message waiting for me at the Embassy. I knew nothing about that country and I just wanted to go home, so I stayed away from the Embassy mansion. I hung around here and there and picked up my baggage early on the morning that I was scheduled to leave.

At the airport, the people from Pan Am were waiting for me. They were so happy that they had a new and valuable Navigational Aid to navigate by. They put me into First Class. I had recently been injured, so I had to walk with a cane. They were very concerned about it. The pilot invited me to sit up in the cockpit with him, the co-pilot and the navigator. It was a very new and exciting experience. I watched the fuel gauges flying very fast as we took off. When we reached cruising altitude, the gauges just ticked very slowly compared to take off.

Teheran was the first stop. It didn't look too bad I thought but at that time, I was only thinking of home and my wife and kids. Next stop was Rome where I had to change to a German airline. There was a lay-over, so I decided to look around Rome. I took a taxi and went all over the city to see everything I could.

My next destination was NATO headquarters in Brussels. An Embassy limo picked me up and took me to a luxury hotel. The next morning, I was de-briefed. It was there that I was told that I should be in Iran for the next three months. They soon found out that wasn't my plan at all. I had decided I was going to Washington D.C. "I am not going to Iran and that's that!" I said firmly.

My wife, Lucretia, was waiting for me there in Washington, D.C. She almost didn't recognize me. My weight had dropped about twenty-five pounds, from one hundred and ninety-five to one hundred and seventy. We checked into the Harrington hotel. We had not seen each other in more than three months. There was catching up to do. The lizards at Karachi airport touched a chord for a second. Maybe I should have brought one back with me.

Our nation's capital is a beautiful city with lots to offer and we took advantage of it. The de-briefing at headquarters was quick. They assured me that they were very pleased with my accomplishments in Pakistan. Now I was known to them and that's what I wanted. They told me that there was a position coming up in Iran and I could have it if I wanted it. I assured them of my interest and wondered how Lucretia would react. I was sure she'd be up for an adventure, as long as we could be together.

44

Neighbors were waiting for us in Charleston W. Va. and were surprised at my trimmed-down appearance. In addition to the change in diet, I'd had a bout with malaria which took a slight toll on me. My wife told me that she must wash all of my clothing as soon as she opened my suitcase. Everything had a "funny smell" to it. I remembered that smell when I first landed in Karachi. After that, I got used to it and couldn't smell it anymore. Remembering the young Pakistani woman I'd seen making manure patties, I realized what the smell was.

All this happened in a little over three months. In a short time, I would go to Iran and start all over again. It doesn't sound too smart, but that's what you do when you're young and in need of money.

Chapter 2: Assignment to Iran

A street in central Teheran, Iran

The Pakistan assignment was to be completed in six months. I did it in three, and demonstrated exceptional ability. Back home, people started to take notice. In March of 1967, I got a call from Washington, D.C. The Office of International Aviation Affairs called me to let me know that I had been selected for a position in Teheran, Iran.

I was overjoyed, to say the least. Now, down to practicalities: how was I going to handle it?

This assignment would involve moving my entire family 6,337 miles away, to a foreign country. My wife, Lucretia, was pregnant and we already had four children. Were they going to turn me down when they found out about my growing family? Our circumstances couldn't be hidden; the FBI was already investigating us.

Neighbors near our rented home in Charleston West Virginia were interviewed about our circumstances. Then, 'Cretia and I were interviewed separately. We could only hope that I would be approved for the position. It was a promotion and at that time promotions were hard to get. Plus, we needed the extra money.

At the same time, I was called to Washington for an interview. Another man had been selected for the position I coveted. I inquired as to why he was selected. They told me that he had fifteen years of experience in Instrument Landing Systems (ILS). I said, "Is that all that he has? I'm certified in everything. Is he somebody's friend?" Wrong thing to say! Since that was my reporting station, they were going to punish me by sending me to JFK International Airport for six months.

I immediately called the Office of International Aviation Affairs and told them that I must be promoted by a certain date or I would be stuck with the assignment to JFK Airport. I was counting on the fact that my reputation, based on the excellent work I'd completed in Pakistan, would speak for itself. It did.

The word came down officially that I was accepted for the job in Iran. We could hardly contain ourselves. The people back home in Pennsylvania, especially Lucretia's father, thought we had gone crazy. "Where is Iran?" they would ask, meaning "Why would anyone in their right mind go to Iran, of all places, when they had a perfectly good life in the United States of America?"

We couldn't listen to them. This was our life and we had big plans. We were both twenty-seven years old and wanted to make something of our lives. No one could dissuade us. We were told that we couldn't take our children to a third world country. It could be devastating for them. We didn't listen. Our youth was a powerful driving force. To us, this was the opportunity of a lifetime and we weren't going to let it pass us by.

Lucretia:

Ever since I was a little girl, I had an intense desire to go places. I can still remember how excited I was, as a very young child, to discover all the places my feet could take me. I walked into town to pay bills and run errands for my mother, feeling very important to be out on my own. A year or so later, I was riding my bike all over the countryside. I just loved that sense of adventure, Plus, I had so much energy; I always wanted to be going somewhere and learning something new. I got into nursing because I liked helping people, but it was also exciting – you never knew what each new day would bring. So when Mike told me we were going to Iran, I couldn't wait.

Mike:

International Aviation Affairs (IAA) was sending information about what we needed to know and what we had to do to prepare for the move. First and foremost were the inoculations the whole family needed. That turned out to be a job in itself. 'Cretia flatly refused to take some of the shots, saying they might be harmful to the baby. That held things up a bit, but turned out to be a blessing later on. Everyone in the family needed a passport. I already had mine from the Pakistan tour. The rest was easy.

Then there was the car. That had to be paid off before we tried to ship it. The information that was sent to us about conditions in Iran would have dissuaded most people from continuing, but not 'Cretia. Once her mind was made up, that was it. She was a nurse and a very good one. That would be a great asset to us. Iran was going to be her new home and no one could change her mind. It was beyond me that my wife had such powerful courage. I was so very proud of her.

I had been an expert marksman from childhood in rural Pennsylvania. Guns were very important to me, as a way to defend my country and protect my beloved family. Naturally a move to Iran meant armament for both 'Cretia and myself. I pored over the U.S. Embassy regulations. We would be allowed to bring a shotgun, a rifle and a pistol. That meant that I could take my Model 12 Winchester shotgun, .308 Model 88 Winchester, a Hi-Power Browning pistol and a P38 pistol for 'Cretia. That would cover all bases.

Soon the movers came and carted off all our possessions. We began saying our goodbyes to the many friends we'd made in the two short years we'd spent in West Virginia. What a sad occasion! Many of our friends worried and warned us we were going to a dangerous place. Most of them didn't know where Iran was. We informed them that at one time it was called Persia. That didn't seem to make much difference.

Then, it was off to our hometown of Hokendauqua, Pennsylvania. We planned to take a very short vacation there, and spend time saying goodbye to family and friends back home. We were to leave for Iran right after our vacation. All of our belongings were already on the way to Iran.

Home in Pennsylvania was a very welcome place for us. Our parents were so happy to see us. The grandchildren, Carolyn, Sharon,

Michelle and Lucretia Ann, were the apples of their eyes. They showered them with affection, and criticized our decision to take them overseas. Their minds were fixed on the dangers of living abroad, but we paid little heed to their warnings. Our new life was beginning and we were very excited about it.

Shooting rats was the sport of the day in Hokendauqua. When we were kids, we always went out and shot them at night, so no one could see us. It was also against the law, but we never got caught – our getaway plans were just too good. I remember one night, years before, when I bagged 96 rats. I would count the shots that missed. Four misses on that night. When I went into the Army, August 1957, everyone stopped shooting rats. When I came home on leave in December of that same year, they were giving free bullets to anyone who would shoot the rats. Seemed like the rats had become very numerous and started invading people's houses. My brother Dick and I went to the dump one last time to shoot rats, just to celebrate old times. It's surprising what excellent shots we were. We'd had many years of practice.

Seeing so many friends from childhood was a real blessing. We had all grown up together, gone to school, knew each other's stories, watched each other's backs. I enjoyed reliving old times, all the crazy escapades we'd survived. Unlike my parents, my friends didn't react in a negative way. They were happy for us to have got a position overseas, something very different from their ordinary lives.

Our families had dinners for us and just plain pampered us. They were so saddened, knowing that we would be gone for a long time. We said all our good- byes and began our journey. Our car had to be dropped off first in Newark, New Jersey. That was simple enough. Newark Airport was our next stop. From there a big helicopter flew us to the Pam Am building at Kennedy airport. That was a new and exciting experience; none of us had ever flown in a helicopter before. The brief flight gave us a quick, breathtaking view of New York City.

The Pan Am 707 flight was smooth and uneventful, but very long. We stopped at London, Italy and Istanbul before landing in Teheran. I remembered landing in Teheran on my way back to the States from Pakistan, so I recalled something about the way it looked. My mind wandered back to that time, six months previously when I had finished my assignment in Pakistan. After all, that tour was the reason that I got the assignment in Iran. Now, we were all looking forward to a new life together in a foreign country.

Everyone from the FAA was waiting for us outside of Customs at the Mehrabad International Airport. We could see the FAA group as we went through Customs. They waved to us, but we didn't know who they were at that time. I'm sure we were easy to spot in a crowd. The people in Washington must have told everyone about the new FAA man with four young girls and a pregnant wife.

They came up and welcomed us as we exited Customs. Everyone was smiling and so friendly. It was great therapy for us after that long trip. What a delightful feeling! This was our new home and it felt so good. Fred Hemp was the Chief of the FAA in Iran. His wife Lorie was a pretty woman and so genuinely friendly. Norm Swenson was my compatriot. His wife's name was Laura. The Swenson's were older people who had a twelve year old son with them. They were so happy to see us. This assignment just had to be a beautiful experience. I could feel it.

Our transportation was there waiting for us, so we got in the vehicle. The driver was an FAA/AID (Agency for International Development) man who was assigned to Iran. We talked all the way to our hotel. I asked him why there were no windshield wipers on the car. Of course he laughed and told me that if he put them on, it would be the last that he would see of them. Hmmm, lesson number one!

We arrived at the Caspian Hotel on Takteh Jamshid Ave. The American Embassy was right across the street from us. We'd have to find our own housing, so we would be staying at a hotel until we got settled. The first thing I noticed was a bullet hole in the window in our room. Now how did that get there? Another surprise!

Our new friends were with us in our third-floor room. We were immediately flooded with information -- what we must do and where to go. Luckily, everything we needed to take care of our immediate needs was close by. After an hour of listening and asking questions, everyone left. They knew that we were tired.

Now we were alone. By that, I mean all six of us. It was an eight hour time difference from eastern Pennsylvania to Teheran, Iran. That would take some getting used to. It was early evening and everyone was tired, so we all went to bed and fell asleep, exhausted. At two o'clock in the morning, we were all awake -- and hungry. We would have to wait. The time difference was showing its ugly face.

The US Embassy had a nice restaurant so we went there to have breakfast. It was like a restaurant in the States, with the same menu. Having breakfast was a pleasant experience. The attendants were all Iranian and they all spoke English. Very pleasant people! The four young girls, with their blond hair, were an attraction to everyone. So many people came up to chat with us; we were certainly getting a lot of advice!

Teheran was different, but it seemed to be a nice place. On the afternoon of that first day we were all up in our room when we heard strange noises in the street below. Looking down, we could see hundreds of men, young and old, singing and marching down the street. They were beating themselves with chains. Our kids were watching from the window, astonished. They had never seen anything like this before, nor had we. It was a religious celebration of some kind. Later we found out it was the Muslim (Shia) holy day of *Ashura*. "Don't go into the street," we were told by the people in the hotel. I could see another difference now. Not the same as the USA! We were learning fast.

A driver and a vehicle were assigned to us. I had to get to my office and get familiar with my new job. Among other things, Lucretia had to find us a house. Of course, the children had to go with her everywhere.

Doshen Toppeh (Rabbit Hill) was the name of the place where the Imperial Iranian Air Force headquarters (IIAF) was located. All our U.S. Air Bases in Iran were located on IIAF bases. Nasser, the driver, zipped me right through the security check point. Nasser was an IIAF Sergeant. We became very good friends. He offered helpful explanations and insights into people and places we encountered throughout that first morning. After dropping me off at USAF Military Assistance Advisory Group (MAAG) Headquarters, he left to take Lucretia and the kids on their errands.

Upon arrival at the new office, I found that just about everyone there was USAF. The Federal Aviation Specialist Group (FASG) had its own office. Norm and Fred were there. They proceeded to tell me how lucky I was. On the Saturday before I arrived, the IIAF had its first C-130 crash and everyone on board was killed. Fred took me to the scheduling board and showed me my schedule. I was supposed to be in Iran and on that military plane. If we hadn't been delayed for two weeks, because of the vaccinations my pregnant wife refused to take, I would have been on that flight. It would have been a very short tour of duty. I thanked God for the delay. I thanked God that my wife was a good nurse and didn't want to get those shots. That saved my life.

I remembered a similar occasion in El Paso, Texas, several years earlier, when I walked away from another scheduled flight. Something told me not to get on that airplane. I was in the U.S. Army then. The plane crashed and killed everyone aboard. Now it had just happened again.

Norm Swenson was from Seattle. This would be his last assignment. He was ready for retirement. Norm was assigned to Shahroki AFB and I would be going to Vahdati AFB. That was much farther away than Shahroki. I was disappointed I wouldn't be working with these new friends. The bottom line was that we were behind schedule so I would have to leave for Vahdati as soon as possible. That meant that Lucretia would have to take care of everything in Teheran. We had brought five hundred dollars with us, but after five days in Teheran, our cash was gone. At that time, there were no credit cards used there. It didn't matter because we didn't have one anyway. The U.S. Embassy made arrangements for us to pay for the room and gave us spending money. We had to watch our money. The Caspian Hotel was too expensive for us, so we moved to the Sina Hotel. It was a little farther up the street from the Embassy. The hotel people didn't see a problem. They just took our passports as security.

Our first impression of Iran was that the Iranian people absolutely loved Americans. Cars would stop to look at our four little blonde-haired girls. They would ask us if they could touch their hair. I remember times when we were looking at things to buy from some of the shops, the merchants would tell us to take what we wanted and pay when we got the money. No signatures, notes or anything. They knew they would be paid, because Americans were honorable people. That was then. A time came, later on, when not-so-honorable Americans came to Iran and ruined all of that. To us, this was just unbelievable. Such trust! We were seeing a very bright side to Iran. Lucretia was stuck with working out all our problems, but kind Iranians helped at every turn.

Blessings kept coming our way. There was a family of entertainers staying at the Sina Hotel. They were Spanish but spoke excellent English. The father and the two teenage daughters did their acts at the *Shu Café Now* (pronounced "no."). That was the largest entertainment center in Teheran. What brought us together was their attraction to our beautiful children. Soon, we became very good friends. During the day, the teenage girls, who were acrobats, would practice on a rope that hung off the balcony at the hotel. Naturally, our little ones loved to watch as they performed all kinds of acrobatics. At night, the entire family would perform at the nightclub -- all except the mother. She was not in the show; she was their manager.

They invited us to join them one night at the club. What a treat it was! The waiter brought us a bottle of fine Champagne. The girls did their act along with the father. He rode different kinds of bicycles and the girls would also do acrobatics on the bicycles while the father was riding it. One of the bikes was so small that it didn't seem possible that a grown man could even get onto it, but he did. What a wonderful performance it was. When the act was over, they came back to our table. There were so many different acts by various entertainers. This place was only for people who were well off. It was a pleasant experience and an introduction into the finer life in Teheran.

I made all the preparations to leave for Vahdati AFB and promised 'Cretia that I would come home as much as I possibly could. That I did. She and the kids would be in that hotel room for sixty two days until we finally managed to get a suitable house. That came about through an American couple we had come to know at the Sina Hotel.

Pat was very outgoing. I would say "noisy," but – her husband, John, was a quiet man. Pat and Lucretia became good friends. She and John had just found a house in Teheran and Pat offered to help Lucretia find one in the same neighborhood. They did find one, almost immediately. It was very close to Pat and John's new house, but it was occupied. We had to wait until the U.S. colonel (who was about to leave the country), vacated the house.

Our four little girls had become a part of the Sina Hotel family. When the day came for our family to leave the hotel, the staff was very sad. They just loved those beautiful children. It was a very touching experience. Our growing family had spent just over two months cooped up in a single room. How did 'Cretia manage everything so well? I don't know. I remember one time she looked at me and started crying. She said "I don't know how much longer I can take this." We hugged, and I hoped that all would work out for us. It did, but I had a lot to learn.

Attempted Murder -- Ab Garm

In July of 1967, Fred Hartquist became my new boss. Four new FAA guys, including Fred Hartquist, came over from Jordan because of the '67 war. He was a GS 15, so he outranked Fred Hemp. I was impressed that he could type 80 wpm; most bosses can't type at all. His secretary was named Sweet and she had a friend named Butterfly. Sweet married an Iranian friend of mine, and we are still friends.

Anyway, Fred Hartquist, my new boss, wanted to go hunting for mountain sheep. Why would he want to go hunting now, I wondered? It was winter. Turns out he just bought a new rifle and wanted to check it out. Okay! I didn't know that he was a hunter but since he was my boss and a nice person, I agreed to take him on a hunting trip.

It was very cold in the high country where the Ibex and Mountain Sheep lived. This would not be an enjoyable trip; we would freeze. I gathered information as to where we could go that was not too far from Teheran. I decided on Ab Garm. That means Warm Water. My friend, Al, who was of Arabic descent, assured me this was the best place. I had known him in the FAA. Al was an engineer from California. We met at the FAA Academy in Oklahoma City. Both of us had attended RADAR school there. For some reason, he left the FAA and went to work for the US Air Force. I ran into him again in Iran. We were both on a plane that was taking us to the site of an airplane crash in Hamadan. We continued our friendship until he became a "snoop" and left Iran to go to Libya. Al told me to go to Ab Garm and look up the barber. He would make sure that we were taken care of. Well, the barber certainly did his best.

Fred and I checked out a four wheel drive vehicle from the MAAG motor pool and started our excursion. He took along his dog whose name was Pedro. Pedro was a Mexican Chihuahua. The dog was always shivering. I wondered why Fred would want to take the dog on a hunting trip. He would have to carry him everywhere we went.

We arrived in Ab Garm about five hours after we had begun the trip. We found the barber. He seemed like a nice person. Ali, that was his name, almost immediately took us into the mountains. Fred had his new rifle but the scope wasn't zeroed in. Now, you can't hunt with a rifle that is not zeroed in, so we stopped on a mountain top and I zeroed it in. Fred held Pedro who was shivering badly. "The dog has to stay in the car or freeze to death," I told him. We saw some mountain sheep running but they were over a thousand yards away. That would be a waste of ammo.

We had no luck that day and we were far from Ab Garm. Ali took us to a place to stay for the night. This place made a dump look clean, and it was very cold. I had that strange feeling about this place and these people. It was an intuition that would serve me well in future encounters with Arabs and Iranians.

We had some of the food that we had brought with us and the people, who were there, had theirs. Those people were a shady bunch of characters. A fire was going and we were told to sleep beside the fire on a wooden "bed." The "bed" was a slanted, wooden platform that resembled the ones that soldiers in the 1700's used. Many years later, I saw beds like this one at Colonial Williamsburg. We got into our sleeping bags but there was no sleeping that night. Watching that gang staring at us was all the warning that I needed. My 9MM kept me warm.

The next morning, we went hunting but again, we had no luck. It was bitter cold and Fred couldn't stand it. Hunting ended early and we headed for Ab Garm. A room was given to us, which was very cold, but Ali had a solution. He put a very heavy blanket on a table and put a charcoal fire in a container under the table. The heavy blanket was draped over the sides of the table and reached down to the floor. Many people died from charcoal fires. I had seen it personally. It's real and does happen. We had to make a decision about what to do. The idea was to sleep in the sleeping bag with your feet and legs under the blanket. The rest of the body was outside the blanket. The carbon dioxide and fumes would be contained by the blanket, and the air that was coming in from the outside would dilute any carbon monoxide fumes that might escape. That was acceptable under the circumstances.

During the night, I had to go to the toilet which was outside. I had no choice, it was urgent. It was a real shithouse. The toilet building was made of animal excrement patties and it had a hole in the ground for doing your duty. It was fifteen degrees below zero. That was an experience that I'd rather not describe. Half naked in -15 degree weather is an unusual experience and I went back into the house as fast as nature would permit me.

In a situation like this, I programmed myself to sleep very lightly. I was able to do that and I think most people could do the same if a situation required it. A kerosene lantern was in the room on a very low setting. It was hard to see but it was possible. About three in the morning I was awaken by something. Something seemed wrong. My eyes opened and I saw a figure come in the door and began sneaking around a three foot high wall. He had a long knife in his right hand. "Here comes trouble; this son of a bitch has something on his mind," I said to myself.

They probably wanted our guns and the vehicle. Strangely, he didn't make a sound and that was surprising, since it was deathly quiet in the room. As he approached us, I got the 9MM Browning out from under the "pillow." That strange feeling came over me. It's hard to describe but it is real. My senses became extremely keen and a calmness and excitement came over me.

As he raised his right hand to begin his stab, I pointed the Browning to within three feet of his face and cocked the hammer. The click sounded so loud. He saw the gun and heard the click. He let out a squeak, then ran. I could easily have shot him. It was a definite kill shot but I knew the trouble that it would cause for us. "Don't kill unless you absolutely have to." That's the law I live by. Actually, it was quite entertaining. These guys weren't fighters. They all looked like mean pussies. A knife can't stand up to a gun, except in the movies. Proficiency in a reliable weapon instills confidence in a person and that is very important. If you don't have it, you do dumb things. Fred was awake and said "What was that? Did something happen?" I answered, "I just saved your miserable ass, Fred." Then I told him what happened. He replied "Oh shit!" I added, "That little bastard of a dog just kept on sleeping." We didn't get any more sleep that night.

The next morning, we knew we had to get out of there. It was so cold the Jeep wouldn't turn over, so we had to build a small fire under it. After an hour of heating the engine, the car finally started, but the clutch snapped. Now we had no vehicle. Ali said that he would tow us to Teheran with his car. It was in fact a funny looking jeep, just a wreck. There was no choice. We had to pay him for it.

We never made it to Teheran. Ali's car crapped out about 20 miles from Teheran, but that was close enough for the motor pool to tow it in. The Gendarmerie stopped to help us, but the major who was in the car insisted that we go with them. He had been drinking. Ali had to stay there. I thought that they would provide security for the vehicle but they didn't. My 9mm was packed away in the vehicle. I never saw it again. Ali stole it. That kind of weapon was worth a fortune over there. I know that it was recovered. They must have beaten the crap out of Ali; I found out he was thrown in jail. When I went to identify the gun that they "recovered" they showed me a rusty, old Mauser rifle. The Iranian person who accompanied me to the Gendarmerie told me this would happen and it did. Lots of corruption over there! The good thing that came out of it was that it enabled me to get a new weapon. That's how I was able to get my Smith & Wesson .357 Magnum which turned out to be a great, great blessing.

Chapter 3

Cultural Differences:

Our Early Life in Iran

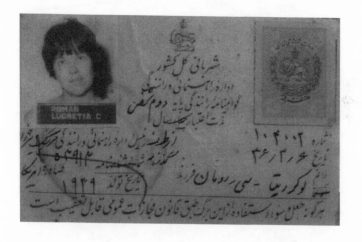

Lucretia, Iranian ID card, exp. 1979

Getting used to a whole new way of life was a
challenge. In everyday life, our ways were so
different. For example, to indicate "yes" in
our culture, we nod our heads up and down.
To say no, one would shake their head from
left to right. In Iran, it was the opposite. Once
you got used to it, it wasn't bad.

While I was teaching a class at Vahdati AFB, several times I asked "Am I right?" I did this to get them to reaffirm the portion of the lecture that was being covered. The students turned their heads away and didn't answer. At the end of the first lecture, Rasul came up to me and said, "Sir, don't say 'Am I right.' " I looked at him, surprised. "Why not?" He looked down at his shoes, politely. "It means 'Do I have an erection?'"

Wow, now that's a big difference! From that time on, I would make note of the words and phrases that I learned in Farsi and made sure that they meant the same thing in English. All of their books, reports and technical manuals were written in Farsi, an Arabic script. Like Hebrew, the words were written from right to left. (Numbers went from left to right.) The back of a book was the beginning.

Lemons and oranges were a different experience. Lemons were sweet and oranges were sour. In Iran, sweet oranges were from trees that had branches from sweet orange trees grafted onto them. They were called "Portugal" which indicates that it was originally brought there from Portugal and they were more expensive than the sour oranges. The sour oranges were called "*naronge*."

The learning process begins with a surprise: 'This orange is sour. This lemon is sweet. What's wrong?' There was always someone around to give you answers.

In those early weeks, our family came to accept that life in Iran was just very different from what we had been used to back in the States. The girls adjusted quickly and thoroughly enjoyed their new life in Iran; they were always telling us of some new discovery.

Fortunately, people in Iran drive on the right side of the road. That is a blessing because everyone drives very badly in Iran. Drivers go very fast and assume that others will get out of their way. You have to start up fast when the light changes, because everyone behind you is frantically start blowing their horns and trying to get around you. A taxi ride was a scary experience at first. Eventually you just got used to it. There were so many old Mercedes cars there and they all seemed to be taxis. They could keep those cars going for a million miles. Teheran had one of the highest traffic fatality rates in the world. Of course, in 1966, no one had seat belts or air bags.

You couldn't use the ordinary hand signals we used in the States either. The hand sign "thumbs up" means "up your butt". The "tally ho" sign means "I'll give it to you in the butt or you can give it to me in the butt". The wave using five fingers spread apart that we use to say hello means "five of the middle finger." Clenching the fist and moving your hand downward to emphasize "yes," means "screw you."

The most common insult is *"Pedar Sag."* That means your father is a dog. Sometimes I would hear "your mother is a dog" or "you are the seed of a dog." Anything referring to a dog is an insult.

Dogs are a subject all their own. Iranians considered dogs very dirty. They would not touch them with their hands. I did see a couple of soldiers pet them with their foot. Dogs wandered the streets of Teheran all the time. Periodically, a team of workers would throw raw meat that was poisoned, on the sides of the streets. The dogs came along and ate the meat. In a very short time the dogs died and a crew came along and picked them up, loading them onto a truck.

In some places, outside of the cities, dogs were very important. They were used as watch dogs and also shepherds used them to tend their herds of sheep and goats. The dogs were fed all at once, no individual servings. Among the dogs themselves there was a pecking order and a lot of fighting. The lead dog always ate first and then so on down the line until the last one ate. Once in Esfahan, near a big lake, we saw a pack of dogs fishing. We had to stop and watch since no one ever saw that before. The dogs were standing in the water and when a fish swam near them, the dog's head would jerk under the water very quickly and most of the time the dog would have a fish in his mouth when he brought his head up.

Iranians were taught from birth certain rules of etiquette called *"Taroof."* There was an old saying that if you were in a person's home and told them that you just killed their son, they wouldn't do anything to you. When you got out of the house, now, that was a different story.

You could not look at another man's wife or talk to her. If you were a foreigner, it might be forgiven. Many a time I was caught in situations that I didn't know what to do. Sometimes they would forget their rules to be polite to a foreigner. On the other hand, some Iranians would pretend to completely forget the rules, because they wanted to be like us Americans – but you had no way of knowing that unless they told you.

An incident happened where an Iranian friend and I were crossing the street. A car ran over my friend's foot. He yelled out something in Farsi. The car had to stop, because it was an insult. My friend asked for an apology. The man driving the car, who had stopped, refused to apologize. My friend went to the window and punched the man in the face and asked for an apology. The man refused. In the *Taroof* system, if the right words were spoken, all would be forgiven. Since the man refused to apologize, my friend kept punching the man in the face. I finally had to drag him away since the women in the back seat were screaming. We ran across the street into a shop. The man in the shop must have been watching and started to yell. My friend told him to stop shouting. He did not. The shop keeper then grabbed a butcher knife. My friend went after him. I interceded. I told my friend that I had a gun and I could stop the fight. My friend refused. He disarmed the shop keeper, then beat him pretty badly. That was a surprise to me but I'm happy that it turned out that way. Of course, I made him run out of the shop with me. Things were getting too hot and more trouble would soon come up. All this happened because of *Taroof.*

The toilets are quite different in Iran. There is no hopper seat at all. Americans called it a "bomb sight" toilet. The toilet is level with the floor. If a person had a problem with stooping, they were in trouble. Also, there is no toilet paper. There is a miniature sprinkler can filled with water that is called an "*oftabeh.*" The right hand is used to hold the *oftabeh* and the left hand is used to clean one's butt. It must be the left hand that is used. You could never give your left hand to shake hands. That was a no -no. Usually only cold water is there to wash hands -- if there is any water at all. Many people there had brown fingernails. This of course presented a problem, especially when unclean hands exchanged paper currency. It is very unsanitary and affected people's health. At one time the twenty *rial* paper note, that was the same value as a quarter at that time, was replaced by a metal coin because the paper note, in dirty hands, caused the spread of a lot of disease. When you opened your billfold, there was a very distinct smell, not a good smell. You could tell the bills had been touched by unclean hands, many, many times.

The work week ran from Saturday thru Wednesday. Iran is a *Shia* Muslim country. Friday is their holy day. Americans also went to church on Friday because if they didn't, another work day would be lost. This work week affects business. In the Western world, days off are Saturday and Sunday. If the remaining days are used to do business on an international scale, that leaves only three days; Monday, Tuesday and Wednesday.

We lived near a mosque. Every day there were prayers sung over a very loud speaker five times a day. Poor people appeared to be religious. The better off people didn't appear to be that way. If they were, they kept it to themselves. Fortunately, the people that I worked with did not stop work to pray. In the 1960's, when I first arrived in Iran, the Iranians celebrated 48 holidays. Americans had eight holidays. Altogether that made fifty six holidays. That was just too much. Long term projects were dragged out week after week because of all these holidays. That was eventually changed.

One morning, while I was riding on a bus from Vahdati to Teheran, for lack of any other type of transportation, some people in the bus approached the driver. They ask him to stop before sunrise so that they could get out and say prayers. The driver said no, so they threatened to beat him up. He agreed to stop. They got out and said their prayers. There was a specific ritual they followed: the men had a prayer stone that is wrapped up in a white cloth. Some of them had prayer blankets that they would spread on the ground. When they bow down to the ground, their head touches the stone that is on top of the white cloth. Some of them have a compass that indicates the direction of Mecca. They must face Mecca. I also observed this ritual on a train -- that was a sight to behold. It is carried out just before sunrise.

Iranians had to take a bath once a week and after having sex. I asked a friend why they must take a bath after having sex. He said that women bleed from the vagina and that makes it dirty. I don't know if that was right or not but that's what he said.

At the age of fifty-five, men received an opium ration. There was a lot of opium smoking in Iran. The opium was called *Taryak*. It looked like a Tootsie Roll. The opium pipe had a long round handle with a ceramic end that resembled an egg. It had a tiny hole in it. The opium kit also had a long stick pin that was used to keep the hole open. There was a brass tray with live charcoal in it. A pair of tongs was used to hold the live charcoal. The charcoal was held in front of the hole. The person smoking would blow on the mouthpiece. The stream of air made the charcoal white hot. That heated up the ceramic. Then a piece of opium was cut off of the roll that looked like a Tootsie Roll and put it above the hole a tiny bit. It would stick there. When it had stuck, they would hold the charcoal close to the opium and blow on the pipe again. The *Taryak* then began to smoke. The smoker inhaled the smoke and held his breath for a minute before exhaling. The ritual took some time. If there was more than one person, the pipe would be passed around until everyone was happy. The richer a person, the more elaborate their smoking equipment. Near our house, one could smell opium burning constantly.

All things considered, our cultures were very different. While I was out learning my new duties, 'Cretia and the children were adjusting to their new life in Teheran. Our new house was located in a nice section of Teheran called Zarrine Club where several Americans already lived. We would not be surrounded by total strangers. I was away most of the time; she had to do everything herself. Keep in mind that she had four children to take care of and was expecting our fifth child. Believe me; I was so proud of her. It made me feel bad that I wasn't there to help her.

The Embassy PX gave us access to all the things that we needed and the prices were cheap compared to the open market. We were provided a driver and vehicle by the FAA, so my wife was able to run errands, pick up things, and get settled in. Our driver was a very nice Airman; Lucretia gave him cigarettes and Scotch, so he was happy to help her. I don't know how she would have managed otherwise.

After a very long wait, our car finally arrived. It was not recognizable when I first saw it. Ivory was its original color, but the car I saw was almost black. Everywhere that you went, there was an exchange of baksheesh involved. That's a payoff. If you didn't pay it, there was always some kind of problem. It was an expected daily transaction. They started my car for me because the battery was dead, and then cleaned the windows so I could see out of it. Driving the car to our house was a nightmare, with crazy drivers and hundreds of horns blaring all around.

It took a lot of work to get the car back to its original color but I made it happen. Just the thought of 'Cretia driving in Teheran traffic scared me to death, but she had to do it. To my surprise, she did very well. I think Iranian drivers gave special consideration to foreign women. First of all, Iranian women were covered from head to foot with a chador. Well, not all of them wore it but the overwhelming majority did. There were a few westernized Iranian women who dressed in the latest fashions. They ventured on the streets in a car, but they knew what to expect and drove the same way the men did, so it wasn't a problem for them. The important thing was we now had our car, so we weren't dependent on other people to drive us everywhere.

The streets were usually good, except when they were doing work on them. One day, while on our way home, we soon became aware of the trenches that were dug on either side of the road going to our home. One ditch came from the left and one from the right and they met near the center. They were about three feet deep. There was just enough room to drive through. The measurement that they used was based on a small car.

Our car was a Plymouth Fury. I made it through the maze until the last one. The trenches were very close together. Both wheels went in. Was I angry! 'Cretia took the wheel and put the car in reverse. The anger helped. I actually lifted the front of the car up enough so that she was able back out. They had left a thick board there so I put it across one trench and was able to drive across. That happened many times to many other cars but it never happened to us again. Helping Iranians out of the trenches was easy. Their cars were small and easy for me to lift. Teheran driving was always full of surprises.

The Officer's Club was a godsend for us. It was like having a class "A" nightclub, restaurant and recreation for the kids at your disposal all the time and the cost was very affordable. You were surrounded by American officers and their families. There was an Olympic-size swimming pool where the kids could learn to swim. They also took classes in water ballet. My wife enjoyed playing bingo there. All things said, it was the beginning of a new, very nice life style. It was a comfort to me, knowing that 'Cretia and the kids were safe and well taken care of.

Lorie, my boss's wife, and Laura, Norm's wife, took 'Cretia to the Teheran American Society. There she learned Farsi and the culture of Iran. They introduced her to some interesting people who became part of our lives and enriched them tremendously.

She also learned how to cook Iranian food. That in itself was a wonderful thing. To this day, we have several favorite dishes that we just can't do without, like *Fesenjoon*, a stew made with crushed walnuts and pomegranate syrup. Another favorite was *Kharesh-e Gharmeh Sabzi*, a green vegetable sauce with lamb, leeks, green onions and black-eyed peas. Iranians often cooked with fruit and spices like cinnamon and saffron. Our children grew up eating healthy Iranian food and they loved it.

Our maid, whose name was Iran, took care of the household and gave my wife more time to care for the children and enjoy our new life. Iran could not speak English but my family learned enough Farsi to make conversation and talk to Iran about our daily lives.

Shopping, at that time was basically at the Embassy store, Post Exchange (PX), and ordering things from catalogues. The military provided free APO mail. The open market offered things that were not available in the PX.

The PX supplied such things as canned goods, meats, goods needed for everyday life, and party rations. The open market provided the fruits, vegetables, eggs, bread and things we needed. Everything purchased on the open market had to be treated before cooking and eating. There was dirt and feces everywhere. You never just picked up a piece of fruit and ate it; it was too dirty. 'Cretia soaked everything in a solution of Clorox and water. That was a must. The solution killed all living things that shouldn't be in the food. All in all, it was a very good lifestyle.

The landlord took care of the grounds and repaired things in the house. There was a law that the rent could not be raised so we didn't have to worry about that. The landlord argued this law only applied to Iranian citizens, but we knew better.

On weekends, partying was the order of the day for most military Americans. Remember, in Iran, their weekend was Wednesday and Thursday. Most of the time, the parties were at private homes. In our first five years, we were involved mostly with American officers, since I had the rank of a USAF major. That meant the Officers Club. That evolved into the "Wednesday night group." This group was already established, but we worked our way into it. It was by invitation only.

Here's how it worked. The party started at the Officer's Club at Wednesday night "Happy Hour." At happy hour, drinks were very cheap. You become happy from the drinks and the low price of the drinks. Since it was the end of the work week and nobody went to work the next day, it was the ideal time for enjoyment. After happy hour, everyone went to the home of the person who had the "flag" for that week. The flag was given to the person who was designated to have the party the next Wednesday.

Those who had the flag went all out to give a great party. Foods were very special and so were the drinks. Women had their hair done and wore very beautiful dresses. The Embassy PX cooperated with us and gave a special booze ration to those who were throwing the party. It was called a party ration.

Women drank all kinds of drinks and I became an excellent drink mixer as a result of that. I ordered a book on drink mixing and studied it very well. Most of the officers drank Scotch so you had to buy good Scotch and a lot of it. Actually, it didn't cost too much more than the regular stuff. There was no beer. Nobody drank it. If it was to be a very big party, the staff from the Embassy would be hired. Usually, there was a hired bartender at every party.

Dancing was a very big part of the party, therefore music was very important. I had made up a tape of the best party music around. Everyone wanted a copy of that tape. The parties would last anywhere from midnight to six in the morning. It was a very big part of the social lives of the Wednesday Night Group and kept everyone happy.

Special parties happened every so often to celebrate a special occasion. For the men, it was same old, same old, but for the women it was special. They would have dresses made and get their hair done at Ingaborg's beauty salon. She was a German woman who had very artistic Iranian women working for her. They knew all the latest hairstyles. Ingaborg and her assistants styled hair so beautifully. Our wives did not look like the same women when they joined the party. All of them were so beautiful. Just looking at the women made the whole thing special and they knew it. For them, it was one compliment after another, all night long.

These were very "civilized" parties with no nasty behavior by anyone in the group. That was a good thing, because sometimes our children were watching. When the party was at our house, we would look up at the steps and there were some of our kids observing everything the grownups did. When people left, they were all very happy. It was an escape back to the American lifestyle.

Membership in the Wednesday Night Group changed constantly. For most of the officers, this was an accompanied tour. That meant that they were able to stay there for two years. After completion of the tour of duty, a lot of them were assigned to Vietnam. A lot of them were wounded there and some were killed. As soon as it happened, everyone knew about it. It was sad because we knew them so well. It was probably those experiences that made 'Cretia resist my future assignment to Vietnam. For the moment, we were enjoying our time in Iran. I was delighted my family had settled in so well, especially when we found out that our tour would be extended from eighteen months to five years. Because of the longer assignment, we would be entitled to a thirty-day vacation back in the States. The kids were looking forward with great anticipation to our cruise, and visiting relatives back home. After a year away, the girls thought of Iran as home. 'Cretia and I were delighted for the opportunity to visit friends and family. We had so much to tell them about our new life overseas, and we wanted to introduce everyone to our newborn son, Michael.

Chapter 4: My First Assignment, Vahdati AFB

Lucretia and Mike, near Dez Dam,
Iran, 1968

Fred Hemp, my initial FAA boss in Iran, and
I were headed for Vahdati Air Force Base. As
I mentioned, the United States Air Force had
no bases in Iran; we were permitted to use
bases belonging to the Imperial Iranian Air
Force (IIAF). A C-130 was on the tarmac at
Doshen Toppeh waiting for us to board.
There was nothing elaborate about the plane.

It was a four engine, propeller driven military cargo plane and that meant no comforts at all. Fred and I boarded and the plane began to taxi. The different noises were very strange and irritating. It was strictly a cargo plane.

The landing at Vahdati was a surprise. It was a Fighter Base and the Fighter planes were F-86's. The F-86 aircraft had made its appearance in Korea, back in the fifties. Here it was 1967, a trip back in time. Vietnam was now deep in warfare, so everyone was accustomed to the newer planes that were in use. This should be interesting I told myself. I was sure that I would enjoy this assignment.

Vahdati was located between the ancient cities of Dezful and Andemesk in the Khuzestan Province. It would be a deep and fascinating exposure to the country of Iran. Dez Dam was very near and I would be able to experience all the workings of the dam. It was a recreation area for the IIAF, a hydroelectric plant and an irrigation source of water. Here it was the end of April and it was already very hot. There were no trees in the desert except for the ones that were growing on the Base. They had planted hundreds of Eucalyptus trees in the area next to the runway. Those trees emitted an exotic aroma and they grew very quickly because the irrigation ditches supplied them with water.

The day was spent settling in and getting to meet the Iranian officers and members of the USAF. The Americans didn't have a room for us to stay, so we were assigned a room on the base. The room had no air conditioning and a very strong body odor. These concerns proved to be quite a problem, considering the extreme heat. Neither of us could sleep, so the work suffered. Finally we were given a room at the American Team House. That was where the men with the USAF stayed. Now life was normalized, as much as it could be under those conditions. Fred left in a very short time to tend to his duties in Teheran. Now it was up to me to get the job moving.

The first Iranian Airman I met at Vahdati was Rasul Damavadi. He would prove to be a very good friend and life-saver. He was a very unusual Airman who appeared to be much Americanized. USAF training in the U.S. runs about a year and the Iranians who were sent for training loved it. Rasul looked like a very young man, but I quickly came to realize he was intelligent and a definite asset to me. The USAF gave me the honorary rank of major and issued me a USAF ID card which entitled me to all the perks of a major in the US Air Force. Protocol encouraged us to fraternize with the officers. That I did, but I also had to work with the enlisted men. People become close when they work together all day long and week after week. Rasul and I became friends. He taught me a lot about Iran.

The Dez River, which fed the Dez Dam, was near the site where I was installing my first TACAN (Tactical Air Navigation system).

The TACAN was at the end of a long runway. That put the site about two miles from the main base. The river itself was about three quarters of a mile from the site in the opposite direction from the base. Water flowed very quickly due to the dam overflow and surprisingly, the water was ice-cold.

The soldiers who were assigned to guard the site were conscripts. That is like a draftee. They were paid about $2.50 a month. These men were surprised that I spoke to them. Not many people talked with the *"Sarbazie,"* as they were called. A *Sarbaz* is a soldier with no rank. Money was a problem for them – they never had any -- so I would pay them to do things for me. That turned out to be a mistake, at least in some circumstances. They sneaked into town at night to buy things for themselves. One of them sought out some of the local prostitutes and of course got himself a dose of VD. He didn't tell the doctors where he got the extra money to treat himself to the entertainment that he bought. They really got to like me because I treated them with respect. That turned out to be a very good thing for me.

One day I had to work very late on a problem and I was by myself, except for the *Sarbazie*. When I finished up, and was ready to get into my jeep, they warned me that I would be shot if I left now. It was very dark. My Farsi was very limited and they spoke no English at all. They talked among themselves and the

86

soldier, Hassan (the one who later got VD), was selected to go with me.

As we were getting near the Control tower, a shot rang out. A guard was in the kneeling position, right on the road. He was aiming at the jeep and preparing to fire another shot. Hassan jumped out and shouted "don't shoot, it's me, Hassan!" He walked out in front of the jeep lights and began talking. It turned out he knew the guard; they were friends. He explained to the guard that I was an American and new to the base; I didn't know about security. The guard let us pass. Hassan then walked all the way back to the TACAN site in the darkness. Needless to say, I was very happy that the *Sarbazie* liked me.

One of the F-86 pilots that I knew told me that nobody went out there at night because they would get shot. He was right! Not long after that, another Lieutenant who was Officer of the Guard went out at night to check up on the guards. One of the guards started shooting at him. He ran from sand dune to rock, to anywhere he could, until the guard ran out of ammo. Don't go out at night!

The *Sarbazie* and I enjoyed each other's company. I would eat with them on occasion when there was no one around. Someone other than a *Sarbaz* being there would be a no- no. They ate out of a large tin can and the food that they ate always seemed to be a dark green mush. They also tried to teach me how to read, write and speak Farsi. It wasn't a

87

complete failure. I didn't have enough time to really learn it all but I got a good idea of things.

There was an incident that happened at a critical phase of the installation. True north and magnetic north points were needed to finalize calibration of the TACAN system. To do this, surveying equipment was needed which I borrowed from the Base Engineer. That was easy enough but I had to go to the top of the antenna and use the telescope that came with the equipment to finalize calibration. The telescope was gone.

I was about to call the officer in charge to find out what happened to the scope, but before doing this I asked the Airmen to talk to the soldiers about it. It turned out that the soldiers had the scope and used it to spy on the girls from Dezful who swam naked on the other side of the Dez River. To me, it was so funny. After all, the soldiers had their fun – and I got my scope back. I had no doubt the girls knew they were being spied upon. If I reported the incident, the soldiers would have been beaten and put in jail. I couldn't do that.

This was my first assignment in Iran. At that time there were virtually no navigational devices in Iran. That meant there were also no people who knew how to design and build navigational devices. I was on my own.

My boss, Fred Hemp, never told me that I would have to do the engineering and all the work that it took to install a TACAN. I guess they just figured I could handle it, based on the work I had done in Pakistan. I remembered my classes at the FAA Academy and the depth at which they taught electronics on an engineering level. I was grateful they had trained me so thoroughly. I had brought many of my books from the academy with me -- and I needed them. During my three years in the Army, mostly at Macgregor Guided Missile Center near Fort Bliss, I had been introduced to many different types of RADADS, (Research Aircraft Data Acquisition and Display Systems) and computers. It was at MacGregor that I received a thorough grounding in electronics and shooting down airplanes. (Certainly more exciting than shooting rats back home.)

At that time, the early sixties, the FAA training classes taught engineering at a highly advanced postgraduate level. We received engineering credits for successfully passing major FAA schools. The schools were very difficult. Everything was intensively math-oriented. Without a strong mathematical ability and skill in using a slide rule (essential back then), it would have been impossible to pass the FAA engineering schools. I successfully passed all available certifications and came to regard my growing collection of technical books as an invaluable resource. As a result of this comprehensive grounding in all aspects of electronic engineering and design, I had become an electrician, diesel mechanic, welder, air conditioning technician and so many other things. I was able to invent and design electronic devices of all descriptions and modify existing devices to suit the needs of whatever project I tackled. Working on projects in a foreign, third world country, you would not get far unless someone on your team had that kind of training. My skills were exceptional and badly needed in the Imperial Iranian Air Force. That was why I had such a positive impact on so many people and events in Iran. I was good at what I did and they needed my help.

At times, the work became overwhelming and I had to get away. While I was walking near the river during a lull in the routine, I realized what a soothing experience it was. Desert and water came together at the banks of the Dez River. Coolness and a constant roaring sound were hallmarks of the flowing water. Water shooting from the overflows of the Dez Dam chilled the water and it held the coldness for a long distance down-river. In the heat of the desert, that was strange.

The Shepherd

One day, I was walking along, looked up, and saw a tall, blue-eyed man dressed like Jesus.

90

He was there with his herd of sheep, looking at me with a calm, peaceful expression. In the pictures we had at home and in school, Jesus was always shown wearing long, flowing robes, exactly like this shepherd. That was not the way a normal shepherd dressed in Iran. He had no fear of me.

That was strange I thought. After all, I was a foreigner, wearing a Pith helmet, along with khaki clothing. Not only that, I was armed. There was a pistol on my side. Blue eyes were extremely rare in that part of Iran. Only people from Northern Iran had blue eyes.

The sheep were all around me before I knew it. They had no fear. After all, their shepherd was with them. He came over to me and said "*Salaam*," which means "peace". I replied with the same word. The newborn lamb that he held in his arms was beautiful. What a stunning picture! This was a strange happening. We talked for a few minutes in the limited Farsi I knew and then, he handed the lamb to me. The mother of the lamb saw this and charged towards me. Quickly, the shepherd shouted something and the ewe stopped dead in her tracks. After stroking the lamb for a few minutes, I gave it back to the shepherd.

As I walked away from him, a strange feeling overcame me. An air of peace settled upon me. It was a feeling that was very powerful. I'll never forget it. In all my time in Iran, I never saw another shepherd like that and I

never saw him again even though I looked for
him.

Father Mulligan

A dark blue *Peykon*, a car made in Iran, car
pulled up to the Team House one hot
afternoon. The driver was a stranger. He had
never been here as far as I could remember. I
went over to the car to see who this strange
person was. He was a short man dressed in a
black suit with a very small silver cross on his
lapel. As the door was opening, the man got
out and immediately introduced himself.
"Mulligan is my name. I'm a priest," he said. I
greeted him and invited him into the dining
room to get out of the heat.

"What in the world are you doing here?" I
asked him. He explained that this was the area
that he took care of. It was a very large area.
As our conversation went on, I found that he
was an Egyptologist. He had spent a lot of
time in Egypt and knew Abdul Nasser,
personally. At that time, Nasser was the
president of Egypt. Father Mulligan also
taught at Cambridge University. I inquired as
to why he was here instead of Cambridge. He
answered, to the effect, that people needed
him here and they did not need him at
Cambridge. He then asked me if there were
Catholics in the area. I told him that I did

know of some. "Bring them here if you can. I'll say a Mass with them."

He settled in and I got the word out that Father Mulligan was at the USAF Team House. The people came to the Mass and they had an enjoyable experience with the priest and many of the USAF people. There were several Catholics in the USAF group.

Our conversations became so engrossing. Father Mulligan did so much work in Egypt. He was into archeology, big time. How I wished that I could have been there with him in Egypt but here he was in Iran with me. I spent every spare moment with him that I could. In our conversations, I asked Father Mulligan if he made any converts in his travels. He told me that he did, but he asked the converts to keep it in their hearts and not to display it openly around people that they knew. The family of the convert would be obliged to kill the family member if they knew one of their own had deserted the Muslim religion. To me, meeting this man was a fantastic experience. I've never forgotten him.

There was an Irish group at Vahdati, installing some kind of missile system. In the evening they were at the upstairs social room. When Father Mulligan found out that some of his countrymen were there, he went over to meet them. They were from Northern Ireland and they hated priests. As he introduced himself, one of them pushed him out of the way. Every member of the USAF stood up, ready for action, the least of which was to throw the guy out. The USAF people there were of many different religions. It didn't matter to them. They just knew that a clergyman had been disrespected.

The leader of the Irishmen stood up and demanded that the guilty man immediately apologize to the Father. You could see the hate and rage on the guilty man's face. I also saw the anger on the faces of the USAF people. Adrenalin was pouring into me. The guilty man saw this, along with the group leader. Our troops wanted to beat the hell out of him. He did apologize, after which the USAF people sat down.

I had been a soldier too, just a few years earlier. That never leaves you. I was so proud of our military men and it gave me a very good feeling. After that incident, that Irishman did not get any respect from the Americans. They knew what a great man Father Mulligan was and considered it was unforgiveable for someone to knock him aside like that. Father Mulligan was a great man and a great priest. He left his mark on many people.

The Dez Dam

The Dez Dam was a spectacular sight
to behold. It had been built in 1963 over a
very old dam, by an Italian engineering firm.
Its function was to provide electrical power
and to make water available for irrigation.
One day I got that "I want to get away" urge,
so I got into my jeep and headed for the dam.
There was only one road going to it so I
couldn't get lost.

When I got to the gate, the guards wanted to
know what I wanted, so I told them as best I
could. They gave up; my Farsi wasn't that
good at the time. A man named Gene Buffim
was called. He was an American engineer
from Redding, California. In a little while, he
arrived and greeted me. He appeared to be
very happy to see me, although we had never
met before. Seeing a new American in the
boondocks does do something for you. From
that time on, we became the best of friends.
Gene just couldn't do enough for me.

Gene's job was to put up the structures that
carried electricity away from the dam. Some
of these towers he designed were on the side
of a steep mountain. Engineering was his
forte and he was very good at it. Gene was
one of those guys who could do everything
and he loved it. He gave me a tour of the

95

entire dam. It was awesome and beautiful. Some of the tunnels were not yet completed. The water from the dam would rush down these tunnels and run into a turbine. The force of the moving water would turn the turbines and generate electricity. Later, Gene took me to his home and introduced me to his wife and family. It was the beginning of a beautiful friendship between our families.

As it turned out, there were many more Americans attached to the Khuzestan Water and Power Authority (KWPA) then I thought. I was introduced to many new friends. These introductions always included an invitation to dinner. They invited me to their duplicate bridge night where I learned to be an excellent bridge player. The people in KWPA gave me a different type of social life then I had in Teheran. I'll never forget the song that I heard while I was spending my time with some of those people. It was Johnny Cash singing "Sunday Morning Coming Down." To this day, I just love hearing that song and it brings back such fond memories. I think that I could identify with some things in the song at that time. That was one of the places that I looked forward to visiting while at Vahdati.

On one occasion, a big whip from the Embassy in Teheran arrived to take his teenage boy on a wild boar hunting trip. He didn't have a gun so I loaned him mine to use. Gene let me use his M-1 paratrooper carbine. It was a semi-automatic weapon with a folding stock. While on the hunt, the boy kept missing his shots. I always fired after his shot and told him that he got it. His father knew better so we kept going and going and going until we came upon a large herd. I just couldn't help myself; the carbine and I went bananas. The Embassy whip finally agreed that the boy got one. Lots of dead wild boar! Gene was so happy that his carbine had finally drawn blood. He kept it for self- protection, not for hunting.

Lucretia and the kids came to visit me, and our families joined together. The kids had a wonderful time playing with the sheep that were grazing in the area. They were exposed to the desert and loved it. The Buffims came to visit us at our home in Teheran and they loved the city. Everything was mutual. When we parted, I missed them.

Dr. Dempski

This was a man that I truly admired. He was a Doctor in the USAF. I kept running into him and in doing so, I kept learning. He had been an orphan, in the care of the Jesuits. He became a Medical Doctor and was also studying to be a Psychiatrist. He was an avid fan of Sigmund Freud. He had a maroon-bound collection of Freud's works, with gold etchings. His duty at Vahdati was to visit the

USAF people and to attend to their medical needs. Sometimes, he was stranded there and we spent some time together.

Iranian people sometimes puzzled me. I remember one time when I had an appointment with an Iranian engineer at two in the afternoon. When I went to his home, he wasn't there. The servant said that he had left for Teheran the evening before. Boy was I pissed! We had reached a critical point in the installation and we needed a crane. Dempski was there and I asked him why this engineer would treat me like that.

What he told me was stunning. "There are many types of mindsets. We are of the Western mindset which is basically Christian. The Eastern mindset does not want to offend anyone. It's all respect, even to the point of copying written mistakes. The Muslim mindset is fatalistic. They live for tomorrow, not today. The Iranian mindset is about sixty percent Muslim, twenty five percent western and fifteen percent Eastern. He didn't want to offend you, so he made the appointment with you." I guess he just didn't want to say no. Oh well! When we did get the crane, the operator finished the work I needed. He then crashed the crane and broke it up. Then he insisted that I pay for it. Ha!

Dr. Dempski accompanied me for a full day of work, to see what I was doing in Vahdati. He seemed impressed with things. His world was medicine and this must have been a pleasant change for him. He was also known for close calls in airplanes. Some people called him a "jinx." One day, I saw a U-8, American airplane coming in for a landing and he was in trouble. I immediately said, "Dempski must be on that plane." He was.

Another time, we were aboard a C-54. The thing that went through my mind was, "I hope we get home." We didn't make it. A training fighter took off before us, flamed out at the end of the runway and crashed in front of my TACAN, killing both people aboard. Now it was our turn. As we were taking off, an engine exploded but fortunately, we were able to land. Dr. Dempski once missed boarding a C-47 at Mashad. The wing broke off and everyone aboard was killed. All were U.S. military people. I guess you could say that he was lucky.

After we got off the C-54 I said that I was going to the train station to get a ticket. He wanted to go along. When the train began to roll, I felt a funny bump, bump, and bump. The car had a flat spot on the wheel. Five hundred miles of that! Dr. Dempski came to Teheran to deliver Michael, the first of our three children born in Iran. That was a good experience. I have fond memories of that man.

Chapter 5
USAF Team House
Vahdati AFB

Two Assyrian Warriors

Persepolis, Iran

The USAF Team House at Vahdati was the place that made life as pleasant as it could be. It was occupied by USAF enlisted personnel with an officer in charge. What could be better? I had breakfast, lunch and dinner there each day that I was in Vahdati. Upstairs, there was a bar with good drinks that were served very cheap. We played volleyball after dinner and at seven o'clock there was a movie. After the movie, all went to the bar and chit-chatted until it was time to go to bed. Once in a while, the routine was broken.

One night, I was coming down the stairs and spotted a very big cockroach. He ran into the mess hall. I was feeling pretty good from the booze so I went into my room and got a powerful BB/Pellet pistol. The cockroaches were waiting for me in the mess hall. I sat down on a chair. There was the big one in the middle of the floor. When I shot it, it flew apart. Then it all began. There were roaches all over the place. I kept shooting and shooting. Pieces of roaches were everywhere. After a while, the roaches that I saw were getting smaller and smaller. I must have killed hundreds of them. The kitchen seemed to be the place that they were coming from so I went in. Then I saw where they were coming from. The drain in the floor was their home. There was no trap in the drain. Finally, when I had killed them all, I went off to my room and fell into a deep sleep. I don't know how long I was in the mess hall but it must have a very long time.

In the morning, when I came into the mess hall for breakfast, the cook was cleaning up the mess. Pieces of cockroaches were everywhere. They were even on the windows. People were staring at me, but didn't say anything. The cook asked me what had happened. Of course I said that I didn't know.

And that was that, except for the BBs that were everywhere. There was only one BB pistol in the Team House and that was mine. What I didn't know was how many people knew that I had it. Anyway, I got away with it.

Occasionally, we would go on a wild boar hunt. Now that was interesting and exciting. Everyone got on the weapons carrier with their hunting rifles. We spent a good while getting to the hunting area, two hours or more hunting and another hour or so getting back. A weapons carrier was the vehicle of choice. The enlisted men procured a landing light from an airplane. It gave off a lot of light. A boar's eyes would glow a bright red color when it was in the light. The people who were firing stood in the rear part of the weapons carrier. We took turns firing. When we got enough boars, it was time to go home.

They gave me the name "*Jube* Jumper." That was because of an incident that happened one night. A hyena was spotted in the light. It was running, and nobody wanted to waste a bullet except me. When I shot, it flew. The only problem was that it landed on the other side of a *jube*, a fairly wide irrigation stream. Since I shot the hyena, I had to go get it. I was the youngest person there and in the military they make fun of you if you're the youngest, or the new guy.

Getting to the hyena wasn't difficult. I ran and jumped across the wide irrigation stream. The

103

rifle on my shoulder made it a little harder to jump, but I made it to the other side.

The hyena was dead and I dragged it to the stream. They threw a rope to me to pull it over to the other side. I tied the rope to the hyena and they pulled it across the stream. Nobody had ever seen a hyena before, including me. They were all looking at the hyena and talking. It was time for me to jump again. The land on my side was slanted upward a little and besides that, I was tired from dragging the dead animal. This time I didn't make it. When I hit the water, I went down. It was a lot deeper than I thought. They had a good time laughing their asses off. From that night on, my name was no longer Mike. It was now *Jube* Jumper.

If you were unfortunate enough to bag a boar, and that was just about every time we went out, you spent the rest of the night cutting it up inside the Team House and then cleaning up the mess. After many months of doing this, I got very good at it. Hunting was a great way of releasing the frustrations of the day and enjoying the desert at the same time.

* * *

Hot was a nice way of saying it. By August, temperatures were now 120+ every day. In the morning, when the sun rose, it was already

104

100 degrees. It was time to get away. This particular night was going to be a hunting night.

J. was an FAA friend who was evacuated from Jordan during the 1967 War with Israel and reassigned to Vahdati to assist me. We became very close friends. He asked to go along with me on the hunting expedition I had planned. Three other USAF people were also going. The desert was waiting for us.

We would be going to Haft Toppeh, which meant Seven Hills. Long ago it was a religious site. The ancient city of Susa (modern day Shush) was nearby. Fr. Mulligan had told us once, when he was giving a talk, that this was where the three wise men came from. He was an archaeologist and loved the desert. I was told that Haft Toppeh was a place where people sacrificed to the gods. There are still remnants of the old buildings. Walking among the ruins was an exciting experience. The bricks that they used were very different. They were about fourteen inches square and about three inches thick. We passed by an old French castle on our way to the hunting area. I had stopped there to check it out one time. The thing I remember the most about it was a skeleton chained to a wall inside the prison.

Not too far away from Haft Toppeh was the tomb of Daniel. Daniel's tomb was a beautiful place. At night it was lit up very brightly and could be seen from a great distance. The walls appeared to be made of green marble. We were not allowed inside. Although Daniel was a Jew, the tomb was not taken care of by Jews. This was a Muslim site. The Muslims believed Daniel to be a prophet. Of course, there were always people there selling old coins. Some of the coins were very unusual, but they were always asking a lot of money for them. At that time I didn't have a lot of money. Daniel's tomb was, in essence, a marketplace. The whole practice was illegal. We didn't stay around there very long. Crowds began to gather when we stopped at places, and that becomes a pain after a while.

The 1967 Arab/Israeli war was fresh on our minds, and because the Americans were on the side of Israel, we were not too popular in places that had high Arab populations. There were Arabs in this location because it was close to Iraq.

On this night, while we were out hunting, we ran into a night patrol. They were not Iranians; this was an Iraqi patrol. We must have gone too far, or perhaps they had crossed the border into Iran. We were riding in an USAF weapons carrier. When we saw the patrol, we immediately hid the weapons carrier behind a huge sand dune.

We knew we were in trouble. Everyone ran to the edge of the sand dune and camouflaged themselves as well as they could in the little time we had. Each of us had about twenty bullets, but there were at least thirty soldiers in the Iraqi patrol. In the little light we had,

106

just the headlights from the trucks, we tried to pick out the ones with automatic weapons. If the shooting started, we had to make our shots count, and keep the incoming fire to a minimum. The trucks kept encircling, and we were sure they were looking for us. After about half an hour, they left. A big sigh of relief went up from our group. We had to be still for hours, until we were sure they were gone. Slowly, we started moving. First we had to figure out where we were.

That night, everything appeared to be calm and quiet. The sky was very clear and bright. As we were chugging along I noticed a very bright object moving in the sky. I couldn't tell what it was, or how high up it might be. I pointed this out to the rest of our group. The driver, Horace, stopped the weapons carrier so we could take a better look. It was a very unusual sight, but I have seen things like that before. It could have been anything. Suddenly, it stopped. Uh oh, what was this? There was no sound. It had stopped and was very bright. This was puzzling. We had no aircraft like that. It didn't move. Conversations began: "What the hell is it?" one man said. "I don't want to think about what it is," said another. Johnnie said, "It's a flying saucer." "Don't talk like that," another man responded. "What the hell do we do now?" someone said. "Is it watching us?" I asked. "Maybe we had better put our weapons down," Horace suggested.

So we did, and sat down beside the weapons carrier.

The "Thing," stayed above us for about two hours. As it was hovering above us, we were talking about this strange thing. The USAF people said that if we told anyone what we'd seen, we would be taken in and questioned, and it would go on our record. At that time it would be considered some kind of mental disorder. Finally, everyone agreed not to say anything about it to anyone, for the sake of the USAF people.

The UFO began to move again. It streaked across the sky and was gone. What a relief! What was it? We had lots of questions, but no answers. If it was a UFO, we wondered, what was it doing all that time above us? Was it watching us? Needless to say, it was a great relief to see it go. It was very strange and eerie, sitting under that UFO. I can't explain the feeling; simply, we were experiencing the unknown for those two hours.

Hunting was over now. We had exceeded the limit on our hunting time. Besides, nobody wanted to hunt after that experience. We did talk about it afterwards, when nobody else was around. I thought it was all over until September of 1976. The UFO sightings at Shahroki Imperial Iranian AFB and at Teheran made headlines around the world. People from the Pentagon were in Teheran the very next day. You could see it on television today. That's another story. It did make our experience much more believable. To this day, I can still recall everything about that experience, as clearly as I did the night that it happened.

In September 1976 I arrived at Shahroki AFB, located near the ancient city of Hamadan. Something was different, this day. As I arrived at the USAF Team House, I was suddenly hit by the realization that there were a great many Iranian pilots around. The tension seemed to be high, as if everyone was on alert. I exchanged greetings with some men and asked what was going on. Then it began:

The evening before, an unidentified saucer-shaped "aircraft" showed up on the air defense radar over Iraq. Its speed was clocked at 4,000 miles per hour. The strange "aircraft" was heading for Iran. Almost immediately, interceptors were scrambled. The object slowed down once it arrived over Iranian airspace. The first formation of pilots attacked the object. These pilots, who were part of the intercept, were sitting at the table with me. They assured me this was exactly what happened, for they saw it.

The first group flew in. Suddenly, their aircraft lost all power. They began to go down. On the way down, they abruptly regained power. The second fighter formation attacked the target. They were able to fire a missile. The missile hit the target but did no damage. What happened next is eerie. The saucer then fired

109

what appeared to be a "crescent" at them. The crescent went through the formation and returned to the saucer. The saucer then took off very fast. That was the end, except that it flew over Teheran near Mehrabad International Airport, where it was seen by many thousands of people.

As I mentioned, top brass from the Pentagon were there the next day. There were reports of the incident in Sunday newspapers back in the United States. I also saw it on television, but it was not at all the same as what I just described. It made me feel a lot better about my experience with the UFO in Haft Toppeh. To this day I have no idea what it was. The incident at Shahroki validated what I experienced on our hunting expedition years earlier, so I feel more at liberty to talk about it.

* * *

I worked on projects in almost every part of Iran. I often flew from one base to another in a C-130 cargo plane. Over the years, I saw a number of C-130 crashes -- not surprising, since I spent innumerable hours, and covered at least 1.5 million miles in these planes. All of the crashes were caused by errors. One was caused by loading too much weight in the rear of the airplane. Another was caused by the pilot experiencing vertigo and another by pilot error during training. It is, in fact, a very safe plane. Their pilots were all from the Imperial Iranian Air Force.

On one occasion, while I was aboard a C-130, it began diving from 30,000 feet. At the time, I was with my boss, Fred Hemp. The aircraft suddenly went into a steep dive. Fred was smiling and talking to me as it was happening. A crew member was struggling to climb to the back of the aircraft, holding a parachute in one hand. Fred said "We have no problems, see? He's going for help." Everyone else on board was terrified. The pilot recovered the aircraft at about 10,000 feet. Something did happen, but no one said what it was.

One time we hit a very large bird which flew into the airplane. It was a Kunge, and they are about five feet tall. Still, nothing happened to us. I observed many landings. A few times I witnessed a C-130 fly through large flocks of small birds. The props just cut the birds to pieces.

It is a very safe airplane but very noisy inside, and uncomfortable. After all, the C-130 was a cargo plane. It had four large propellers driven by turbo jet engines. Its main use was transporting cargo and people.

* * *

I also spent a lot of air-time in the C-47, a World War II aircraft. The USAF used them

111

in Iran to transport people and supplies to Americans stationed throughout the country. You could still find coal dust in the cargo connections, from the Berlin Airlift in 1948. I was constantly reminded of its age.

Going from the desert to the mountains was not a pleasant experience, especially in the hot weather. Turbulence was very severe in that setting. You had to be strapped in or else you would be bouncing around the inside of the plane. One of our C-47's was in this turbulent situation while flying from Mashad to Teheran. One of the wings broke off and everyone aboard was killed. I lost a good friend that day. The reason for the crash was the age of the aircraft. Metal fatigue occurs when aircrafts age and also from stress on the plane.

* * *

Precision Approach RADAR's (PAR) were needed to bring an aircraft down to the runway in the 1970's. If a plane can't land, you don't have an all-weather air force. If it can't land, it crashes. This had happened many times, before the PAR was installed. Three fighters crashed into the snow, one right after another. When an aircraft takes off, he must be able to land on that runway. As an aircraft is landing, he is in contact with the PAR operator. The operator tells the pilot if he is left or right of path, and below or above path. The pilot then takes corrective action and the operator tells him when he is on path. This will bring the pilot down to the point where he lands, or has to break off the approach. A safe landing is the end result we are looking for.

One of my jobs was to survey the runway and transfer that data into a photo map that is seen on the operator's screen. Making the map is a very tedious job that requires extreme accuracy. Everything must be exactly perfect before the drawing goes onto a photo sensitive glass plate. After the glass map is completed and installed, we check out the map and see if the optical angle from the runway is what appears on the map. To do this, I was on the runway at the touchdown point and we had a three way conversation: the pilot, the operator and me.

When the operator says "on path," I must see that it is, in fact, true with the cross hairs in my transit. I used a helicopter for this. We could tell him to go up or down, left or right and verify that everything is the same. It's usually a fun part of my job. This particular time, it was not fun. The Control Tower and the Instrument Flight Rules (IFR) room are not the same. The IFR room is where the PAR is actually located

On this day, the Control Tower was monitoring four F-4's, which were approaching the point where I was set up with my transit. F-4s are pretty big airplanes. They are fighter jets. They were coming from the hangers and would take off. This had happened before. A runway has two ends. Each end has a number designated to it. If the aircraft is approaching runway 27, he is heading in the direction of 270 degrees. The opposite end of the runway is 9 and that would be 90 degrees. It was my assumption that the aircraft would travel down the runway away from me and then take off. The Control Tower knew that the PAR was being checked on that day.

Unfortunately, on this day, things did not go as planned. All four of the aircraft turned before they got to where I was, formed a straight line and kicked on their afterburners. Now there were eight jet engines with afterburners on, taking off very close to me. That was a huge noise; it was literally a controlled explosion. The noise was so loud; it was like being in the middle of the explosion. I was knocked over by the blast. My body started to vibrate. It began to get very painful. As I lay on the runway, I was in agony. I could feel myself beginning to go into a state of unconsciousness. Then, the planes were gone. I could taste blood and my ears were ringing. I could not hear anything. Vehicles began to approach me but I could not hear them. IIAF people came to pick me up, to try to help me. They took me away.

It didn't take very long to recover, but the ringing in my ears wouldn't go away and it took a while for my hearing to come back. The next day I was back at work, but the runway coordination was better. Everything we had accomplished the day before had to be done over again. Many days in Iran had their dangerous moments. You might say that it came along with the job.

*　　*　　*

Most of the equipment I installed on Iranian Air Bases was donated from the U.S. military. The U.S. government gave Iran old vacuum tube equipment. Equipment was changing all the time, so it was good public relations to give away outdated stuff. The equipment was free but the Iranians had to pay for everything it took to install it on their air bases. Equipment needed remote monitoring, generators in case power went out, cables, radios, a whole system. In addition, the Iranian government had to pay the US about $100,000 for each American expert sent over to install the equipment. They had to pay as well for spare parts, upgrading equipment, and so on.

In the 70s when I was working with the Shah, technology exploded. The Iranians had been using F86s in the 60s. These were Korean War fighter planes, really old junk. Then they bought F5s. There were two kinds of F5s, a training plane and a fighter. Next, the Shah bought the F4s. This was a huge plane, heavy, with 2 big jet engines on the back. Most impressive were the F14s, flown out of Esfahan. This was a complex fighter used on aircraft carriers. It flew high and incredibly fast.

The Shah sent Iranian pilots over to the U.S. to train to use these modern planes. Once they were in the United States, Iranian pilots experienced freedom. I knew what that was like. I'd spent most of my time in Iran with the military, whether I was working for the FAA or the IIAF. Iranians knew they were not free. Their private and public lives were strictly controlled by the mullahs. Life in the Iranian military was even more constrained. The pilots were under contract and had to return to Iran. Some married American girls. When they returned to Iran, those who had married Americans went to jail for a few years. After that, they were allowed to go to the United States, to be with their spouses.

Chapter 6

The Desert at Dezful

Aqueduct (Qanats) near a deserted village

Central Iran

The desert in Iran was fascinating. There was so much to explore. I had my own jeep and could go wherever I wanted. It was identified with US military vehicle tags and that attracted attention but the *Jandarmeri* treated me with great respect. The *Jandarmeri* was a type of military police unit that was all over the country. They wore uniforms that were like that of the Army and they carried infantry weapons.

In a very short time, the Base became a boring place. It was a routine that never ended. Actually, it was two worlds. One life was with the U.S. Air Force and the other was with the Iranians. To the USAF personnel at Vahdati, this was just a one year tour, but I didn't know how long I would be here. I was so eager to learn about this strange new life.

Dezful was the biggest city near the base and it was very old. It was called the "City of the Blind," because there were many blind people in that city. The place was living evidence of how people lived thousands of years ago. In the Bazaar, I watched as the people did things just as they had for eons. It was fascinating. They hammered out many different types of wares. With their primitive wood lathes, they were able to make all kinds of things. Here I was in the 1960's, watching cars go by, and in the shops it wasn't 1967. Nobody spoke English but they were attracted to me because I was strange to them. I tried to speak Farsi and they liked that. As I became more proficient with the language, it was a lot more fun.

Here are some of the everyday things that happened: while walking in the center of the city, people would come up to me in pursuit of money for a service. A holy man approached me. An Iranian friend was with me. The holy man asked if I wanted him to pray for me. I asked my Iranian friend, what he wanted. He told me that for a hundred *rials* he would say prayers for me. I told him to tell the holy man that it would take a lot more than that to do me some good. I said that I would give him two hundred *rials*. That made the holy man very happy. He had a charcoal fire with him and he added incense to it. The smell was very pleasant. Then, he started singing. People drew near to watch this. I must say that he did a good job for the fee. It was very nice.

As we walked on, another man approached us. This one was different. His name was Reza Kaftarbaz (meaning, the man who played with pigeons). Reza, as I was told by my friend, was a pimp (*kosskish*) and he wanted to take us to his place; that made him a *jahkish* also. A *jahkish* uses his house for prostitution. "I have some young ladies of the night there," he explained.

Reza explained to us just how nice these ladies were and because of this the price was high, 300 *rials*. Once again, people started gathering around. This time, they were laughing in a very polite way. They must have known Reza and what he was. They were being entertained. I thanked Reza but I had my friend tell him that we didn't have time to go with him right now. He kept following us and tried to dissuade us from leaving, but to no avail. The crowd kept on laughing.

One day while I was in Dezful, I got the surprise of my life. While riding in my jeep through the town, I saw an American walking on the street and he saw me at the same time. He waved at me so I stopped. After a greeting, we told each other who we were and what we did. He was a U.N. doctor who was working at Dezful at that time. He was a very interesting person, so I invited him to join me and some of the other Americans at the Team house for dinner and a movie. It thrilled him and he accepted the invitation. We just kept on talking all the way to the Base. When we got there, I introduced him to the officer in charge and all the men that were there at that time. He was sort of a celebrity to us.

We had dinner and there was a lot of chit chatting with the doctor. At seven o'clock, the movie began. He sat beside me. During the course of the movie, he put his hand on my leg and began to squeeze. Uh oh! He was one of "the boys." I very graciously picked up his hand and placed it on his lap. I didn't want to hit a doctor. What a disappointment! After the movie, I took him back to Dezful and said good bye. I never saw him again.

As I was going back to the Base I thought, 'He must be having a good time here in Iran because most of the people are bisexual.' It was considered very manly to give it to another man in the butt. When I got back to the Team House, I went directly to the bar upstairs. While I was having a drink, I told the sergeant sitting beside me that our new acquaintance was one of "the boys." A big mistake! The rest of the sergeants gathered around and began razzing me: "Why did you bring one of the boys to the Team House?" they asked. "Did you have something in mind"? "You have a wife in Teheran. Can't you wait?" It went on and on. What a night!

The Dez River borders the city of Dezful. A young woman worked by the bridge that crosses the Dez River. It is a very old bridge. I'm talking two thousand years or more, at least that was what I was told. The young woman's father didn't want to defile his daughter, so he used a procedure that would circumvent the disgrace. He would perform a marriage ceremony before the person had sex with his daughter. The man had to pay first. After the sex was finished, he would then divorce them. An interesting situation! The Iranian people at the base liked the arrangement, but they would laugh when they talked about it. I found out later they called it *sigheh* or temporary marriage. Shiites accepted the practice; other Muslims did not.

There was also a place on a small hill just before you reached the bridge going to Dezful. It was called "The Caves." It was the place where most of the local prostitutes did business. A prostitute was called a *gendeh*. All the Americans were warned not to go to The Caves because of the exotic diseases distributed there. The diseases were given

121

away free, but the services were not. One of the renegade USAF people did not listen and went there for a visit. He got himself something really bad. He didn't get rid of it.

In the cities and towns there were always children around who were begging for money. When I gave them some money, we were mobbed with other kids. All of the larger towns had their beggars. In the villages, it was different. No villagers ever approached me for money. The head of the village forbade it. They were very proud people even though they were very poor. They wanted to share their things with me.

One incident comes to mind. Some villagers were serving me breakfast while I was sitting on a large stone. They always asked if I wanted more. When I finished eating, I got up to walk away. A young boy came over to the place where I had been sitting. He began to pick up crumbs and eat them. When I saw that, I felt terrible. I would have gladly shared the food with him. The village chief also saw what was happening. He yelled at the boy and hit him and then came over to me to apologize. What can you say? I tried to apologize but he wouldn't let me. The boy had just shamed the village in their minds

Outside of the city, things were primitive and wild. A man riding on a donkey passed us by. The donkey was pulling a wooden plow. There were sheep and goats in the distance, feeding. The giant Kunge birds, about five feet tall, were all over the desert. At times, I saw as many as ten thousand birds or more. My friend told me that these birds were very good to eat.

I decided to take one home with me. I really didn't know just how big the birds were at that time so I adjusted the telescope for two hundred yards and got one in the cross hairs. The bullet never got close to the bird and when I fired, thousands of birds, that I thought were herds of sheep, took to flight and covered the sky. What a sight that was! The jeep speedometer registered three tenths of a mile from the spot from which I took the shot to the spot where the bird was standing. Later on, I learned that the drumsticks of the bird were eighteen inches long. There was an incident that took place near the base. One of those birds was hit by a C-130. It came right into the airplane. Fortunately, nobody was hurt and the plane was able to land.

We saw a stone doorway entrance standing alone out in the middle of nowhere. "What is that?" I asked my friend. He said that he didn't know. We walked up to the entrance. It went down into the earth and we could hear water down in the darkness. As we were looking down into the stairway, a man started walking up the steps. He turned out to be the one who took care of the "Qanats" as they were called. He told us that his job was to inspect the Qanats.

These Qanats are tunnels that bring water from the mountains to the desert. There are tens of thousands of piles of dirt that look like giant ant hills in the country of Iran. The "ant hills" are dirt from holes that are dug from the ground surface to the water below, to be able to gain access to any section of the tunnel. All of the holes are connected with an underground tunnel. While flying over the country you can see present day "ant hills" and remnants of those that were there thousands of years before. Those had collapsed or gone dry. By digging a series of holes, and connecting these holes, they use gravity so the water fills up each underground lake. The water eventually comes to the top and flows like a stream, providing villages with water. The people who care for these Qanats walk through them and repair whatever was necessary to keep the water flowing and clean. There are fish that live in the Qanats that have no eyes. It's always dark down there, so there is no need for eyes. There is no end to the wonders that the desert has waiting for you.

One day, I had a surprise. My neighbor, J., showed up at Vahdati. He was attached to the USAF Engineering branch. He wanted some entertainment, so we decided to take a ride on the desert on the outskirts of Dezful. It was not really a hunting trip. You might say that it was a sight-seeing tour. We took along an Iranian Warrant Officer I knew. Not to be

unprepared for surprises, I took along my rifle
and my 9MM. It was still light and the heat
had gone down quite a bit. All in all, it was
very comfortable.

As we were burning along, I saw what I
thought was a very big wild boar. We stopped
and put it in the cross hairs. It was huge. After
the first shot, it began to run. It ran for one
hundred yards and fell over dead. Now the
problem was how to get to it. It was on a flat
area, many feet below the place where we had
parked the jeep. After riding around, we
found access to a pathway that would let us
reach the downed boar. As we approached it,
I said "My God! I just shot a cow!" As we got
closer, I could see that it was in fact a boar.
Wow! I had never seen a boar so big. It must
have been over six hundred pounds. It was a
heart shot; the bullet had passed right through
its heart. The three of us could not move all
that dead weight so I took my K-bar knife and
began gutting it. The sight of all those guts
was awesome. Now we were able to drag the
carcass to the jeep. It took a lot of work but
we were able to get it on the hood of the jeep.
We were not prepared for this. Another
problem; I was not able to see the road from
the driver's seat so we had to take the top off
the jeep. Still another problem; I had to drive
standing up in order to see the road. That, I
could not do by myself. Someone had to
control the gas pedal, the shifting and the
clutch.

That was funny. It took a while to get to the Base, but we made it. When the guard at the gate of the Base saw it, he just started to talk. "It is so big," he said, amazed. We talked for a while and then headed for the Team House. By now, it was late. Nobody was awake. This operation had taken a lot of time and it was just beginning. The first step was to hang it to the second floor banister. We were able to do that with a lot of work and energy. Fortunately for me, my companions helped. I stretched out the boar to twelve feet. The nose touched the floor.

It took me the rest of the night to skin it, cut it up and clean up afterwards. We finished at four in the morning. Then I had to get rid of the skin, the head and the feet. It was very heavy. The head alone was awesome but I was able to take it to the desert outside the Base and dump it.

It was a very thrilling experience that I'll never forget. My regret was that I couldn't weigh it. It might have been a world record. Only the three of us saw it, besides the gate guard, before it was cut up. The rest of the USAF people saw the huge hams and were awestruck at the sight of them. Many of our friends enjoyed those hams at their big parties in Teheran.

The Arabs

By this time, I was very familiar with the desert and the towns around the base. People in Andemeshk knew me as Mike the American. I could go anywhere by myself and function rather normally. I became a very popular guy. Very few Iranians had any form of transportation. They would take a taxi. There were busses in the major cities like Teheran, but on the Base, there was no transportation at all for the Iranians. People often just hitchhiked, paying the driver some money. You would see an ordinary car crammed with people, squeezed on top of one another. They really packed them in.

The Iranians on the base loved to go to Bala Rudd (The name 'Bala Rudd,' just means 'up the road'). It was a truck stop, a place to eat and drink. They served beer there. It was a word that was used constantly at the base. Now why was that? It was a truck stop but that isn't all that it was. In the outposts of Iran, there wasn't a lot to do in one's spare time. It wasn't like the USAF Team House. We had entertainment there to occupy our time. The Iranians didn't. Beer was served at the train station in Andemeshk, but there were no real bars as we know them. In some of the big cities, there was entertainment of all kinds, Teheran being the best. There was a large International community there. But this was not Teheran. There was really nothing to do in their spare time. And the thing that was foremost on the mind of the young Iranian Airmen was women.

Some of the Airmen asked me to take them to Bala Rudd. I had promised I would, sometime. One evening, after dinner, I kept my promise. When we got there, we all ordered beer. They got up and started to talk to the waiter. Before I knew what was happening, they were taking the cook, who was a woman, by the arm. They asked me if they could borrow the jeep for a few minutes. I gave the keys to them and off they went with the woman.

Before they left, however, they talked to the other customers at the truck stop. I didn't have a clue what they told the people; they made some kind of announcement and everyone looked at me. I just smiled; I had no idea what was going on, and who was I to interfere? These people had a boring life and sometimes I had to work them very hard. Maybe they just wanted to have fun.

Something was very strange; everyone kept on staring at me, after the others left. When I smiled, it seemed to make things worse. No one left their tables; everything in the truck stop just came to a halt. My table was higher than the rest of the tables and almost isolated by distance. Everyone could see me. What was going on? I hadn't a clue. It seemed as though they were waiting for something to happen or were in a strict behavioral mode.

An hour passed. Nothing changed. Thirty minutes later, the men returned with the "cook." She was in fact the cook, but she was also a prostitute. The Airmen were all smiles and so was the cook. They said that it was time to go.

As I got up, I asked them why no one was moving and why the people had were giving me dirty looks. Then they told me. "We would have had to wait for a long time for the woman because she was the only woman there, so we told them that we were taking the woman and that the American had a gun and that he would shoot the first man who got up," they said.

I couldn't believe what I just heard. I felt like such an ass. I had been used. Everything that appeared to have been so strange became very clear. Of course I had to make myself known as to my feelings and I did it in a loud voice. Now everyone was looking at us and talking wildly. I knew it was time to get out of there in a hurry. We ran for the jeep and everyone piled in. When we got to the jeep I burned out of there. There were a lot of people running after us yelling. There were no favors for a long time after that.

I had befriended a civilian who had come to Vahdati. He was inspecting the Ammo Dumps. The assignment was not scheduled to last very long. His name was Jeremy. He was a very nice, peaceful person. His Farsi was very good. In our conversations, he had told me that he fought at Iwo Jima. He was a Marine. I liked Jeremy. He was a very interesting person.

One day, Jeremy asked me if I could take him to see the desert and possibly to go on a wild boar hunting trip. It would only be the two of us. Most of the time on a boar hunt there would be three or more, which was an unwritten rule, but I decided to take him anyway. One rifle was not a lot of fire power, so for added insurance I took along my Browning 9mm Hi-Power pistol. It held thirteen bullets in the magazine and one in the chamber, and of course you always took along an extra magazine. It made me feel better to have more firepower since he didn't have a weapon. You couldn't trust the desert environment. There were just too many variables.

We gathered up the things that we would need besides guns, the most important of which were water and flashlights. Darkness had not set in yet when we began our jaunt. Heat was the order of the day and today was no exception but it wasn't bad, in fact it was very pleasant. Desert air feels so good if it isn't hot. By not too hot, I mean less than 110 degrees. One does get used to the heat and when you do, 80 degrees feels cold.

Usually, you don't see boar before it gets dark but that isn't always the case. We drove around the desert but tonight there were no wild boars to be seen. What we did see, after many miles of driving, was a camp. This wasn't the usual Bedouin camp. There were no horses or mules to be seen. About twelve men were gathered round a fire, talking quietly. I could see by their dress and their faces that they were Arabs. My friend wanted to stop and talk with them, but I said that it wasn't a good idea. I had a very uneasy feeling; something wasn't right. Jeremy was insistent, so we stopped by to talk to these men.

Their politeness was unbelievable. This is the usual behavior in Iran but I could see by their faces that they had no good intentions. My Browning was hidden underneath my shirt which was hanging over my waistline. What they did see was my .308 Winchester rifle that was slung over my right shoulder.

As we got closer, I noticed that they were all staring at the rifle. A thought burst into my mind: 'they want the rifle.' People in Iran couldn't have guns. They were allowed to own old-fashioned powder muskets, but a modern rifle or pistol was not permitted. A rifle like mine was worth a fortune and even more valuable if it was to be used for things other than hunting. Only very wealthy people had any modern firearms.

Jeremy was ecstatic. He walked among them, speaking Farsi to them, and smiling from ear to ear. They invited us to have tea with them. He said yes, but I begged off. Jeremy sat down with them. He had some kind of a shawl with him and he draped it over his shoulders. They all sat round the fire and chatted but they were always looking at me. I stood apart from the group and kept smiling at them. Their looks were not very nice. It was an artificial friendliness and I could sense it. The chattering kept going on and Jeremy was having a ball. I didn't see any real weapons but they could be hidden.

I thought of the time two years earlier when I was stationed in West Virginia. It was the winter of 1965. I was at an FAA facility in the mountains, and I was alone. There, I was attacked by about 25 wild dogs while making my way from the facility to my Jeep on snow shoes.

It happened after I had finished my work at the site. I had no other choice but to shoot the dogs. They were hungry, and I could not make it to the Jeep, nor to the building I had just come from, without the dogs catching up to me.

The first two shots missed. I was huffing and puffing as a result of running so hard with snow shoes on. Now I had just enough for each dog, with the two clips. What a scary feeling it was. I couldn't get away, and the gun was only thing that could save my life. At first I was sitting with the pistol between my knees in a sort of sitting position to steady my aim. They started to go down, but the rest kept on coming. Then I got the lead dog and the pack turned and ran away. Without their leader, they were nothing. The thought rang in my mind, 'If something happens, I must get the leader first.'

That's what I was thinking as I watched Jeremy speaking with the Arabs. Availability of bullets and the number of them that were quickly at your disposal can mean the difference between life and death. Then, before my eyes, something changed. The leader of the group started saying things to them that I could not understand but Jeremy could. They all got up and looked at me. I smiled at them. Then Jeremy got up and came running towards me. Now he was frightened. He got behind me and was almost crying. He was frightened. "They are going to kill us," he said. They were in a group coming towards us in an encircling movement. My smile didn't break. I'm sure that they sensed that something was not right. Then I pulled back my shirt and put my hand on the Browning. Now there was fear in their eyes. This was an automatic pistol, not a repeating rifle. It's true that a rifle is much more powerful than a pistol but reloading time is a serious factor and in a situation such as this one, many bullets is far more critical than a single shot.

My smile changed to a mean glare. People can sense fear. They had no idea what was going through my mind but to me it was an overwhelming thought. 'I must make every shot count. Get the leader first.' But the leader faded off to the side. I could still see him though, so I edged to the right to keep him in view.

"Pedar Sag," I spat out. I was looking directly at the leader, telling him his father was a dog, an insult of the highest degree in Iran. Maybe I subconsciously wanted him to do something out of anger and pride.

He had just been insulted in front of his men. Things were getting hot now and I didn't want to give them time to think. He had been insulted in front of the group but he didn't do anything. Now I thought, "Don't just spray a lot of slugs," because reloading another magazine would be out of the question unless I was very lucky. It just takes too much time when there is very little of it to spare". We are talking about fractions of a second.

I brought the Browning half way out and they all stopped. I told Jeremy to head for the jeep. Now I got the Browning out with the business end pointed and moving across them and I stopped at the leader. They were scared. The leader started to talk and was being apologetic but I wasn't listening. I was going to shoot him if I had to. It was such a strong urge. I was full of adrenalin and wanted to fight. I backed towards the jeep. Jeremy was already there and in the seat. Now, I didn't want to leave. I had control of the situation and wanted to do something. Jeremy was yelling for me to get into the jeep. 'I must leave,' I thought.

As I stepped into the jeep, I switched the Browning to my left hand. I started the jeep with my right hand and off we went. 'What a stupid move that was,' I thought, and said it to Jeremy. He was so happy. What could easily have been a tragedy turned out just fine. As we sped for home, wild boars were the last thing I thought about. I kept telling Jeremy what a dumb move that was and of course, he kept agreeing. He was laughing; he was so relieved.

That experience was burned into my mind and had a strong influence on my behavior and movements from then on but the thought echoed through my mind, "Why did I try to anger the leader?" I shouldn't have done that. I wanted to shoot him. Why did I ever even stop there? People do dumb things and I did my dumb thing for that day but I felt good that we got out of there all right. That gun served me well until it was stolen and I replaced it with a .357 Magnum.

Chapter 7
Stories From The Desert

Bactrian camels, Iranian desert, 1972

There are many dangers in the desert: heat, poison water, quicksand, camel spiders, scorpions, a variety of snakes and poisonous things that crawl around, like hellgrammites. There are comical sights like walking frogs. And there is incredible beauty.

The heat is the most dangerous. You can become dehydrated in an hour if it is really hot. Just riding in an open jeep is terrible. The temperature does reach 135 degrees

137

Fahrenheit and it can go higher. That is the temperature in the shade. When you are in the sun, the ground is much hotter. It gets to 170 degrees (F), more or less, on a hard surface. If you touch an object like a car in direct sunlight, you will burn yourself. You have to have water to drink and to pour on a towel. While riding in a jeep that has open sides, one must cover his face and chest with the towel. If you don't have a towel, you must take off your tee shirt and soak it or dump the water over you. It actually gets you cold. Most people are used to sweating. You don't sweat there -- at least you don't appear to sweat. The evaporation rate is tremendous. It is essential to be aware of the heat and what it can do to you.

An incident happened to me far away from Vahdati. We had a small group of three. It was in the mountains in the desert. An Iranian captain, who was a close friend, was with us. We hired a guide who knew the area, so he said.

It was hot but not overwhelming. I'd say that it was one hundred and fifteen degrees. The guide assured us that there was a water hole on the way to our destination. Dumb as we were, we believed him. As it turned out, he was in it for the money and really didn't know enough to care about us. What he didn't think about was, 'What happened to them would also happen to me.'

When we got to that point where the water was supposed to have been, there was no water hole. I was furious. He was a liar and I actually wanted to kill him. The Captain begged me not to do it. The guide sensed my anger and hid behind the Captain. "Why not, he just killed us all!" I said to him. "We have no water and we can't get to any. What can we do?" I added.

I told him to ask the guide if there was any other water close by. He asked him and the guide said no. We were almost at the top of the mountain and I had just shot a mountain goat a minute before the water incident. It was a far shot, about six hundred yards, and the rifle jammed after the first shot. The shell casing would not come out of the chamber but I was able to open the bolt.

The whole herd ran but the one that was shot just started walking up to the top of the mountain very slowly in a daze. If we got him, I thought, we could drink its blood. The Captain had a good rifle he but couldn't hit it. At six hundred yards, you had to estimate the height above the target to hit it. His scope was not calibrated like mine. I tried but it was not zeroed in for me, so I missed also. There was nothing that we had with us to get the spent shell from the rifle. My shotgun was with me today so I decided to open a shotgun shell with my knife and pour a little powder down the barrel. Then I found a very small, dry stem of a shrub. I then lit the stem and put it

139

down the barrel. I quickly laid the stock of the shotgun over it and put my weight on it. There was a small explosion but all that it did was blow the shotgun stock off the barrel. Now we had to get close to the sheep that was still walking slowly up the mountain so we could use the shotgun.

We went from one large boulder to another, seeking shade and following the goat. My tongue began swelling and the back lower half of my brain started hurting. I was dehydrated. The Captain had some canned Iranian rations in his pack. We opened them and shared the liquid from the canned fruit. There wasn't much but anything was better than nothing.

We met the goat at the very top of the mountain but almost at the same time, I saw water at the bottom of the other side. To hell with the goat, now we had a chance. I had learned from some Iranian people in Bandar Abbas how to get down a mountain fast. It was a technique that took coordination and strength. It was a controlled falling. It would be dangerous for me in my condition but I got a surge of adrenaline and was sure that I could do it. I started jumping, turning, twisting and going like hell down the mountain and got there very quickly.

Immediately, I ran to the water. It was a very small lake. This was a preview of paradise. I just drank and soaked my head in the water. My head was very hot. The others got there about a half hour after I did. They did the same thing that I did. It was an overwhelming experience. We were going to live.

It's so hard to explain the level of joy that I experienced. Death had just been cheated. The sun was still very hot so we stayed there until the sun went down. Then we headed for our home base. We were as full of water as one can be and very cool. Elation is not a strong enough word to describe our state of mind. We all were very close to death a short time before, but we managed to survive. Alive! Alive! Alive!

* * *

What is quicksand? It is created when running water flows through the sand. It could be at the bottom of the water or at the top depending on water depth. Along with that, it could be underneath a crust of sand. As the heat gets intense and prolonged, the top looks like ordinary desert sand, but underneath there is still running water, so if you break through, you begin to sink.

A German friend of mine had a strange motor cycle. It had a rotary engine. I think it was called a Wankel engine. During one of his exploits in the desert, he lost his cycle in quicksand. He was lucky that he wasn't lost with it, because he was riding on the motorcycle when it hit the quicksand. If he had been alone, he wouldn't have made it. We all felt so sorry for him.

D., my neighbor, liked to go with me into the desert outside of Teheran. Sometimes we would take motorcycles and sometimes it would be my Land Rover. On one trip, the quicksand got us. It was the type that had a thick crust over it. Fortunately for us, the tires broke through the crust but the crust was strong enough to support the body of the Land Rover. There was nothing that we could do at that time to save the car. We were far away from Teheran, but we had to get back that night. It looked like it was going to rain. The walking and running started. It was getting dark and we would have to walk all night.

What was the problem? If it did rain and if it was a heavy rain, the stream would rise and the top would become quicksand. If that happened, the Land Rover would sink. We would not be able to pull it out once it was submerged.

In the far distance, we could see light. It was a truck. We could hear its diesel engine. After waiting a couple of minutes, we were able to plot the direction which it was heading. Our only hope was to run in a direction that would intersect a road. There had to be a road, so we ran as fast and as long as we could. Luckily, we were able to find the road before the truck passed us. What was a truck doing out here? The driver saw us while we were trying to wave him down. He stopped and asked what we were doing out there. We told him and asked where he was going. He was going to Teheran. It was a mining truck. There was a mine of some kind out there.

After a long, slow ride, we got to south Teheran. It was very early in the morning and there was hardly any traffic. Teheran is a big city and it would take a long time to walk home and time was something that we didn't have. It was starting to rain. Fortunately, we were able to flag down a car and got him to take us home for a price.

Both of us were exhausted. We had to get some rest before we headed back to the desert. At five o'clock, a new day started. D. had an old jeep. He was able to find some plywood, a jack and shovels along with an assortment of other things. One of D.'s Iranian friends wanted to go along to help us. It was raining fast. Our only hope was the ground would soak up the rain before the heavy water flow began.

Teheran is a city built on a slant. South Teheran is low and north Teheran is high. The water from the city flows out into the desert into dry rivers that are actually underground. When it rains, they are above-ground rivers. That is what our problem was, beating the river before it rose high enough to trap the Land Rover.

143

We were able to find the jeep by finding its tracks. We knew the general area by memorizing the skyline the night before and noting direction. Immediately, the work began. One put down the plywood while the other two began harvesting "tumbleweeds." We had in a short time, gathered a small mountain of the stuff. The Land Rover had one wheel jacked up. The plywood made that possible. We then packed the tumbleweed into the hole that was made by the tire. The process went on and on until the tire, when let down from the jack, didn't sink down. After all four tires were finished, we put a piece of plywood in front of the rear wheels and another one in front of the front wheels. We were able to drive the vehicle across the plywood. Then we put sheets in front of those sheets that were already down. We kept doing this until we got out of that area.

As we drove along what we now knew was a river, we noticed water on top of the sand. What luck! We had made it in time. If it had taken an hour longer, we would have lost the Land Rover.

* * *

Dust storms are a hard thing to explain. Those who experienced them know what I'm talking about. Temperature and winds cause temperature changes which in turn bring about strong winds. These winds pick up dust and sand and crank them up to awful speeds. If you are unfortunate enough to be in the open when it happens, you can expect punishment.

It's hard to breathe because the dust gets in your lungs and you have to cough. Unfortunately, when you cough, more dust gets in your lungs and you've got to do something. Something must cover the nose and mouth to get cleaner air. This is essential. Any skin that is exposed will feel stinging from the sand in the wind. The best thing to do is to get to shelter but it's so difficult to see. If there is no shelter, lie down and wait out the storm. It's a little taste of hell. I know. It happened to me more than once.

One other thing happens that is a phenomenon. When it remains hot for a long time, dust rises in the air and blots out the sun. I saw this happen for two weeks. You actually cannot see the sun. It's just a bright area in the sky. No airplanes landed at the base for that period of time.

* * *

Poisoned water never bothered me. I kept my eyes open, and there were usually dead things around or near the water. Also I had been forewarned about the possibility of poisoned water and usually had my own water with me.

145

I did see a lot of it but it never caused me any trouble so I have no real bad experiences to write about. If I did, I probably wouldn't be writing now.

* * *

Then there were the Camel spiders, as they called them. They look like a tarantula only it was the color of a camel. I'm sure that's how it got its name. It was poisonous. I had seen them, but they do a good job of hiding. While we were working on the TACAN one day, one of the Airmen that worked with me was bitten by one and began to yell. I immediately tried to kill it so that it wouldn't be able to bite another Airman or get away. It fought like the devil. Even when it was pretty well broken up, it was still fighting. It was five inches long. You had to be very careful and be aware that those spiders were around. The Airman was taken to the hospital immediately. Fortunately, everything turned out all right.

* * *

Scorpions were commonplace in Iran but you didn't see a lot of them except in Bushehr, a city located on the Persian Gulf. The desert met the sea almost abruptly. The sea had its

146

creatures. There were a lot of swordfish there, and plenty of sharks. While I was there, a soldier was assigned to take me around to the various places that were strange to me. He didn't speak English at all, so my limited Farsi had to carry me through.

The soldier never stopped talking to me. One of the funniest things that I recall was when he tried to act as a translator. He had asked a native resident where we could find a good place to fish and what kind of fish were there. The soldier asked him a question and the man answered. I could hear what the man said but the soldier would tell me what the man said.

I kept thanking him and he was happy. This was not a normal situation. I was standing at the shore line and the soldier was standing on a sort of pier. Something wasn't right. There was a small stream flowing into the gulf where I was standing. I started sinking fast, going down into the water. It was quick sand. The soldier was looking at me and he just might as well have said "What are you doing?" That's what he was thinking.

Finally I said "Help me out of here!" He came running over to me and tried to pull me out. It just doesn't work that way. It's not that easy to get someone out of quicksand. It was like being pulled out of a large suction cup. After a lot of maneuvering I got out without my boots and got away from the quicksand. The boots would not come out then but I was able to recover them later by crawling like a

147

snake and working the boots out of the quicksand.

There was a large stone wall along the sea and on the seaside, it was a garbage dump. Rats were all over the place. There were thousands of them. It was like a big show. Cats were there, constantly catching the rats. It never ended. To the people there, it wasn't worth looking at. This was an ordinary event that went on day after day.

There was an American there at the place where I was staying. He had been there for some time on a different program than I. As we were talking at the outdoor eating area, there were very large snakes crawling around. It didn't bother him at all. He gave me some advice, "Put pieces of bread on the floor of your room, otherwise, the rats would crawl onto the bed at night". He was right. The rats were there, so I followed his advice.

On that first night in Bushehr, I walked out of my room and I couldn't believe what I saw. There must have been ten thousand scorpions, like a moving carpet, walking on the paved walking area. My first reaction was "What the hell is this?" I was told not to be afraid, just walk over them. This I did. Crunch, crunch, crunch! What is the first thought that would go through your mind? That's right: 'what happens if I fall?'

Don't fall! And walk with your feet going as straight down as possible, otherwise, you

148

could kick one up on yourself. I know I killed
hundreds and hundreds of them, just walking.
It's something that you just don't get used to.
I'd call it a cheap thrill. I've never forgot that.

* * *

I was never told that there were giant snakes
in Iran but then again, I wasn't told about the
lions either. One night, I was coming home
from Ahwaz. It was already dark and I was
speeding along in my jeep when something
really got my attention. A snake was crossing
the road right in front of me. It stretched
across the entire road. It had to be twenty feet
long. Can you imagine the feelings that fly
through your mind all at once? You're driving
and then all of a sudden, a shocking thing
makes its appearance. A giant snake! I
slammed on the brakes. Too late! The snake
got caught under the wheels.

There was a big bump as the tires went over
it. The head part and the tail wrapped around
the jeep in a bang. The jeep was a canvas
covered type so the noise could be felt as well
as heard. Why the canvas didn't break, I don't
know. I got it with both the front and back
wheels locked. My first thought was that I had
killed it. When the jeep stopped, I turned
around to get a closer look at this monster. It
wasn't there. The snake must have been hurt

149

but not enough to stop it. I jumped out of the jeep to get a better look. The marks of the tires and traces of the snake were there on the road. There was a constant noise. It was still there but I couldn't see it.

My .357 was in my hand, not to shoot the snake, but to be ready in case something happened. The desert is full of things at night. I got in the jeep again and edged into the desert slowly. It was there and I caught a short glimpse of it. It was erratic. Its prime motive was to get away and it did. It was all so eerie and exciting but I was getting too far into the desert. It was time to break it off. The time had come to leave. Things might become too dangerous and there was nobody with me to help. All was not lost. It was a once in a lifetime experience and I loved it. There are many night creatures in the desert and I thought that the snake must be one of them. It would be too hot for something so big to be able to stand the heat.

Walking Frogs

At Vahdati AFB, I saw a strange creature. Every once in a while, I would see something run across the road in front of me that wasn't identifiable because it didn't have a familiar form. When I saw it or them, whatever the case was at a particular time, I couldn't determine what this creature might be. When I remembered, I would ask someone what it was that I saw. No answer. Maybe they thought I was seeing things.

It became apparent that they did not know very much about this desert. This went on and on until one day a large group of these creatures ran across the road in front of me. I was close, so I stopped the jeep and ran to see what these things were. Lo and behold, it was a group of large frogs. They weren't hopping, they were running or walking. Never, have I ever seen a frog run. They hop.

Thinking about it, the road would be too hot for a frog to have its belly on the hot road. In the summer, the temperature of a road could reach as high as one hundred and seventy degrees Fahrenheit. That would cook a frog. My curiosity got the best of me, so I followed them. The frogs went to a small pool of water and jumped in. There were frogs around the pool and they were hopping. The riddle was solved. The frogs walked, ran and hopped. Now I was happy, but nobody believed me. They had to see it for themselves.

Hellgrammites

At the Chemist's, what we would call a pharmacy, there was a display of poisonous creatures, each preserved in its own liquid-filled bottle. There was a practical reason for this display; if a person was bitten by one of these creatures, the person could point it out and get the correct antidote. I never paid too close attention to the bottles. At this point in time, I was living in a big house in the city of Andemeshk which was shared by a man from Philco Ford. This was in 1967. Life was good then. I was able to bring my family to visit for a while. It was a very clean house and was kept clean by our "*badji*" which is their name for maid.

One night while I was asleep, something awoke me. In fact, there was something crawling over me. I waited until it had crawled over me and then I jumped out of bed and turned on the light. There it was, a Hellgrammite, about six inches long and about an inch wide. A Hellgrammite is a crawling millipede that is usually seen in water. It has pinchers on its head. These were big pinchers. I wanted to show this creature to everyone, so I got a dust pan to pick it up and found a string to tie around it. Then I went into the bar area, found a tall glass and filled it with Scotch. After it was filled, I put the Hellgrammite in the glass. It did not like the Scotch but now I had it to show to everyone. The next day, I went to the Chemist's to look at the bottles. Sure enough, it was there and labeled poisonous. There were a lot of other things out there in the desert. It would take years to discover just a few of the creatures.

Chapter 8: Shiraz

Entrance to the ancient city of

Persepolis, Iran

Along with my assignment at Vahdati in April 1967 I was also assigned to the airbase at Shiraz. Two months later, in July 1967, after things were set up at Vahdati, I boarded a plane for Shiraz. The plan was to install both TACAN facilities simultaneously.

To my surprise, the people who greeted me at the tarmac were an IIAF major and his wife. They had a brand new Volkswagen and they invited me to join them. He spoke very good English; his wife spoke none at all. She was a very beautiful woman with classic features like the women in ancient Persian paintings. Omar Khayyam came to mind. The Major insisted on taking me on a tour of Shiraz. My answer was an excited "Yes!" I had heard a lot about Shiraz.

What a beautiful place! The City of Roses; that's what they called it. Roses, beautiful roses, graced the divider on the road from the airport to the city itself. Once seen, you will never forget it.

Not far from the city was the ancient capital of Persia. Its name is Persepolis. It was constructed over twenty five hundred years ago. The ruins were a very alluring place. Very near was the tomb of Cyrus the Great. Right at the ruins, there were two huge tombs carved into the mountain side. You could still see the marks of the chisels that they used to hew into the solid rock. There were two large tombs inside the "cave." Of course, they were empty. The chiseled marks were very thin. The manpower that it took to do that work must have been amazing.

I visited the Persepolis area at every possible opportunity. I remember looking at the names of British soldiers from the eighteen hundreds with messages that were scratched into the structures there. That was the only English writing to be found in Persepolis.

Shiraz itself became my favorite city. The Major took me here and there to try to show me everything. We saw the tomb of Hafez with its elegant pillars and a monument with perpetual fire roaring from the top.

What was puzzling to me was the behavior of the Major's wife. She would turn around to look at me, smile, and then she would stick her tongue out at me while I was sitting in the back seat of the car. Since I didn't know what it meant, I just smiled back at her. She kept doing that all day long.

It was important that I check in at the U.S. Army Team House. They had a room reserved for me and I didn't want to lose it. When I told the Major that I must go to the Team House, he answered "Of course". It was getting late and I was tired. We had spent almost all of the day on a C-130, followed by some sight-seeing. To my surprise, he told me to check in quickly and then we could go to his house. As much as I wanted to say no, I couldn't, so after I checked in we left for his house.

After we arrived, we had tidbits of food. There was American music in the background. As soon as the tidbits were eaten, I was invited into the parlor. They served me Scotch. 'How can he afford to buy Scotch?' I wondered. On the open market, it cost thirty dollars a bottle. Americans with official military status, like me, could buy Scotch for three dollars at the Embassy store, but this was a major in the Imperial Iranian Air Force (IIAF). He didn't have those privileges. Then he asked me if I would like to dance with his wife.

Now that hit me like a ton of bricks. The Embassy indoctrinated us on dos and don'ts. That was a taboo. 'Don't look at a man's wife,' was the rule of the culture. I quickly answered, "Thank you, but no. She is your wife." His reply was, "Don't you think my wife is beautiful?" Now I didn't know what to say. Was this some kind of test? I hesitated then answered, "Please don't be offended! You have a beautiful wife but she is your wife. You should dance with her."

He smiled and began dancing with her. Then he broke off the dancing and said "Now you can dance with her." I didn't know what to do. She came over, grabbed me and began dancing. 'What the hell is going on?' I thought. She was trying to crush me with her body, French-kissing me with abandon– and the Major just smiled. 'Oh shit! I'm in trouble now,' I thought. This is just too much. Iran was new to me. I had only been there for a month and a half. If I did something wrong, I'd be out of the country in a flash. After the song was finished, I got another drink and told the Major that I was very tired and I had a lot to do the next day. I needed to get some sleep. "Please take me to the Team House," I asked. Reluctantly he complied.

Next morning, a driver came to take me to the base. All the people with whom I was to work politely introduced themselves. The

156

equipment was very old; I had never seen some of it before. After a few days, we had a plan. I had to assess the needs at Shiraz and get things moving there, but the staff at Vahdati was always waiting for me to guide them and keep their projects on course too, so I had to balance both efforts -- and I had to get back soon. Things would grind to a halt there, if I was away too long.

After a week's work, in Shiraz, I left again. I planned to spend the weekend in Teheran with my family, then go on to Vahdati. By now, the never -ending C-130 flights were routine. Teheran was my home and I loved being with my wife and family, but we had so little time together. My life was in the "boondocks" as it was referred to in the military. In May, we heard President Nasser was massing troops along Israel's Syrian border. Then he signed some kind of agreement with Iraq. It was June 1967. Little did I know that it would be a long time before I returned to Shiraz.

The June 1967 war between Israel and the Arabs changed everything for me. A team of FAA people had been working in Jordan. When the '67 War began, they were pulled out and transferred to Iran. Two of them were stationed in Shiraz, to work under me. Getting the electronic equipment working was part of my job. These two men would install the electronic equipment and look after the generator and physical things in general. They continued where I left off, until they couldn't go any further.

On one of my escapades, I was assigned a C-130 to check out false replies and unlocks on all the TACANs in the country. This was exciting. Now I could do what I really loved. The first thing that I did was to set up my various pieces of test equipment in the C-130 and then we were off. It took a week of flying to get the pattern of areas that gave false replies. There was a definite pattern. It seems that all of the TACANs gave a seven mile false reply along with the real reply on an approach. If there was a distance unlock, the receiver would go into search and lock on to the false reply and the indication to the pilot would be a seven mile error. If the weather was good, he would see the error but if the weather was not good, he might well lock on the wrong pulse and get the seven mile error. That would be very dangerous. My notebook soon was filled in with all the details and I even drew pictures. It was fun.

When I got back to Vahdati, I duplicated everything that I could with my ground equipment and came up with a solution that worked on every system. I came up with a modification which made each system work with one hundred percent efficiency. It made me feel so good.

I got to know the crew very well and they would even let me fly the plane. That was fun. It was a four engine, propeller plane that used turbo jet engines. When people wanted to hop a ride, the pilot would say "Ask Mr. Roman. He is in charge of the plane." I couldn't refuse them, so we always had company. The people were fascinated with what I was doing and would come to stand by me and watch. What a beautiful assignment! At week's end, we landed in Shiraz and I scooted off to my hotel.

Now, I had come in on my usual C-130. The plane's ID number was #105. While I was in the hotel, a pilot who had flunked out of fighter training school was training as a C-130 pilot. My plane was available, so they had him take the C-130 up, to practice maneuvers. Unfortunately, while coming in on a training landing, the pilot trainee banked to the right instead of the left. The trainer had cut out the engines on the left hand side during this landing, to make sure the pilot could recover the airplane. The trainer assumed the trainee knew he was to bank to the left. But the trainee banked to the right; that was his mistake. The plane was too close to the ground to recover, so it crashed.

I was outside the hotel and saw black smoke pouring skyward. It was at the Base. Immediately, I jumped in the jeep that was assigned to me and sped to the airport. A C-130 had crashed and had killed everyone aboard. As I looked on, I noticed the number on the tail: 105. That was my airplane, the same plane I'd been in all week. Tears began flowing. All my new friends were dead. There was hardly anything left of the airplane except the tail section and it was still burning.

Shortly thereafter, I was notified that someone was trying to get hold of me on the radio. It was my next-door neighbor, the LC (Lieutenant Colonel). It had been reported that I was killed in the crash. My wife was being notified of my death. It wasn't easy to make a telephone call in Iran, but I had to do it. I immediately headed for the telephone center to call 'Cretia to tell her that I was not dead. When I got there I was dismayed; the place was packed. I would have to wait for hours. I couldn't let 'Cretia think I was dead. What was I to do? The poor woman would have a breakdown, not to mention the kids. Thoughts raced through my head. I had an idea. There was a rich retired Iranian Colonel whom I knew. I ran over to his house, and asked him to help.

When he showed up at the phone center, my call got through immediately. 'Cretia answered the phone and I told her what had happened. I don't know what was going through her mind and I never brought it up again. Happiness and sadness came over me. 'Cretia knew that I was alive but I was also grieving for all the friends I had just lost.

For the first two years, I was based in Vahdati. I made frequent trips to Shiraz to take care of things there. This changed in late 1969. My permanent station was then changed to Shiraz. There, someone had started work on a specific kind of RADAR (radio direction and ranging) project, called a RAPCON (radio approach control). The project was not completed, but the buildings were already in place when I got there.

The first thing I did was to get myself in trouble. The IIAF was building a new fighter runway that was parallel to the existing runway. The original runway was used by both military and civilian aircraft. Right away, I saw a problem: the Precisian Approach RADAR (PAR) was not in the right place to serve both runways. As it was, it would only serve the existing runway.

The MAAG was visiting the base at that time and when they asked me if there were any problems, I told them about the mistaken location of the PAR. They were shocked and thanked me for what they said was considered critical information. The Commander of the base called me to his office and thanked me for aborting a large time delay and a loss of a lot of money. All of this made me feel good, at least for a while.

After a couple of days, I got a radio call from the boss. I had put the FAA behind on its schedule, so a Letter of Reprimand was put into my Personnel File. What a nice reward! The MAAG found out about it and had the letter removed.

Priorities are a must when moving to a new place. The retired Iranian Colonel that I spoke of earlier owned a nice building. The lower floor was a restaurant and the upper floor had some nice apartments. The Colonel was delighted to see me, and immediately gave me a room. Now I was living! I had a completely furnished, comfortable home away from home all for myself.

The Colonel and I became very good friends. He had an interesting life. He told me that when he was younger, his father owned forty-nine villages. His job was to ride to each village and ensure that things were being done properly. The interesting thing was that he had a wife in each village. Can you imagine, forty-nine wives? Those days were gone; that was when he was a much younger man. "What was that like?" I asked, burning with curiosity. "Just like Paradise," he replied sagely. He had just one wife now. The Colonel made life so pleasant for me in Shiraz.

The US Army Team House was the recreation spot for Americans working in Shiraz. You could watch movies and they had a very nice bar room. You always ran into other Americans, so there was a social life.

One night, a Greek Song and Dance group performed for us. A U.S. Army Colonel came down to the bar. We knew each other well. In fact, he was the Commander of the Unit in Shiraz. He said "Hi, Mike!" I responded with

162

"Good evening, sir." He had on nothing but an expensive oriental silk bath robe. The front was wide open; everyone could see he was stark naked underneath. He got a bottle of Scotch and left. Nobody said a word.

During my stay in Shiraz, I made some very good friends at the Team House. I never forgot them. They were all separated from their families for over a year. Lonesomeness breeds very close companions. Most of them were into Armor, like tanks; some were Special Forces. Getting away from the work was necessary. Some days were so busy I didn't stop to eat. I'd plan what I had to do tomorrow.

When I could get away, I enjoyed hunting wild boar, and there were plenty of opportunities. On one particular trip, I and a friend named Clyde were in the mountains near Shiraz. It was winter and snow covered the mountains. No hunting rounds were available to me, so I had to use NATO .762 full metal jacket bullets. These rounds went right through an animal. There was a little hole where the round went in and a little hole where the round came out.

The shot had to be well placed or the animal would get away. My rifle was loaded with these bullets. My friend went to one location near the bottom of the mountain and I went to another near the top.

As I was lying in the snow on a peak, I detected movement below. I couldn't see what it was, so I kept still and watched the animal come into view. It was an enormous, snow-white boar. When it came within two hundred yards, I zeroed in and fired. The boar just turned to look around. This I couldn't believe. How could I miss? Very quietly I reloaded and carefully aimed for the heart. This time, it jumped and ran into the bushes. There was a lot of movement and noise. The bushes moved for about two minutes and then the boar rolled out into the open. The snow was red with blood. It kept rolling around so I lit up a cigarette and waited. When the movement stopped, I went down to see the boar. The bullets had actually hit two inches apart. It was a big one, and too big for me handle alone. This was a real problem. How could I get it down? I had no idea where Clyde was. I kept yelling for him, but no answer.

As I thought about it, I dressed out the boar and removed the head. I had an idea. It was a funny idea, but I had to try it. There was snow on the ground and lots of it, so I dragged the boar to a steep part of the slope, like a ski slope. Then I got onto the carcass and began to push off with my foot. I was moving faster and faster. Soon, I was flying along and holding on to the front legs and using my body weight to steer. It worked! Can you imagine riding a dead pig down a mountain? I actually did it.

When I finally stopped, there was my friend Clyde. He was laughing and laughing. It must have been a sight. Together, we managed to get the boar into a truck and headed for Shiraz. An unusually funny day! It did something for me. Clyde lived in Shiraz, so he kept most of the meat. The rest, I had to take to Teheran.

Very shortly, I was in contact with my wife in Teheran. As I related the happenings of the day, I mentioned that I would like to have the white boar's pelt made into a white carpet. Her reply was sort of shocking, "If you bring it home, I'll throw it into the garbage as soon as you leave." "Why?" I asked. "I'll not have the hide of a dead pig in my house," was her answer.

There really wasn't much of a choice. I dumped the skin alongside the road going to the airport. It was a very heavy skin. What a disappointment! I never saw a white Russian boar again. That was my first and last.

My assignment was such that I would now have to spend a full year in Shiraz. On most of the weekends, I was able to get home but it was costing me a lot of money. Most of the time I had to fly on Iran Air and it was expensive. It was getting to the point where we were falling behind on our bills.

My dear wife decided to visit me in Shiraz.
She brought along her friend, A., one of our
neighbors back in Teheran. Now that I had a
nice apartment in the city, there would be no
inconveniences with visits. The trip from the
airport to the city was a new world for them.
The roses along the road were an impressive
sight. There were literally miles of flowers.
They liked that. My apartment was on the top
floor of a building that had four stories. The
restaurant was on the ground floor. This was
the place that the retired Iranian Colonel
owned. He is the one that helped me at the
time of the C-130 crash. The fourth story
also had a flat roof that you could walk on to.
The view was magnificent. They could see the
city both at day and at night. There was a
perpetual flame monument that was near the
room and we could walk out on the roof at
any time. The flame in itself was a beautiful
sight. It was very close. You could smell the
burning gas which was tapped from the
ground. It was not the usual type apartment
setting.

 Everyone in Teheran was curious as to what I
did out in the field, including my wife. She
wanted a better idea what my work was all
about. The next morning, I took her and A. to
the Air Base to let them see for themselves.

At first, they were awed when they saw all the
scopes, as we called them, that the controllers
use to control air traffic. The room itself was
huge. There were lots of scopes and the

166

screens were very large and had a yellow, orange glow. They could see the RADAR sweeping around in a circle and the blips that were aircraft showed up very brightly. The Precision Approach RADAR (PAR) was very different from the Surveillance RADAR. One side of the scope showed a sweep that went up and down and the other side went from left to right. The Controller had to tell the pilot of the aircraft, which showed up as a blip on both lines, to go up or down or left or right. In doing that, the aircraft came right down to the runway even if the pilot couldn't see it.

Then I took them to see the different RADARS that produce those blips on the scopes. They had never seen that kind of thing before. The PAR was very impressive because both the vertical and horizontal antennas were inside the building and were bobbing up and down and left and right. Nobody knows the complexity of Air Traffic Control, so one never talks about it. You really can't explain it very well, unless the person that you were explaining it to could actually see the RADAR devices. Their question was, "How could you do all of these things?" At least, they understood that I installed all of these things, made them work and trained the people how to take care of the equipment.

The Control tower was also a visiting spot for them. They liked looking out over the airport from such a high place and listening to the pilots talking to the controllers. It gives a person a new perspective of flying. After a day of that, their minds were saturated. It was time to go to other places.

Persepolis was the first stop. Of course, that is a first-hand look at antiquity. Archeologists were there, doing their thing. 'Cretia and A. were amazed at how new some of the statues and carvings looked and also with the size of the city. The tombs were quite elaborate. We spent quite some time looking over the ruins. They were impressed with the names of the British soldiers that were carved into some of the walls. There were black marble statues of birds. They were actually heads of birds. One head was on the front and one head on the back. It was a two headed bird and was very shiny black. Many years later, we saw this same statue in the museum in London. I guess they took one back with them. After seeing Persepolis, the other places that I took them seemed minuscule but still very nice and interesting.

At the end of the sight- seeing, they wanted to go on a boar hunt. All that they knew about boar was the great meals we provided when it was our turn to host the "Wednesday Night Gang's" blow out parties back in Teheran. Wild boar is very delicious and everyone looked forward to eating it.

So, I got together everything that I needed and put it into the jeep. Security and safety for

168

them was my first concern, so I took along a rifle with two magazines and plenty of extra bullets. My shotgun was a must. I took that and many, many rounds of 00 buck shot. That's for people and large animals. Needless to say, my .357 was always with me. Now we were "loaded for bear." We got into the Jeep and sped off to the country side.

Outside the city of Shiraz was a vast, semi-arid desert. They were both impressed and probably a little scared. They knew that they were in a wild and dangerous place and had to put all their trust in me. My armament gave me a very confident feeling. If we needed the guns, I would not run out of ammo. They were in my care and I would not fail them. It was a whole new world for them.

Darkness set in and that made the desert seem more mysterious. The sky was very beautiful. Teheran is as polluted as Los Angeles so you can't see the real heavens in that city. But out there, in the country, the sky at night was breath-taking. So many stars were visible and they were very bright. A. and my wife were amazed. They were apprehensive, being in a dark place with strange noises but the beauty of the night made up for it.

The only light that we had was from the headlights of the Jeep. The boar came out. We spotted a group of them. I had brought with me some new bullets that were supposed to be very good at killing. After taking aim, I fired. One boar was hit but kept on running.

169

Once again I fired, then again and again. All were hits and the boar finally went down. That was the end of the boar. When we got to it, I was shocked. All the hits were good, but the bullets never opened. They went right through like Full Metal Jacketed bullets. It was a bad performance for the bullets, I thought. The women were shocked to see such a big animal lying on the ground, dying.

All in all, I think they enjoyed the new experience. I'm sure that they were puzzled as to how we found our way back home. I always used mountain silhouettes and the stars to guide me in the desert but I didn't tell them that.

The visit ended all too quickly and I was sad to see my wife go. I missed her as soon as I put them on the airplane. The visit was a time that I could never forget. I was able to share something very unique with Lucretia. Very few people experience this sort of thing.

Now, I had to get back to the routine of everyday life in Shiraz.

* * *

Clyde was a very close friend. He had served in the 101 Airborne in WW II and saw a lot of action. He was wounded at Bastogne by a German machine gun. It was winter and bitter cold. Then, while he was laid out with the other wounded soldiers in a church, German SS came in, screaming and yelling. They shot all of the wounded, including him, with sub machine guns. Somehow Clyde survived those experiences and woke up two weeks later in a London hospital. While he was recovering, he met a nurse and fell in love. But, fate was not on his side. She was later killed by a V 2 rocket. He had a lot of scars, and heartaches to prove his experiences. Clyde and I worked together on many projects. He was a man's man.

Today, Clyde was in a rare mood. We had been hunting the night before and we got some boar. We were on our first break from working on the ASR power equipment. As he sat down, he began talking to the IIAF people. Clyde wanted to have some fun. He told me that he was going to con them into telling him about their queer experience in the States. Normally, Iranians don't talk about these things, but when you get close to people, they tell you everything.

To understand this writing and its intent, one must go back to the mindset of that time. Homosexuality was hidden in the '60s and '70s. Homosexuals were referred to as queers, faggots, the boys and homos. There were many other words or referrals relating to that sort of behavior. It was classified as a psychiatric disorder. Some people would beat up queers and take their money because the homos would not go to the police. Times were different; nobody talked openly about homosexuals back then. People used to laugh at faggots and joke about them. They beat up homos in the States when I was growing up. The queers didn't report it to the police, because the police would beat them up too. Back then, the police even went on queer raids, in order to beat up a whole bunch of homosexuals at once. This was back in the late fifties and early sixties. Everything was very different back then.

Iranians who were assigned to work with us had all gone to the U.S. Air Force Base in Biloxi, Mississippi for training. This was the USAF training school for electronics. The men would land at a Commercial Airport and then be transported to the Base. "The boys" would meet the Iranian airmen at the airport and offer rides to them and many other favors, to induce them to become friends with them. That led to many things. In actuality, it was a seduction. The gays knew the weaknesses of the Iranian men and used it to their advantage. The Iranian airmen just thought that most Americans were gays because these guys were always after them and giving things to them that they wanted and needed. Of course the gays expected payback which was always sexual in nature. These stories the airmen told to us, below, were in fact payback.

Clyde told the Iranians, "Last night, Mike and I went hunting for wild pigs." One of the guys inquired how many we got.

"I can't remember," Clyde replied, his eyes twinkling.

"How can you forget that?" they asked, curious.

"Well, after I shot the first one, I got really excited. I threw my rifle in the air and ran to the pig and screwed it." he said.

"What! You screwed the pig! How could you do that?" they shouted. He was playing with them and they believed him.

"There's nothing better than 'pig pussy,' why it's the best thing in the world," he answered back. I sat there, just shaking my head.

"You do that!" one of them yelled in a very loud voice.

"If you knew how good it is, you would do it too," said he.

Now they didn't know what to say. "Did you find your rifle after you threw it in the air?" one of them asked".

He answered back "What the hell do I care about a rifle, after having that great sex? No, I didn't find the rifle, but it was worth it," he answered back.

"Can you tell us where you were hunting?" one of them asked.

"I was so ecstatic, that I don't remember," was his reply. Now there was silence. Then they began talking to each other in Farsi. They believed what he had told them, and now they wanted that rifle.

When we went back to work, I advised him to tell the IIAF people that he was just kidding; otherwise they would tell everyone he was a "pig fucker." He laughed and said to me, "Who cares? It was a great joke."

Clyde was sitting on the edge of a very large fuel tank that was not yet finished. He said "Now that I told you about the pig, I want to hear about some of your queer escapades". He singled out one of the Iranians, an airman, and said "We haven't heard a queer story from you at all. You must have done something while you were in the States."

The airman replied, "I don't do things like that." Clyde insisted. "You're lying. All Iranians have a queer story. You did something while you were there."

After thinking a while, the man answered "Something happened while I was there, but it wasn't a queer story." He went on, "I had a very dear American friend who took me everywhere. One long weekend we went to Florida for a short vacation. Our rooms were side by side and I heard him crying one night so I went to his room and asked him what was wrong." "What did he say?" asked Clyde. The Iranian airman explained, "My American friend said, 'I went to the doctor and he told me that I had this disease and the only cure for me was to have someone give it to me in the butt.' So I told him, 'I am your friend and I will help you.'"

Clyde then asked, "Well, did you help him?"

"Of course," the Iranian airman replied "He was my friend and he needed help." That was it! Clyde went into a laughing spasm and it was genuine. He laughed so hard that he fell into the fuel tank. I didn't do such a bad job myself. The tears were pouring down my face. This guy actually believed what the queer told him and he followed through to do what he thought was the right thing, in helping a friend.

Well, he was helping him, but not the way he thought he was. When we explained to him what actually happened-- after the laughing spasm -- the Iranian airman was shocked. After the explanation, he realized what he had done. Heartbroken and angry, now he knew that he had been used. He was one of the few Iranians that I knew who was a Christian. We felt sorry for him after it was all over.

To our surprise, another young man said that he wanted to tell us what happened to him in the States. Clyde's story about the pig must have torn down barriers. Here's what he said. "A close Iranian friend and I were in a bar one night, drinking. A man at another table invited us over. He was with a very pretty girl.

He bought all the drinks. When they had too much to drink, the man said that one of them could take the pretty girl home with him, or go to her place. The other would have to go home with him. They would have to draw for the short match. Unfortunately, I lost." They actually did prefer women.

Then I asked him what he did. He answered that he went to the man's home and gave it to him. "The man kept getting up in bed and spraying perfume in the air," he said; "I finally realized what I was doing and left and walked back home. I felt so bad about myself and what I had done."

Nobody laughed this time. We decided that we'd had too long a break and went back to work. Clyde really got them to talk. That day was not boring. There were so many stories on that subject that I could write a book on it. Being in the military in a foreign country, we were exposed to a lot of people who didn't have anything to do in their time off. At night, they'd talk about women, maybe go out and get some *gendeh*.

* * *

Shiraz was a year-long assignment, plus intermittent trips. All in all, I spent a lot of time there. My main priority was to try my best to get home on the weekends. Shiraz was about seven hundred miles from Teheran. I checked on the C-130's first to see if there was one going to Teheran on Wednesday. If there weren't any available, I would go on Iran Air. That cost me lots of money but I had no choice. After all, I had a wife and seven children. Three of my children were born in Iran.

In Teheran, the weekends were very heavenly. On Wednesday, we had the "Wednesday Night Group." That meant wild parties. On one occasion, I could not get home so I got on the radio and was able to get a message to the MAAG. I asked them to tell my wife that I was unable to make it home. She must have mentioned it to the neighbor who was a US Army LC (Lieutenant Colonel). What happened after that was a huddle in their group. The end result was that they were able to get a C-54 to get me right away. That's a four engine cargo plane that was modified to seat people in comfort. As I had mentioned before, I was very close to the military.

It was my birthday and they were having a big party for me at my home. That was cute. I was next to the runway in my Jeep when they landed. I had been working late and they called the base on their radio and asked them to advise me that they were coming to pick me up and take me to Teheran. The pilot opened a window in the cockpit when he saw me and told me to get my ass aboard now. There was an Iranian Airman in the Jeep with me so I told him to take the Jeep. He did, and I ran to the aircraft.

When I got aboard, the pilot said, "I don't know where you get your pull, but they told me to get my ass down here and get you back to Teheran, <u>now</u>". They didn't say why but when I got home late, I soon found out. The party had already started and as I came through the door, they all yelled "Surprise!" and began singing "Happy Birthday!" I almost cried but I didn't. The women were hugging and kissing me and the officers were shaking my hand. There was a lot of genuine love in that group. Americans clung to each other in that foreign land.

Everyone enjoyed the music, dancing, food and dessert through the night. The waiters left at about ten and the bartender left about midnight. He was an Iranian friend who was in the IIAF. 'Cretia depended on him for some things. He took very good care of the family if the need arose while I was gone, and that was most of the time. All the guests had a wonderful time. We loved the circle that we were in, in Teheran. The party ended at about three in the morning.

The weekend turned out to be a wild one. Being home was so beautiful to me. All our kids loved our way of life. I could see them watching us at the parties from the stairway. They were always smiling. I could feel their happiness. "What would life be like without kids?" was a thought that went through my mind. They were all such beautiful kids. Even today, they remember those parties.

But the weekend was not over. On Sunday morning, I left early to catch the plane that would take me back to Shiraz. Gala Morgie was the name of the airport that was very close to Mehrabad International Airport. Gala Morgie was only for military planes. There were cooks that made breakfast for you and you could drink coffee until the airplane was ready. Guess what? I was the only passenger so I sat in the copilot's seat.

This morning I could feel the effects of the wild weekend. An American Army Major was flying the U-8. It was a twin engine plane meant to carry six persons at the most. The Major looked at me and said "You had better get some sleep. You look like hell." I agreed with him. He had just finished a tour in Vietnam so he was new to the skies of Iran. A few minutes later, I was in dream land, sound asleep.

A few hours later I was awakened by an unusual sound. Someone cocked a pistol. Like an experienced mother tuned to the softest peep from her newborn infant, that click could draw me out of the deepest slumber. In an instant, I was on my feet, ready for action. The pilot was holding his own pistol, pointed at the floor of the plane. He appeared to be checking the pistol, something you might do in preparation for an emergency landing. All these thoughts ran through my head at

179

lightning speed. "What are you doing?" I asked. "We're lost. I have no idea where we are," he responded, oddly calm. Now I was wide awake.

If the pilot was lost, we were in danger of running out of fuel. That meant a crash landing. First responders at crash landing sites are the wolves. They work very quickly, leaving a grisly horror behind them. I looked out the nearest window. All I could see were mountains and low cloud cover, no recognizable landmarks, nothing. I immediately grabbed the map and got into the general area to try to match the heights of the mountains. What a job it was! There were so many mountains. The pilot said that we had better find a landing place. Where? I asked him if we could go higher. He answered, "We're running low on fuel." My reply was that if I couldn't identify the closest mountains, we would never know where we were, and they would never find us even if we did survive.

The plane climbed and we went on oxygen. Then I saw it. There was a train moving down there. I only saw it for a minute and then it was gone. In a couple of minutes, I saw it again. It was going in and out of mountain tunnels. I scanned the map, found the tracks and the tunnels. "Here we are. We're going the wrong way," I said. Now we knew where we were. We made a quick turn and headed for Shiraz.

180

When we landed, there was very little fuel left. You could never have found two happier people that day. I will never forget it. I've been close to death many times but this was indeed different. The train saved us.

Chapter 9

Kerman, Hamadan, Yazd, 1969

Towers of Silence

Old Zoroastrian burial pits, near Yazd, Iran

Kerman

When we parted in Vahdati, Rasul asked a favor of me, "If you would, please help me become an officer." I promised him that I would do my best to make it happen. I did what I could to get him assigned to the isolated city of Kerman, so he could study to get his high school diploma. That was one of the requirements for becoming an officer. My influence with the senior officers in Teheran helped, and he got the assignment. The schedule called for a relatively long time before the installation work would start in Kerman. He could use that time to study. Fate is such a strange thing. I had no way of knowing this assignment would save my life.

A year later, in September of 1969, I was assigned to Kerman. I had no idea where Rasul lived. There was no Air Base in that city. The pilot of the U8 twin engine US Army aircraft dropped me off on the side of the runway. There was nothing to do but pick up my travel bag and other stuff. I began walking down the runway towards the Terminal. There was a truck coming towards me so I flagged him down. The driver stopped. He looked surprised; Americans were a very unusual sight in Kerman.

He took me to the terminal and directed me to a man who appeared to be in charge. The man's command of English was limited, and I spoke little Farsi at that time. Of course, he immediately ordered that tea be served. I was a celebrity. While drinking the tea, we talked, and I explained to him just what I was doing there.

After much ado, he called the *Jandarmeri* and explained my situation. I had a letter with me that I presented to the police when I arrived at their headquarters. Again, tea was served. They took me to the commanding officer. More tea! Finally, after much entertainment, a tired Captain arrived on the scene. He spoke English very well.

Again, I explained what my mission was about. Rasul was the man that I had to see. He directed a driver to take me to the home of Rasul. The Captain told me that he was a broken man who hated what he was doing. When I asked why, he really didn't say too much except "this place is disheartening."

We found the house. As I entered, there was Rasul, studying on the floor. His home was a very modest place. He introduced me to his pretty young wife. I could see that she already knew about me. Rasul and I talked about the "old days," and then we went off to get me settled. Being an American in Kerman was a strange experience. You were noticed by everyone. People everywhere would come close to see this foreigner. Very shortly, the whole town knew about the American.

Rasul dropped me off at the only decent hotel in Kerman. The manager spoke English very well. That night, it seemed as though anyone who spoke English in Kerman was there at the hotel dining area. They introduced themselves and just talked and talked. That night, I met so many people; I had lots of invitations to come to visit.

A young millionaire took up a lot of my time. He had spent some time in California, so Americans were not strangers to him. "You must come to my plantation," he insisted. I accepted his invitation and he set a date for the visit. He owned a very large pistachio plantation. Pistachios are a money crop there. From the size of the plantation, it was easy to see why he was rich. The red carpet was there and he rolled it out for me. Touring the place was a joy. A stream flowed through the place and of course there were many hundreds of trees. Strangely, I never met his parents and he never brought up the subject. He was twenty eight years old. That is very young to be in charge of such a big business.

That night, an older woman from Romania who owned a carpet factory took me for a moonlight tour of the plantation. We hadn't been walking more than a few minutes when a man with a club attacked us. He came at me first. I ducked and got the club. It was about seven feet long. I didn't want to hit him, even though that was my first inclination. There was a shout. It was Houssain, the owner. Something was said and the man ran away. He turned out to be the watchman. Houssain apologized to me and that was that. All in all, it was an enjoyable visit.

There was a British archeological team who were excavating somewhere near Kerman. They were staying at the hotel. One day, the leader of the team invited me to join them at dinner. Everyone there appeared to be very polite. We engaged in pleasant conversation -- that is, until they began drinking wine.

This was 1969 and people around the world were excited by the spectacular Apollo 11 moon landing just accomplished on July 20th. It was the first time a man had set foot on the moon, a truly historic occasion, so we were proud it had been an American astronaut. During the course of the meal, a younger member of the British team stood up and said "What's so great about dumping a Yank on the moon? It's the past that's important."

This was too much for me. There wasn't a prouder and more patriotic American that ever lived than I; at least that's what I thought. I was ready to take them all on right then and there. I stood up at my place at the table. The anger in me was like fire. Everyone there stared at me. They all knew that the young Brit had said the wrong thing. And he wasn't the only one; another man affirmed what he said. There might have been more, but my anger was instant, so I can't remember exactly how many spoke.

The leader of the group stood up and said "You will all apologize to the young American." They all did apologize immediately. That ended that. I never did find out exactly where and what those British archaeologists were digging for. One thing I did know, Englishmen where everywhere in Iran. The taxes required to support their

Socialist system were so high, the only way to escape the taxes was by working outside of their country. We Americans had a saying; "If you turn over a rock, you'll find an Englishman."

I was told by the hotel manager one morning that there was to be a very big wedding celebration at the hotel. The young couple invited me as their special guest. At that time, I had never been to an Iranian wedding and I was looking forward to the experience. The wedding day arrived and I was privileged to see all the preparations. Three big truck loads containing enormous rolls of carpets arrived. The whole area was soon covered with carpeting. I assumed that the people getting married were from very wealthy families. I was disappointed that I didn't have the right clothes for the occasion.

The Governor of the Province was there, along with many people from Teheran. As a special guest, I was introduced to him; fortunately, he spoke some English. We had a conversation going, but there were so many wealthy people, who wanted to speak with him as well. He invited me to his mansion and turned to speak to some other people. The head of the *Jandarmeri* found me and held my hand. He wouldn't let go of my hand. We had met before, on the first day that I arrived in Kerman. He wanted people to know that he was friends with the American. Many people

188

were standing in sort of a line to talk with me. What a day!

Now the strangest thing happened. We had been imbibing various drinks all along. It was a very formal event and was most enjoyable. Then the announcement for dinner was made. This I had never seen before. All the people rushed over to the tables and started eating immediately. No one left. They all stood at the table until they had finished eating. I was not able to get a thing to eat. When they were all finished, they saw me standing there by myself. They realized that I had not got any food, so people insisted that I go to the table and fill up my plate. There was some rice left, but I really didn't get anything to eat.

That night there was a party. I was asked to attend, so I did. When I got there, I realized that it was a Hashish party. Everyone was happy and laughing. I knew that I couldn't stay there, so I left a short while after I arrived. Trouble was sure to happen there. What a day!!

A couple of days later, I was out for a break. I was driving around the outskirts of the city. Suddenly, everything started to shake. I could actually see the city of Kerman, swaying. My first impulse was to stop and watch. It was an earthquake and I was in the middle of it. Actually, it was a nice feeling for me. It really was enjoyable. I've been in small earthquakes, but never experienced one of this magnitude. There was a strange, rumbling noise that came

189

along with the movement. When it all ended, I had an elated feeling. After all, it was a new experience for me and it really didn't affect me in my jeep. Some buildings fell down and many had cracks in them, but it didn't seem that bad.

During the mission in Kerman, I was nearly murdered by an American who worked with me. A few days before it happened, I was working in the TACAN building. It was my responsibility to install all the equipment, make it work and then Flight Check it. The two men who were assigned to help me had just come from Zahedan which was a very undesirable place.

They had spent a month there and they were wild. They would not help me with anything. Their perception was that I was in the building doing all of the complex work and they were doing the "grunt" work. That surely brings on jealousy. The equipment that I was putting into place was very heavy. A few of the equipment racks were 1200 lbs. After I had moved the last of eight enclosures into place, my back went. The pain was extreme. I fell over. The soldiers put me into a chair. I was then moved into my bed in the hotel. Teheran was notified. An air evacuation was ordered, but didn't come for days.

After two days, I was able to walk again but that was about all. I still couldn't lift anything. An Iranian lieutenant took me out to the site where I began doing an inventory. I went

190

outside to check on a few things. One of the Americans, who didn't like me, decided he was going to beat me up. Normally, he would not have had a chance, but in my present condition it wouldn't be much of a problem. I think he knew that. He came at me fast. I was able to get off a punch and he went down. That surprised me because, in the Army, I used to fight in the Ring. To throw a good punch, you need to use all of your body from your foot up to your fist. Otherwise, it is just a jab. His friend, unknown to me, decided that he was going to kill me.

Rasul was there, along with a soldier who was assigned to guard the site. Rasul ordered the soldier to shoot the man that was about to hit me over the head with a sledge hammer. I could not see him, since he ran up behind me with the hammer raised in his hands, over his head, but I understood the order to shoot. I turned around quickly and saw him. At the same time, he realized that he was about to be shot. I shouted to the soldier not to shoot. The man had lost all his color. I shouted, "I just saved your life you stupid bastard. What the hell is wrong with you?"

The truth was that Rasul had just saved my life. I didn't report the incident because I knew it would get distorted. These two guys had just come from a month long assignment in Zahedan, which is a real shit place. An American Army Colonel from Shiraz, who became close to me, told me about that place.

He got very sick from actual feces in the water and had to be evacuated. The guy who tried to kill me used to drink a tall glass of Scotch before he went to bed, so you never knew what state he was in.

How utterly fantastic! The man that I had done a small favor was there now at the right time and because he was there, I am alive today. Was that what it was all about? I don't know. He saved my life and because he did, he eventually became an officer, as a result of my influence. Sadly, Rasul lost his life during the war with Iraq. If I hadn't used my influence, he would most probably be alive today and I would be dead. I often think about that and I grieve for him. I will never forget Rasul.

The evacuation plane finally arrived and took me to Teheran and the American Hospital. The injury put me out of action for two weeks. Many months passed until I felt better, but I never fully recovered from that back injury.

Hamadan

The closest major city to Shahroki AFB was Hamadan. It is a very ancient city. Very long ago, it was the summer capitol city of Persia. The autobiography of Xerxes is carved into the mountain above Hamadan. I visited the spot and saw it. Very impressive! It took me far back in history to the time of Xerxes and Esther. After one sees something like that, it impels you to read about those people. While reading, it's a much different feeling and a beautiful experience.

The tombs of Esther and Mordecai are in that city. During the Yom Kippur war in 1973, the Supervisory Evaluation Team, of which I was the leader, was at the base evaluating, along with the USAF. The USAF was an important part of that team.

We took a trip to Hamadan for a break. Jewish people live in the building and attend to the historical Biblical Shrine. It isn't anything special in appearance, just an ordinary home. Jewish people are not liked in that city by some of the people. They dumped garbage over the walls of the site and some men pissed on the walls around it. As we walked past the tomb of Esther, the Jews who attended the shrine came out to us, pleading for us to come into the shrine. They were pulling at our clothes and crying. It was about the war and they knew that Americans were friendly with Israel and helping them in that war. The USAF uniforms made us very visible. There were some Iranian military men, who were also in uniform, with us. They came along but it was obvious that they weren't welcome. Some of the Iranians were glaring at the Jews. We were taken to the coffins of Esther and Mordecai. The coffins were small, not ossuaries but small coffins. Of course, we had to remove our shoes because this was considered a very holy place. I was in awe. The coffins were covered partially with very fine cloths. All that I could think of was Queen Esther and the Jewish feast of Purim, which is still celebrated by Jews today. That holiday originated in the Book of Esther.

The Jewish people there were praying and crying. There were only a few of them, mostly women and one elderly man. We all stayed there for quite a long time because we were awe struck to be in such an old and holy place. They did not want us to leave. They treated us like royalty but it was obvious that the Iranians were not welcome. As we left, all of the Americans had a very good feeling about the visit. Many times my mind goes back to that day especially when I read or hear about the Book of Esther. To me, that was the greatest attraction in Hamadan and an awesome experience for me.

There was a Catholic church in that city. At one time, some of the Americans stationed at Shahroki would go to church there on Sunday. That was very unusual because most Americans would go to church on Friday. Sunday was a work day. Once, I was invited to go along with them so I sneaked out of work and joined them. The Mass there was an unusual experience. The air about it was so ancient, even though it was very similar to the Mass in the States. There were hardly any men there. They must have been at work. It was just the opposite of the Muslims. The only ones in the Mosques were men. There was the scent of incense in the church and it smelled so pleasing. We were the center of attraction and looked so out of place but we smiled at everyone and they smiled back. They appeared to be happy that we were there. I know I was.

In the center of town was a statue of the Shah mounted on a horse. Many streets came together at that point. One of the streets that came to that point was nicknamed "The Horses Tail." I wondered how it got that name, but the explanation was not long in coming. The Horse's Tail was the street where all of the prostitutes lived and conducted business. It derived its name from the tail of the horse on which the Shah's statue was mounted. The horse's tail pointed to that street. The Horse's Tail was a very busy street. At that time, there was a very famous prostitute who set up a business hut there. The Airmen at the base would always talk about her. Her name was Nargas. At times, one of them would shout out loud, "Nargas, I love you." All of the Airmen would talk about how beautiful she was. One of them claimed she was the most beautiful girl in the world.

On one occasion I was in Hamadan with some of the IIAF NCO's and they insisted on taking me to see Nargas. It was the first time that I really saw the Horse's Tail. It was a slum. They knew exactly where Nargas' place of business was. They went directly there and knocked on the door. When she opened the door, I could see that they were not making this up. She was indeed a beautiful woman. What in the world was she doing here? It was a slummy room. We were invited in but I couldn't get myself to go in. At least I was able to see that Nargas was real.

Yazd

There is a city deep in the desert of Iran that is radically different than any other city in that country. Yazd is its name. People in Iran say that is the place that ancient Persians fled to escape the Muslims who conquered and overran Persia in the 700's. Zoroastrianism was the religion of Persia at that time. They were the followers of Zoroaster who founded the religion. Muslims called them Fire Worshipers. Incidentally, Iran is a relatively new name for the country of Persia. It was changed to Iran by Reza Shah the Great in the middle 1930's.

FAA assigned me to Yazd, to install a TACAN. That was a boring job after installing so many of them, but the city itself was a fascinating place. The hotel where I stayed was different than any other that I saw in Iran. It was in a wilderness sort of environment with cabins among the trees.

There was a nice restaurant that served good food and drinks. Veal was the food of preference in Yazd. No other city had that much veal. Mutton and chicken were the most popular meats in Iran. The main staples were rice and bread.

There were two giant burial biers in the city. Zoroastrians did not believe in burying their dead. Bodies were placed on iron bars on the top of a giant bier. There were two biers in town; one for the rich and one for the poor. The place for the poor was very big, about the size of a football field. The one for the rich was more beautiful, but half the size. The idea was that once a body was placed on the bier, birds of prey would come and eat the bodies. Bones and body parts that were not eaten by the birds fell into a deep pit that was below the iron bars. Piles of bones were scattered around outside of the walls. It was evident that a lot of the bones had been there a very long time. The reason for this type of burial was that many Zoroastrians believed in ritual exposure. They believe the elements of earth, fire, water and air should not be contaminated by people. That I didn't understand. If a person is buried in the ground, the body is contained in a box and decomposed in it. With an open bier, the body parts were exposed to the air, fell into a pit and rotted in an open space, giving off a putrid odor. The parts that were eaten by the birds were dropped to the ground anywhere in the form of fecal material.

The Shah had made it a law that this practice must stop. There was a cemetery near the bier for new burials but there were only five gravesites there. I tried to get into the bier to see what it was like, but the doors were made of very thick steel and the walls were very high. There was no way of getting in.

While I was at the bier, I saw a film crew. They were in the process of filming a movie. It was a French crew. They had a giant fan that was blowing dust. The actors were speaking their parts. The name of the film, I found out, was "The Queen of Sheba." I had seen her sitting at the filming site but didn't know who she was. Interesting!

That night at the restaurant, I saw her, the Queen of Sheba, drinking a bottle of wine at her private table. She looked a lot older than she did on the set. She invited me to her table and offered me a glass of wine. Since I could not speak French and her English was poor, there wasn't much conversation. When the glass was empty, I thanked her and left for my cabin.

She was a very pretty woman. On the way to the cabin, a figure popped out of the trees and on to the road. I almost hit her. It was the "Queen of Sheba". She didn't know that it was me driving. She smiled in a sort of a "Thank You" and continued on her way.

Nothing really interesting happened to me in that city. It was just so different an experience. Oh! There is one thing that was interesting. One of the soldiers, who happened to be my driver, told me about the delicious melons that they had in Yazd. He insisted on taking me down town to a place where they had these fine melons. As we were going past one corner I saw the strangest sight. I couldn't believe what I saw. I asked the driver to back up. He did and I looked again. It was a woman, breastfeeding a child underneath a tree on the street corner. That wasn't the strange thing. What was interesting was that the child was lying about a foot from the mother. Her breasts were very long but flat and it looked like the breast was grey. I took a second look, signaled the driver and we moved on. That was different!

Chapter 10

Family and Friends in Iran

Lucertia, Mike, Helen Gladis, Agnes,
(Lucretia's mom & aunt), R. & A., Teymor

Teheran, Iran 1971

Lucretia:

Reza Shah, the Shah's father, changed Iran.
Traditionalists were upset because he was on a
mission to modernize his country. Mullahs
had been paid by the British to maintain a

minimal British standing army. After all, the mullahs' salaries were paid by the state. Reza Shah reorganized the Iranian Army and established an Iranian Navy and Air Force. He shot some of the mullahs and gave people more freedom. He took land from the rich and gave it to the poor. He got a bad reputation for siding with the Germans during World War II and had to abdicate.

His son was Mohammed Reza Shah, the current Shah. The Shah's third wife, Empress Farah, wanted to help her husband continue the improvements his father had begun. She especially wanted to help Iranian women. Most women didn't work then, and girls usually didn't attend school after 8th grade. Under Farah's influence, girls were educated to university level.

I was pregnant with our seventh child, Christel, due in October 1971. This was near the end of Mike's tour with the FAA. Iran held a very special celebration that month. They called it a "Twenty-Five Hundred Years of Monarchy Celebration." This was a celebration of the 2,500th anniversary of the founding of the Persian Empire by Cyrus the Great. Empress Farah was at his side during the lavish celebrations as he greeted kings and world leaders including Emperor Haile Selassie of Ethiopia, Princess Grace and Prince Rainier of Monaco, King Farouk of Egypt, King Constantine and Queen Anne Marie of Greece, President Giri of India,

Cardinal Maximilian Von Furstenberg , the
Vatican representative and U.S. Vice President
Spiro Agnew.

Reza Shah was of the Pahlavi family, lauded as
King of Kings and Light of the Aryans. The
Pahlavi Crown had been made for his
coronation in 1924. Now, his son was to wear
it at the 1971 Monarchy Celebration. The
crown was very heavy, with 3,755 jewels,
2,000 karats. All these kings and world
leaders gathered in one place was an
impressive sight. Haile Selassie, Emperor of
Ethiopia, delivered a message to their imperial
majesties on behalf of the royal guests. It may
have been the last time all the kings of the
world were together.

Teheran, Shiraz, Persepolis and all the major
cities were decorated with thousands of lights.
Towers were covered in lights. They put up
pictures of Persia's ancient kings. Scrollwork
design, like paisley, was everywhere, on
screens, lights, walls.

My mother and her older sister, my Aunt
Agnes, came to visit us. Now, Mother had
travelled abroad before -- she had been to
Rome and other places -- but this trip was an
adventure. They were allowed to travel as far
as Brussels, but then they were told they
would have to disembark. It turned out they
didn't have the right visas to go on to Iran.
Someone had told them they could get the
visas when they landed in Iran, but that wasn't

203

true. They had to stay an extra day in Brussels while we got their paperwork sorted out.

We asked our friend, R., to help us and she did wonders. She arranged for someone to meet them when they landed in Brussels. They were taken directly to the Iranian Embassy. My mother was upset because their passports were taken from them, but they were told the visas would be ready the next day, and they could pick up their passports then. A flight was arranged for them to leave the next day. R. had contacts in the Iranian embassy in Brussels and told them to give my mother and aunt the visas they needed. R.'s contacts actually got them permanent visas, which was very nice.

R. was an Iranian-Jewish woman who made it her business to become a close friend of mine. Mike and I knew what R. was about, but we also found it was useful to know her, because she really was a big help to us in many ways.

Back in Iran, R. kept track of everything my mother and her sister were experiencing; she knew the whole process. She told us they would be coming in on Sabrina Airlines. They flew into Iran that evening, October 15, 1971 and saw the lights glittering everywhere, like jewels. It looked like Teheran was on fire, because of all the lights for the monarchy celebration. Mother and Aunt Agnes couldn't stop talking about it. "It looked like a fairyland," my mother said. Little did they know, it was only the beginning. We took

204

them to a different section of the city every night, and they saw all the lavish displays.

Instead of the bleak desert they expected, my mother and aunt were introduced to a fashionable metropolis. We went to a whole variety of nightclubs, the Inter Continental Hotel and the Teheran Hilton among them. We had passes from R. to the Bank Markazi (which we called the Bank Melli), to see the crown jewels, and the Pahlavi crown. The crown was later taken out to be worn in the celebration. It weighed over 75 pounds!

I took Mother and Aunt Agnes, to the bazaar. I warned them people would pinch their butts, because it always happened to me, every time. I never went to the bazaar by myself. Despite the pinching, I loved the bazaars, the smells, all the spices, cinnamon, mint, saffron, sumac, other Oriental spices, all the unusual Middle-Eastern smells, fruits and vegetables, gorgeous colorful Persian carpets with detailed birds or flowers depending on which town it was from. The carpets from Tabriz always had birds, ones from Esfahan had flowers. Little villages would have brown or beige tribal carpets. Then there were the brasses and etched designs on trays, done by hand. You would see them in the marketplace etching designs on cups, trays, and decorative items. It was all made by hand.

Lalazar, a Jew, was a man R. knew. He sold us beautiful jewelry. R. told us not to buy our carpets at the bazaar, but to buy them from her friends.

There was a lot of noise in the market, lots of people shopping, all different kinds of people, not just the Iranians, but Americans, Germans, French. You would hear all these different languages, French, German, Farsi, English, other dialects. It always helped to know some Farsi, when bargaining for items. There were rosewater candies, cakes, ice creams for sale in the market. You could walk around with delicious ice cream served in a paper cone with a stick to eat it. You'd get nuts in the nut shop served that way too.

Iranian music was played too, mostly someone singing accompanied by horns, flutes, percussion instruments, like tambourines. It wasn't like anything else, Iranian music. Sometimes they would sing American top ten songs, in Farsi, and you could recognize it by the melody. This was mostly at the nightclubs; you didn't hear American songs in the marketplace.

My mother bought some brass camels. Here's how you shopped in Iran back then: the first thing, as you enter a shop, the shopkeeper would offer you some tea. He showed Mother and Aunt Agnes how to drink their tea with sugar cubes. You put the cube in your mouth, then you would drink the tea through the cubes. The merchant spent at least 15 minutes displaying hospitality, so my mother felt she had to buy something. Later we went to a shop with a great variety of nuts. The nut shop gave you samples; I know we bought plenty of nuts. The spice shop was another place that offered you tea, and we bought some saffron there. It was very expensive in the States, but here you could buy pounds of it for $4 a pound. Iranians cooked with lots of cinnamon and nutmeg and saffron. They would sprinkle red sumac, (This is not poisonous. White sumac is a poison), on the rice, and it tasted so good. There were Chelo Kebab houses, restaurants all over, lamb kabobs. My mother and Aunt Agnes discovered Chelo Kebab and loved it.

My friend introduced them to an elegant Iranian dish called *Gormeh Sabzi*, made with lamb, dark green vegetables and spices. We would call a local Chelo Kebab house, place our order, and it would be delivered to the house on a silver tray with a silver cover, very elegant. They would serve it there, with butter, bread, red sumac, everything you needed. The bread, *Taftoon*, was made with wholemeal. It was rolled and patted out in a great circle, about 12 inches in diameter. Your plates would be filled and served; then they would take away the silver platter. The cost was perhaps $2 for all this. My children would order kebab on their own. If they didn't have money, the restaurant would just tell us later, and we paid them. They trusted us because we were Americans. At this time, 1971, Iranians still liked Americans. Our friends in Teheran and I didn't make much of a big deal about the 1967 War with Israel; it didn't affect us.

My mother and aunt were pleasantly surprised when I took them to modern Iranian department stores. Years later, back in America, they were always talking about the trip to Iran, because it was so different from what they had expected. They thought of Iran as a hot, empty, backward country, and were astounded by the modern culture, and all the advantages we enjoyed there. My mother was about 55, my aunt was 58 at that time. I thought it was brave of them to come out to an unknown land. But it was an adventure, and they loved it.

We lived on Kuche Zarrine. Mr. Zarrinal owned all the homes in that area so the neighborhood, six or seven long streets, was called Zarrine Club. Mr. Zarrinal was very wealthy; his name meant "Golden Horseshoe." All the roads came to what we called The Circle. There was the pharmacy, the jewelry store, the chicken store, a store for fruits and vegetables, an "everything" store where the kids used to buy little toys, and the bread ovens where they baked *Taftoon* bread. The ovens were like a dome. They would mix the dough, no leavening, then throw it in the ovens. It baked quickly. There was also a bread called *Barbari*, which was baked on stones. The bread was fresh, baked three times a day, every day, without fail. Bread was a very important part of Iranian life.

Iran, our *badji*, or maid, helped me clean the house and take care of the little ones. Merchants would come to the house, singing out the names of the products they were selling, like the Nafti, the man selling fuel, or the man selling camel dung for your gardens. Others would sell delicious red beets, roasted steaming hot, wrapped in newspaper. One man came around selling bitter green fruits, unripe apricots, which the kids loved. They dipped them in salt.

The children liked to run around on the top of an eight foot stone fence which surrounded our property. They called it "running the walls." They rode their bikes all around the neighborhood. The taxi driver knew them, so I allowed them to take a taxi and go into town for Christmas shopping. They often went up to The Circle to buy things. The next door neighbors had a deep swimming pool which they used often. Ours was quite shallow. Of course, all the kids all learned to swim very well at the Officer's Club. Carolyn and Sharon were on the swim team. There were all kinds of activities for the kids: swimming, softball, bingo and more.

Mike:

Most of my time was spent away from the family. When I came home, it made the kids so happy. I felt elated when I saw them. When

209

we arrived in Iran, we had four kids. Carolyn, who was the oldest, began school while we were still living at the Sina Hotel. The school bus would pick her up and let her off at the hotel. It's difficult to imagine an American family with seven kids growing up in a foreign country like Iran. Because we were there for such a long time – ten years – they thought of Iran as home, and their life there as normal.

As they grew, they knew very well that their dad was into guns. I had to keep my skills fine-tuned at the highest possible level, so my older children were involved too. They would stand about six feet in front of me and clap their hands. I would draw my revolver and "dry fire" with the gun pointed far off to the right of them. They loved to try and clap their hands quickly, before I fired. They had a ball. Reloading bullets was also a big excitement for them. They just had to learn how to do it, so they watched me and then asked if they could do it. They learned very quickly.

An embarrassing moment occurred one afternoon, while 'Cretia and I were talking to a friend. The kids came home from school and ran into the room next to our large foyer. They immediately began to load .357 bullets. Our friend was awe struck. It was such a routine for them and they did it so perfectly. Sharon especially loved it. They were always so precise in measuring the amount of powder that went into a bullet. It was an embarrassment to me because I wondered what our friend would think of us.

The kids didn't stop there. There was a pellet gun that I used to fire off practice rounds. This was a semi-automatic. I kept it in the house. One of the neighbors, a woman, who lived right next to us, used to come over the wall that separated our compounds. She smoked cigarettes and would talk to me and watched me shoot. One day, she asked if I could shoot a cigarette out of her mouth. I answered yes and then did it. The kids then wanted me to shoot things off their heads. That became one of their great joys. It became an embarrassment because when their friends came, they wanted to show off. I did it a couple of times so their friends wouldn't think they were lying. One day I told them that they could not do that and told them why, so they stopped asking.

The kids liked it when the camel drivers came along. One time they wanted a ride on the camels. They tried to explain this to our *badji*, Iran, but the camel drivers sold her some camel dung instead. Later, the kids managed to explain what they wanted. The next time the camel drivers came through, they knew to give the kids a ride on their camels. The kids loved it. The camels' faces looked like mice.

White rats were a big part of their lives. The kids had them as pets. They would take them to school and give them away. The school sent home a notice, asking us to stop sending white rats to school. One white rat was the boss; he'd get out of his cage and be on my pillow waking me up. The kids also kept gerbils; they got out, too. Dave would take those white rats and put one in his mouth. The kids would laugh to see the white rat in his mouth; of course, he couldn't talk then.

The Iranian boys in the neighborhood would sometimes tease my older girls. A boy put a broomstick in the spokes of one of my daughters' bicycles as she was riding. One of her sisters beat the boy up and he ran away. I wasn't around much and didn't usually get involved in the kids' daily lives. One day was different: I was there, standing in front of the house where the children played. An ambulance came down the street and ran over one of my children's bikes. They crushed the wheels. My daughter, Lucretia Ann, came running down the street, yelling, "They ran over my bike!" I chased after the ambulance, grabbed driver by the throat, opened the door, pulled him out and pinned him against a tree. A soldier yelled, "a man is dying, we have to get him to the hospital." I threw the man back in the car and walked towards my house. The driver's wheels squealed as he took off. I threw a screwdriver after them, like a knife. The screwdriver's tip hit the windshield and made a noise like an explosion. There were ten thousand tiny pieces of glass, everywhere. The driver had glass in his ears, nose and mouth. He slammed on the brakes and got busy spitting out glass. Then they took off for the hospital. Later, they came to my house, begging, because their officer said they had to pay for the damage, at least $100.00. I agreed to pay for the windshield if they paid for the damage to the bike. After that, I never saw them again.

Lucretia:

The four older girls, Carolyn, Sharon, Michelle and Lucretia Ann were all in school by 1971; they attended the Teheran American School (TAS). The bus picked them up right at The Circle. They had a lot of friends nearby and enjoyed sleepovers and parties.

The Gulf District was a great big entertainment center with a lot of basketball, soccer, several baseball and football fields and a golfing range. Later it became a German club. High school teams played games there and the Non-Com Club had dances for the young people. All the kids had a great time there, parties at Christmas and Halloween. The kids had a good social life there, and so did we. There they had a great deal of freedom, and I had help with the house, which made our lives so much easier.

The Teheran American School was excellent. The teachers there were Iranian, American, German, all different nationalities. So were the kids, actually. As long as one parent was American, the children could attend the school. The school had teams for football and basketball. My older girls were cheerleaders. The football teams were called the Vikings, and the Raiders. The basketball team was the American Eagles. They played against schools like the Iran Zamin, the International School, the U.S. Hospital School, other schools in Teheran.

I had considered sending my children to the International School, but it was all the way downtown, and there were sometimes incidents down there. TAS was closer and in a safer area, I thought. There was a Jazz Band, Concert Band, football marching band, wind ensemble, yearbook, all the activities you would have in the States. They learned modern dance, tap, ballet, but they would also learn the Iranian traditional dances like, "Jump Over the Fire."

The Teheran American School, like the other schools in Teheran, celebrated all 48 Iranian holidays. For New Year's, the children had 13 days off. On the 13th day everyone had to get out of the house because your ancestors would come back and take over. So the kids wanted to leave, go on a picnic, anything, that day. We saw families picnicking all over Teheran, even along the median strips on the highways.

Their education was better than in the States. It was based on the Indiana Education system. One of their favorite teachers was a young man, Mr. Jim Fosnot. He was the art teacher. He taught them to use a pottery

214

wheel, molding clay figures, designing jewelry. Mr. Fosnot taught at TAS for twelve years, longer than we were in Iran. He and his wife were blonde hippie-types from California. He was also Carolyn's swim coach.

They had chess teams at the Teheran American School. The school's standing on the Chess Ladder was high. Their team competed with other schools, guided by their teacher, Mr. Row. The girls also learned how to play pool. I remember Sharon was tops at foosball.

We lived an hour from the ski slopes, on Mount Damavand, where Reza Pahlavi made a ski resort called Abali. It was very inexpensive for us, but the Shah put a lot of money in it, to make it perfect. There were ski lifts, everything you'd expect in a nice ski resort. The girls learned to ski very well. The boys were starting to learn, but they were young, and we weren't there long enough. There were two other ski areas, but they were farther away, Shemshak and Dazim. We went horseback riding there too, in the snow, on a path.

Christel was three years old and developed a bad case of the croup. When I left that morning she seemed fine, but she got worse during the day. The maid called an eighteen year old neighbor, Tom Hancock, because Christel was having a hard time breathing. He actually saved my youngest daughter's life, because she was not breathing when she

215

arrived at the hospital. I might have been at the Officer's Club that day. When someone finally notified me, I went right down to the hospital. Christel was there for three days. For some reason, when Christel came back from the hospital, she announced "my name is Mary." We never understood why, because she didn't know anyone named Mary. The incident affected us deeply; we thought perhaps an angel had spoken to her.

Mike: On Fridays, American Christians went to church and we were no exception. Sunday was a work day in Iran, so that left us with Friday which was the Muslim Holy day. The Friday routine was to go to Mass at the Catholic Mission in the northern part of Teheran. Afterwards, our family went to the Officers Club for breakfast. All the kids loved it. On Fridays all they could think of was steak and eggs. They loved steak. It was prime, shipped in from the U.S.

The priest, Fr. Williams, was an older man who had recently been released from prison in China. He had spent many years there and was very thin. He couldn't have been fed very well in that prison. One American Army Colonel, (who wasn't a Catholic), found out that Fr. Williams had no money. He was influential in getting him a job as an auxiliary chaplain for the US military. He became a much-loved person in the American community. Everyone felt that he was a very holy man. Father Williams cared for all the Americans.

The Mission was very rustic at first but the Americans changed that. New buildings went up and the American community showed how much they cared for the church and its grounds. It was here that we first met Sweet Livvy as I called her. She was petite and very pretty. She was about fifteen years older than us and had three children. Her daughter, Beverly, became very close friends with our oldest girl, Carolyn. That turned out to be a lifelong friendship.

Nine months after we had met Livvy, I was on the roof of our house and heard a voice yelling "Hi neighbor!" The roofs in Teheran are flat and used like an outdoor patio. Many people slept on their roofs in the hot weather. When I looked to see who was calling, I saw Livvy there, two houses down from me. She was now our neighbor. What a pleasant surprise! From that time on, she became a big part of our lives.

My first boss, Fred Hemp was leaving for the States. His tour in Iran was over, and I decided to throw a party for him and his family. It was the first party to which we invited Livvy. During the celebration, I threw Livvy into our swimming pool. It turned out to be a no-no; she showed us what happens to people who do things like that. She was a fighter. I never did that again. She was a lady, except when she began to fight and that was that.

Our kids were over at her house with her children all the time, or Beverly was at our house. Her husband, Raymond, worked with an American oil company and he was away most of the time. When he did come home, he was there for a week. A lot of the time I was able to get home on weekends but that wasn't always the case, so I was able to spend very little time with Raymond in the early years.

All the officers and their wives played Bridge. If you couldn't play Bridge, you set back your social status. In Vahdati, there was an American community next to the Base. It was the Khuzestan Power and Water Authority. The people were not Iranian and they were into Irrigation. All of them belonged to the Duplicate Bridge Club in that closed community. It was there that I became very good at the game of Bridge and that expertise went with me to Teheran. Livvy knew how to play bridge so she was in our Bridge club.

Bridge was mostly played in the neighborhood block of Americans. It was from house to house. One time at Livvy's house the game was on. Livvy was bidding and I was on the opposite side. My partner got the bid. Livvy doubled her and I re-doubled Livvy. Now my partner was playing, and I was the Dummy. I looked at her hand and asked why she redoubled. She pointed to two kings which could easily be finessed. At that, I started laughing. Livvy said angrily "What's so funny"? By that time she had had a couple of glasses of wine. Since she was so tiny, it didn't take much; she was feeling good.

She was really angry, so she jumped on me while I was sitting in the chair and brought me down to the floor. Then she started to hit me with her fists. To me, it was so funny that I began laughing. I could see my wife and another neighbor with their mouths open in awe. She was getting tired and realized what she was doing. It was then that she got up, shook her hair, sat down and continued playing. No one could believe what they had just seen. Livvy acted like it never happened. After all, she was a Lady.

She and her husband attended parties with us and we had a close social life. We had lots of fun together. Livvy was aware that I had a gun and was afraid of it so when we went to her house, I didn't take it with me. On one occasion that turned out to be a near catastrophe.

Dave used to borrow Livvy's son's motorcycle to go with me to the desert. That was fun for me, to have another person with a cycle to do things with me. His wife was the one whose family had a farm outside Varamie, a village about 40 minutes from Teheran. We went there a lot. At one time, Livvy, my family and some friends went there with us to have a lamb roast. While we were there, Livvy wanted to go for a ride on the cycle into the desert.

As we were riding through a very small village, we were attacked by the village dogs. I ran over some, kicked many others and almost flipped the bike. That could have been disastrous. Shooting was out of the question because of the villagers, but if we went down, it would have to be that way. All the while, Livvy was laughing and enjoying the hell out of it. We made it out of the village and rode away until all of the dogs faded in the distance. Then I stopped for a breather. My heart was pounding. Too much adrenalin! Livvy exclaimed, "That was so much fun!" The woman had such confidence in me. Needless to say, we went back a different way.

Livvy had parties and dinners at her house and she had a different group that she was attached to. Livvy spoke three languages which made her a valuable asset to her company. She was Assistant to the President of the company that she worked for (a man named McCullough) and of course they had lots of social functions. At one of these functions, the guy who was sponsoring it put on a show for me. When the time came to leave, I went to get our coats in a room that was set aside for that purpose. As I opened the door, there he was, naked, on top of the maid, who was also naked. They were screwing away and didn't seem to notice me, or didn't care. I had to close the door and let them finish since they were on top of our coats. That was quite a surprise.

Livvy asked "Where are the coats? Why didn't you bring them?" "Bob is screwing the maid in there, so we have to wait until they are finished" was my reply. She scoffed, "Mike, you are always trying to be funny. He would never do that." Then she opened the door to get her coat and saw the same thing that I saw. She gasped and put her hand over her mouth and said, "Oh my God!" She was in shock. As for me, I just couldn't stop laughing. After five more minutes, they opened the door and came out. Never said a word!

We got our coats and left. My beautiful felt hat was squashed. Somebody must have squealed, because he was fired shortly after the party. Livvy couldn't stop talking about it. She was disgusted with his behavior. It was a very unusual thing to see.

There was another party at her house one time. For some odd reason, a Canadian, who someone said was the Ambassador, was there with his wife. She wasn't wearing shoes; she was smoking a cigar and drinking. This was a very big woman. She seemed to be looking at me a lot. Then she asked me to dance. I said that I would but not right now. Her hand came at me and she picked me up off my feet with one hand and said "Now!" Wow! That was an unusual experience. There's a first time for everything. After the party was over, we went to a night club. I didn't want to go but everyone insisted. At the nightclub, the group ran into a Turkish guy who was attached to INTERPOL. She seemed to like him and that was good. Now I was free.

After getting home from a hunting trip, I decided to pull Livvy's tail, so I told my youngest son, Mark, that he was going to take Livvy a present. First, I called her on the phone and told her I was going to send some mountain goat up to her. She said "Thank you!" clearly delighted that she was going to get a present. Then, I put the Ram's head into a big bag and told Mark to take it to her. This he did, and came right back home. He was followed by a furious woman. She burst into the house with the bag and swung the bag as hard as she could yelling, "You pathetic, sick reprobate!" The horns hit me on the knees and it did not feel very good at all. She then stormed out of the house. To my surprise, she made a very beautiful painting of the ram and gave it to me. To this day, I've kept that painting. An unusual woman!

On a beautiful summer day, I found myself sunning beside Livvy's swimming pool. She was in the pool and edging along the side of the pool while talking with me. To my surprise I suddenly discovered that she could not swim. I had taught hundreds of people to swim while I was in the Boy Scouts so I thought that I would give it a try with her. I talked with her and told her what to do and in no time, she was swimming. Never had I seen anyone learn to swim that quickly with no "hands on." I asked her why she had never learned to swim. Her answer was short and simple; "Nobody ever taught me."

When 'Cretia and the kids left Iran, I was by myself and spent most of my time away from home. Since Livvy was our closest friend, I had to tell her that I could not go near her anymore because of my dangerous status. The last thing that I wanted was to see her hurt or killed because of me. Her response was "Mike, I don't know why you worry about things like that. You have that big gun with you all the time. You can just shoot them." Something shot through me then and I almost cried. This woman had so much confidence in me. She was not the least bit afraid. It was very touching. She did throw a birthday party for me at the Inter Continental Hotel and invited some close friends. While my friends were near me, I was afraid and kept a very close watch.

One night she invited me to go with her to play Bridge at her boss's home. I declined but she insisted and reminded me of "that great big gun," that I carried. We went to his house and played cards. He became very angry because we beat him and his wife at the game. He asked me to leave. As we were leaving the house, my senses perked up to make sure there was no danger. Livvy kept yelling at me and said that she couldn't take me anywhere without causing trouble. She hit me with her purse. I wasn't able to get into a conversation in my state of alertness. She asked, "Are you listening to me?" So you see, she was never aware of the danger, or didn't care. What a woman! We are still in close contact with Livvy and her family.

She and Raymond were there together when I said my final good byes. That was a sad occasion; after all we had been together for nine years. She and her family enriched our lives in Iran and we had great times together. We will never forget them. To this day, we are close friends.

Chapter 11

The Caspian Sea and Varamie

Map of Iran

So many things happened at the Caspian Sea. My family vacationed there, along with our American friends, but I also had assignments there. My first boss, Fred Hemp, invited me to go along with him to the Caspian Sea. His daughter worked as an English instructor at the Imperial Iranian Air Force (IIAF) Language School. She taught Iranian Airman and Officers to master the English language. It was there that she met an Iranian citizen who also taught English. He was not her boyfriend, even though he would have liked that to have been the case. He spent several years in the States, going to school. Teymor was his name.

His father was a Chieftain whose domain was in the south central part of the country. He fathered a child at the age of eighty five. Teymor and I became good friends. I got the impression that he didn't care for the Shah. Earlier, in Iran, there was a redistribution of land and I think that his father was affected in some way. Teymor had a house up in the mountains near the Caspian Sea. That's where he spent his time when he wasn't working. He had no car, but there was bus service. The place that he owned was rather rustic, but comfortable. During my stay in Iran, I paid Teymor a lot of visits and enjoyed every one of them. He was a very gracious person, as were most Iranians.

Russian Vodka is an essential item to the Iranian palate, especially those who lived by

226

the Caspian Sea. On our first visit to Teymor, he introduced us to the real Iran. He brought out, what he said was real Russian Vodka.

It was a clear colored bottle with a label on it that had a picture of a lemon --and that was the only thing on it. There was no writing. When we took a sip, it couldn't be swallowed. That vodka must have been close to two hundred proof! "How can you drink this stuff?" I asked Teymor. He couldn't, so he put on a show for us. First he lit a match and then took a swig of the vodka. Then he blew the vodka out of his mouth while he held the match close to it. There was a big blue flame that shot into the air but then he breathed in too quickly and inhaled some of the fire. That wasn't funny. It must have hurt him but he just laughed, with tears running down his face.

Caviar was a vital part of our introduction to this area. We learned to buy our caviar at the Caspian, because it was so much less expensive there. Teymor took us to a fisherman and told him what we wanted. He showed us a can that held one kilo of fresh caviar. If it had a hint of salt, it was old. I had never tasted fresh caviar before. The night before, it was still inside the sturgeon. Small amounts were served at parties that I had gone to in Teheran, but I had never seen a kilo before. Caviar was always served as a delicacy in an elaborate setting. This stuff was inside a large, unmarked can. Fred showed me how to eat it. He just dug into it with a teaspoon, savored it in his mouth for a bit, swallowed it, then chased it with a sip of vodka -- not the real strong stuff. I tried it and in the end, I ate what I thought was a lot. Caviar is very rich and you can only eat so much of it. The Caspian: vodka and caviar!

The IIAF put in an airstrip at Nowshahr, a small town in the Caspian. Since it was a military base, now they needed a TACAN to be installed. This was the first time that I was there with IIAF people. That made it different. Most of my time was spent with them and that meant going to places that I had never seen before. One of the places was a bar and restaurant. We would go there at night. There was a giant bug whacker set up to get rid of the pesky bugs and there were a lot of bugs. I had never seen one of those devices before, so it was especially interesting to me. We would sit there, drink beer and watch the bugs being eliminated by the tens of thousands. It was hypnotizing. When the bar closed, we left. Sometimes we were the only ones left in the place. I must say, it was very tranquilizing and eliminated the effects of the day's work. The routine was a good one and I really enjoyed it.

The installation went very well. The FAA flight-checked it, so I set it up to FAA standards but it didn't work; we had false replies. So I set it up my way, which meets USAF standards, and it worked beautifully.

Ducks were everywhere around the Caspian. The locals hunted ducks in a primitive manner; it was astounding to watch. In order to see it up close, you must be out on the sea at night. We went out specifically to watch the hunting. Here's how it was done: there were no weapons involved. Many people were in boats out there and they were all doing the same thing, gathering ducks. There was a bright torch in the front of the boat. One man was beating on a drum. They would sail the boat into groups of ducks that were everywhere. The ducks would fly into the air but couldn't see because of the darkness. The bright torches blinded them, while the light drew them towards the boat. Another man in the boat had a giant net and was sweeping it in the air above the boat. Some boats had two men with nets. The ducks would then be trapped in the net. As the people took the ducks out of the net, they would wring their necks. One manned boat caught many, many ducks. There was no comparison to regular American shotgun hunting. People in the Caspian area ate a lot of duck and none of the ducks had shotgun pellets in them.

On one occasion, I was treated to the upper echelon style of hunting geese and ducks. We went to an exclusive hunting lodge. I never knew that places like this existed in Iran. It was not anything like I had seen before. The guides took us out into the Caspian and placed us in blinds. These blinds were giant barrels, submerged in the water and placed among the reeds. The geese and ducks could not see us. We just waited for them to come over. Then we would shoot as many as we wanted. Many of the birds were just wounded and would try to swim away. The people knew I was an expert marksman, so I was given a .22 rifle to shoot the wounded birds. They could not do it; you had to be very accurate. I shot a lot of them. We stayed out there most of the day. In the evening, a boat would pick us up, along with all the game that was floating around. We then went to the lodge and enjoyed a sumptuous meal.

Very early the next morning, I was taken to an isolated blind in the inland waterways. This blind was not in the water. It was a structure built out of wood and was camouflaged. I was by myself and they advised me not to shoot until the General shot first.

It was still dark and the sky was absolutely breathtaking. There were countless stars overhead, shining bright. What added a touch of glory was a beautiful comet, dazzling in its brilliance, directly overhead. I had never seen such a big, bright comet. Hunting was the last thing on my mind. This sight was incomprehensible. My mind was enjoying the sight and I just wanted to keep watching it.

Morning began to break and I could hear the ducks calling all around us. Then a shot rang out; the hunt had begun. I started to rake the birds that were in front of me and they all began flying away. As it got lighter, I could see a lot of floating birds along with several decoys that I had shot. What are they going to think of me? I never knew they had decoys.

As the day passed on, I kept shooting ducks. I reached thirty five and then the number began to dwindle. What was happening? Then I saw a very strange creature grab one of the ducks and drag it under. I had no idea what it was but it was huge. It ended up eating twelve of the ducks. After shooting more ducks, my final count was thirty two when they came to pick me up.

On the way back to Teheran, there was a landslide which blocked the road. Now, we had to wait. It was a very large landslide so it would be a long time before we got started again. The joke began: Iranians are very impatient when they are on the road. It was a two lane road, so everyone began moving into the second lane. My first thought was, "What if the people on the other side of the landslide were doing the same thing? We would go nowhere." Needless to say, that's exactly what they were doing.

When the road was finally opened, we went exactly nowhere. "Can't they think?" I wondered, not for the first time. It took a very long time to get out of there, The Land Rover made it easier for us, so we weren't delayed as long as the rest of the people. Landslides were very common in the mountains and a lot of people were killed as a result of the drivers' impatience.

The natives there were involved in many trades. One of the most interesting was making yogurt or *mast* as they called it. While on top of a mountain one day, I was introduced to a band of shepherds. There was a central place where the yogurt was being made. An old man was in charge of protecting the lambs from the wild animals. The shelter that they were kept in was made of wood branches stacked on top of each other to form a small sheepfold. I was left alone with the old man as others did their thing. The man offered to make tea for me and I accepted. He boiled the water in a wooden pot. It didn't burn because of the water in it. I had never seen that before. The old man was one hundred and one years old. He was still working at that age and was smoking too. One thing that I couldn't help but notice; the air smelled like sheep dung. When you walked, you could feel it squishing under your feet. I never got used to the smell, but it didn't bother them.

The other men started pouring milk from the sheep and goats into a very large hollow tree. This was where they fermented the milk. There was another group that took the *mast* (yogurt) out of the hollow trees by extracting a leather-covered wood plug, close to the bottom of the hollow tree. They poured the *mast* into goat skins and then loaded the skins onto a mule. Then, they would guide the mule down the trail, to the bottom of the mountain for the market. None of this was very sanitary! Everyone in Iran had *mast* every day and even mixed it with water to drink. That was called *douk*.

There was no way of contacting Teymor, so every visit was a surprise .He was always very gracious when I popped in on him. Once I did that while he was entertaining a few Bankers from Teheran. They were in a quiet discussion when I came in the door. None of them seemed to speak English. It was the beginning of a pipe party. As they smoked, they became very friendly -- and began speaking perfect English. Everyone insisted that I take a few puffs. I couldn't decline. This was a men's social event and everyone there had to participate. So, that included me. If I didn't, they would stop and everyone would be insulted. After that was over, Teymor started telling them what a great hunter I was and everyone then insisted that we go on a boar hunt. This happened to me so many times, everywhere I went.

Everyone got into my vehicle and the hunt began. It wasn't long before I spotted the prey. One shot and one was down, and then another. As I approached the first one, I noticed that it was still alive and very active, especially when it saw me. I decided to save a bullet and stab it to death. With my K-Bar in my hand, I attacked the wounded boar. He wasn't ready to quit, so it became a fight. The sad part was, I was really enjoying it. The first stab was in the upper front chest. The knife hit solid bone, so I lowered the thrust in the next stab. This time I used both hands, with all my body weight behind it. It hit home and that was it. The guests enjoyed the show and clapped for me. We loaded the boars and headed for home. It was a crowded vehicle.

Frogs are so numerous in the swamps of the Caspian. Iranians do not eat frog legs, so there is no market for them. The International set loves frog legs, caviar and snails. Since you couldn't buy frog legs and we were having an International party, I had to head for the Caspian. Dave, Michael and I took my small boat to an inland swamp. This was a new experience for us. It turned out to be very easy. We harvested about a hundred frogs with a net and a pellet gun. It was a messy operation though, and we didn't smell good afterwards. I decided I didn't care for frog legs. The people who attended the party loved the frog legs and fresh caviar but I never ate one of the frog legs and never wanted to either, from that time on.

Getting away from work was a godsend. As a family, our favorite vacation spot was the Caspian Sea. The MAAG had a reserved location on the IIAF vacation area at Chalus on the Caspian. The kids just loved it. The Caspian is a beautiful swimming place. The sea is very smooth. It is not very salty at all. It is actually a giant lake, the largest in the world, and it is below sea level. The mountains that surround the sea are covered with giant *platan* or plane trees, some of them thousands of years old; the forests are full of wild animals.

I had a friend who lived there and we would visit him. He had an orange grove that he constantly nurtured, importing and grafting fruits to improve the flavor. As I've mentioned previously, native Iranian orange trees, called "Naronge," produce sour fruit. In order to get sweet fruit, branches had to be grafted onto the tree. Sweet oranges were called "Portugal," because they had been imported from Portugal centuries ago. Grafting nursery stock was a thriving business in Iran. Lemons were also grown by the Caspian and elsewhere in Iran, but native Iranian lemons, "Limu Shirin," were sweet.

Once in a while, we were able to stay at the American General's house. Compared to the ordinary cabins, it was luxurious. There was always caviar to be bought. Compared to Teheran, it was very cheap, about thirteen dollars a kilo; that's two and two tenths pounds. In Tehran it was more than twice that amount on the black market. In the U.S. at that time it was seventy dollars an ounce. The kids loved it. If you can imagine them eating it by dipping corn chips into a can of it, well, that's what they did. I would eat it with a teaspoon. The can of caviar that we were eating was worth thousands of dollars. Caviar is black in color normally, but sometimes we were able to get the gold caviar. That was the kind that was only for the Shah. It was a crime to sell it.

On one of our getaways, 'Cretia and the neighbors wanted to go on a hunting expedition. Hunting to me was just an everyday event. I could do it or let it go. All of my guns were with me and we managed to get a light. You usually didn't see wild boars in the day. They hide in the swampy areas. Hogs don't sweat, so they stay in watery places during the day and come out at night. That's when they do their damage. In the Caspian area, people have small gardens. The hogs can destroy a lot of gardens in one night. When they are done with a garden, it looks like it has been plowed.

While on the hunt, we were waved down by a villager. He asked us to come right away and shoot some hogs, so we did. The man was so grateful that he insisted that we have dinner at his house. However, he first asked us if we were Russians. When we told him that we were Americans, the man flipped out. His joy was overwhelming. Now we just had to eat at his house. There was no way to refuse.

They went all out to treat us. They went beyond their means with everything. We knew that they were poor but this was their culture and I'm sure that everyone would know about it for years and generations to come. We spoke Farsi to them and they just loved it. It was a memorable night for us also.

The next day, I took the kids to Teymor's place. They also wanted to hunt, so I took them to a place where the boar lived. This time we would be hunting boar at close range, so I took my Model 12 Winchester filled with "00" buckshot. Up close, it is a devastating weapon. When we were in the swamp, I realized that the place was filled with wild boar. They were all around us but we couldn't see them. It was time to go. This was too dangerous for the kids. That didn't make them very happy.

Swimming in the sea was very pleasant. As I mentioned, there wasn't much salt in it. Iranian woman and kids were swimming close by, laughing and waving. Many wore nothing at all. I assumed there were times when modesty didn't matter. Swimming must have been one of them. The Caspian was the nicest place in Iran and we all loved it. What would our life have been without it?

Varamie

Some of our closest friends, Dave and his wife, S., enjoyed spending time with us at the Caspian Sea. We often returned the favor by visiting them at their farm outside Varamie, a small village east of Teheran. Crops were grown there, along with figs and other fruit. Dave was also raising pigs. The villager that took care of the place didn't like the pigs. Muslims are not allowed to eat pork and consider them very dirty animals. It was a good place to have fun, because of the vastness of the arid region surrounding us. I took my motorcycle there countless times. My wife and kids would occasionally come there to get away from Teheran.

There was a wild river a distance from the house that was on their land. That's the place where we had all our fun. For some reason, there were no fish in the river. The water was undrinkable. At different times of the year, flocks and flocks of wild geese and ducks, all different kinds, would swarm down that river and of course, we liked the ease with which we were able to hunt them. They might have used the river for navigation.

Dave bought an airboat, for some odd reason, and we took it to the house there in Varamie. He wanted to try it out, but I was the one who was selected to do the dirty work. I had piloted many different kinds of boats but never an airboat, so this was a good opportunity to learn. We headed for the river and put the boat in the water. As a standard precaution, I stowed my shotgun in the bow. That decision would prove to be a life-saver.

There was a large propeller in the aft of the boat. The propeller assembly was raised above the boat like an airplane engine and the rudder was in the back of the air steam from the propeller blades. It was, in fact, an airplane propeller with a screen around it so it wouldn't kill anyone. When we got it in the water, I started it and took off up the river. It was fast. I had gone about a half mile up the river when the engine stopped. It was out of gas. He never thought to fill it and I just assumed it was full. After all, why would he ask me to test it with no gas in it?

Now the fun began! The river was raging at this time of the year and there was no way to control the craft. I was moving down the river in the swift current, with no control of the boat whatsoever. A short distance down-river, there was a sharp turn; this was the dangerous part. The fast-moving current hit a solid rock wall, about seventy feet high, at full force. The water went up the wall from the force, and then turned about sixty degrees. My thought was that the boat would be propelled forward with the next big wave, hit the rock wall and then swamp it, if not tear it apart. "What a place to get submerged in icy waters," was the thought that screamed in my mind.

There was nothing I could do but wait. The boat was going very fast. Crash! To my surprise and delight, it hit the rock wall bow first, but the frail bow did not tear apart. The boat turned around one hundred and eighty degrees, shot left, very hard, and headed towards the shore, spinning wildly. The massive force propelled the boat up on to the shore. Dave was there and watched the whole thing happen. I got out of the boat and reached for my shotgun, but it didn't budge. It was wedged between the bow and the front seat. That's what kept the boat from smashing apart. What a godsend! It took a while to get the shotgun pried loose and to my surprise, nothing was wrong with the gun. Then I said to my friend "It's time to kick your ass. There was no gas in the tank. You could have killed me." Dave said, "Go ahead, I deserve it." After hearing that, I couldn't do it. It must have been quite a show.

Actually, I had a small boat of my own that I used for duck hunting. It was small and made of fiberglass. It fit on top of the Land Rover so it was easy to transport. I had promised little Michael I'd take him duck-hunting sometime. Dave came to my house very early one morning and said, "It's time to go. We need some ducks." I didn't want to go, but I had promised little Michael.

We put the boat in the water and my friend got in the boat. Little Michael didn't want to get in the boat. I insisted that he get in with Dave and cast off. Almost immediately, the boat started listing. I shouted to my friend to throw me the line and he did.

The boat was filling up with water. We pulled onto land and inspected it. There was a big hole in the bottom that looked like it was burned in. If it hadn't been so dark when we loaded it onto the Land Rover, we would have seen it. Little Michael and his friend had built a fire in the boat, accidentally burned the hole in it and had been too scared to tell me. So much for my boat! This would be a walking day.

We walked down the river and then diverted farther away from it. Two hours later, we were back on our original route. Something was different. There were very large tracks that had followed up. These were lion tracks. I had heard that there were lions in Iran, but not here. I had also heard that the Shah had brought in many wild animals that had reproduced very quickly so he had brought in lions to control the other animals' numbers.

Now we had one stalking us. I had a shotgun loaded with shells for ducks, but this was a lion. I had to come up with a plan to make sure that nothing happened to little Michael. The area that we were in had too much cover for a lion to hide and there would be very little reaction time. We had to cross the river immediately and climb up the steep walls so we could get an idea where the lion was. This we did, in double-quick time. Now we had to find a place where the river was deep, so Dave and Michael could jump off the cliff into the river -- if it came to that. We knelt there, scanning the desert with binoculars. There was no movement.

My plan was to shoot the lion in the face, blind him with the shotgun pellets and the finish him off with the .357. If something

241

went wrong, Dave and Michael would have to jump into the river and run to the Land Rover. Where the hell was he? I could feel that he was watching us. There was movement up the river, on the other side. It was the lion. He was waiting for us but we had screwed up his plans for us by climbing up the cliff. He decided to move on.

Keeping alert to everything in the desert was a must. Today, it saved us from who knows what, or maybe it saved the lion. We waited for an hour to make sure that he didn't change his mind and then moved down the river to a rickety bridge. The bridge was in bad condition but we could walk across it. After crossing, we ran for the Land Rover. Now, we were safe and aware of a problem that we never knew existed before today.

There was another surprise that came about a little later. One day, Dave and I were out exploring. We weren't doing anything in particular, just burning up gas in a place far south of Varamie. I remember I had a cross bow with me. We were checking out the range and accuracy of the weapon. It was not good for the desert because everything is so far away from you. We stopped the vehicle on top of a high hill and spotted a herd of camels. I had never seen camels, in a herd, so far out in the wild. There were no Nomads around. We just had to see this up close.

Dave went down first and skirted the camels. Then it was my turn. Every camel was

watching me. When I got into the middle of
them, all of them were looking at me. I was so
close to them. These camels had no work
scars on their bodies. They were wild. Then I
heard what sounded like a well gurgling. It
was a very low and mean-sounding noise. It
was coming from a very big, double hump
camel. No doubt about it; he was the leader
and he didn't want me there. He started
coming at me. Immediately, I took the rifle
off my shoulder and started yelling to my
friend. "What do I do? I don't want to shoot
him". He told me to do something that I
thought was dumb, but I did it and as I
thought, it didn't make any difference. He
kept coming at me, only faster now. I was
stepping backwards with my rifle pointed at
his nose. He was close. The time had come to
shoot him I thought, but I held off as long as
I could. Suddenly he stopped, as though he
had reached a boundary line.

Now there was another line of camels to my
left and my right, looking at me. These all had
one thing in common. They had all been beat
up. They had bloody marks on them. I was
sure I knew who had been beating these
camels. This was an exile place for camels
who had tried to take over the herd. It was an
interesting experience, being in their midst.
Now I knew there were wild camels in Iran.
Nobody believed me but that didn't matter.
They were there and I had spent a little time
with them.

Wild dogs were always a problem. They seemed to show up when you least expected them. If you didn't have a gun or a safe place to retreat, you were screwed. Dave had an old jeep that he used to get around in. We were in that jeep one day and were attacked by about ten wild dogs. Their plan was to kill and eat us. My friend was driving much too slow. The lead, a very big dog, jumped into the back of the jeep. I was able to shoot it point blank with the .357. The dog was dead instantly and fell out of the back of the jeep. When the .357 went off, all the canvas covering the jeep popped off, in all directions. My ears were ringing from the blast. That .357 had a lot of power. The dogs didn't like it. These incidences were very common but the setting was always a little different. It was a simple reflex to reach for my gun. The need to shoot and kill to save myself and others happened so many times, it would be redundant to recount each incident. Living through each experience was exciting, though. I kept most of this to myself, not to worry my wife and family.

One night we ran into a wolf. He came after us and was shot with the rifle. When I went to check on him, he jumped for me. I swung the rifle and hit him in the head. It was a hard blow and it killed him but it also broke the rifle and scope. I should have shot him two times instead of one and saved myself all the time and expense of fixing the gun.

East of Varamie was a very unusual, beautiful place. We found it by accident while riding by. The first thing we noticed was a Glass Waterfall. It actually looked like glass, with water running over it. Farther up, on a high mountain, was another beautiful waterfall. We just had to see this. Dave had borrowed Livvy's son's motorcycle, which was exactly like mine. You were able to climb mountains with these cycles.

First, we went to the Glass Waterfall. The substance looked like thick glass, but it was natural. Where did it come from? It was a dam with an overflow. There was a large reservoir, a lake created by the dam. There had to be something in the water that made this glass glow like that, but I couldn't figure out what caused it.

Our next objective was the upper waterfall. It was much higher and further away. We climbed the mountain, which turned out to be a mesa, with our bikes. As we were riding across the top, something felt very strange. I stopped and asked my friend if he had a strange feeling too. He said yes. Near the place where we had stopped, I saw a hole in the ground about three feet in diameter. There was cold air coming out of it. The next thing to do was to throw a stone into the hole. We couldn't hear it hit the bottom. Wow! We were on top of a hollow mountain. All we had to do was to hit a soft spot and nobody would know what happened to us. They would never find our bodies.

The only logical thing to do was to walk the bikes to the edge of the mesa and ride on the edge. The ground had to be thicker there. It was scary. We made it to the upper waterfall and savored the natural beauty. Then we took a different route down the mountain and rested. Now we knew what made the glass waterfall. In the course of tens of thousands of years, water in the mountain had dissolved the minerals in the mountain and as the water seeped over the edge of the dam, it created a glass wall. There was glass on the bottom of the water also, so the creation of the lowest point caused the dam to grow higher and higher and made the water basins grow larger and deeper.

We were driving along the road and saw a whole string of camels. I raked the whole caravan as we went by, shot at them with a BB gun. I got them all. I didn't kill them; I was only using BBs. The camels went bananas. They went after the camel drivers, thinking they had done it. They wouldn't stop until the drivers took off some clothing and gave it to the camels, so they could tear the clothing and take their anger out on the clothes. It was the funniest sight. Of course, the camels weren't mad at us, so we were safe.

Chapter 12: Tabriz

F14s at Esfahan, Iran

It was May, 1969, and things were getting very hot between Iran and Iraq. Military action was on the horizon. All U.S. military people were pulled out of Tabriz, in order that they might not be involved in a possible military conflict. Tabriz is located in the northwestern part of Iran near the Iraqi border. The Kurds, who were Sunnis, had been an irritation to the Iraqis and occasionally launched protests, because they wanted to be an independent state. There were millions of Kurds living in western Iran and eastern Iraq, so they were in the midst of the war zone. This happened to them pretty often. Ayatollah Khomeini was in Iraq and who knows what he was up to now. Iraq had a large Shiite population and he was

247

with them. He had no love for the Shah. The Shah had kicked him out of Iran.

The Imperial Iranian Air Force (IIAF) needed Tactical Air Navigation (TACAN) in Tabriz, to guide pilots to the base there. TACAN was essential for a pilot to know where he was, which way to go and how far he was away from his destination. The FAA Chief asked me how long it would take me to put one in. That was a question that was very difficult to answer. Where would I get skilled people to assist and the equipment I needed? Certain equipment had to be moved to Tabriz to get the job done. I told the chief, if I had everything I needed, I could do it in about a week, working long hours.

That alone was hard for me to imagine, under these circumstances, but it was possible. Then we needed to Flight Check it. That would require an FAA Flight Check crew to fly in and do their checks. I told him that this would be a very difficult thing to do under time restrictions. War doesn't wait. It had to be done right now. The MAAG had pulled out all of the stops. Tabriz was hot. I had to get it done now and I was the only one there that could do it.

The next day, I was on a U-8, a twin-engine US Army plane. Our first stop was Shahroki AFB, which was far out of our way, to pick up the equipment and pieces that I would need. We loaded everything and headed for Tabriz. As I looked out of the cockpit before landing,

I could see that this was an armed camp. Tanks, antiaircraft guns and hundreds of military people were in constant movement all around the airport. The Army Major who was the pilot said "Lots of luck, Mike. You'll need it." We had a nice landing and there were IIAF people there waiting for me, but no Americans.

This was the start of a maximized effort. As the U-8 took off again, I felt that I had been deserted by everyone and I had a strange feeling gnawing inside of me. It was a passing feeling. There wasn't anything I could do, since I was in the middle of it all right now. Introductions were made. At least I knew some of the people there. After all, I had already been in Iran for more than two years. I was pretty well seasoned to that country and its culture. I also knew a lot of Iranian people who were there.

Work began immediately at a feverish pitch. I won't go into details but for every effort, there was an impediment. Improvising was the order of the day and became very common place. American FAA arrived two days later and got right at it. It was a godsend to have them there. When I told them what to do, I didn't have to show them very much.

In the midst of all of the work, military activity was also carried out, at an equally feverish pace. Tanks were being dug in. Anti-aircraft guns were all over the airport. Camouflaging never seemed to stop. The antiaircraft guns were always going off. I could see soldiers running, then stopping and standing at attention as they were constantly being challenged by sentries. It was dangerous out there and would be very easy to lose one's life by straying from the TACAN site. Escorting vehicles would bring us in the morning, take us to lunch and dinner and finally take us home.

I would work later than the rest of the people because I had to get the electronic equipment working. In addition I had to direct the physical installation itself. The TACAN was a high-power vacuum tube piece of electronic equipment which had not been checked out. It was well used, in very poor condition and had major problems which took a long time to fix and stabilize. Early in the morning, I had to begin again. Hopefully, I would not burn out.

The IIAF fighter planes were there, sitting on the runway all day long, loaded with armament. Sometimes, they would take off. When they returned, the armament was gone. I didn't know exactly what was going on. That was not a good feeling, I thought. On the other hand, maybe it was better that way. I knew a lot of the pilots; I would wave to them and they would wave back. The pilots were from all over the country, from other bases. Our work location was on the side of the runway near touchdown. All of this entertainment was free.

The commander of the fighter group came over to see how things were going and asked how much longer it would take. He told me how grateful he was that we were doing this. The commander's name was Lieutenant Colonel Amir Hosein Rabii. He would later become commander of the IIAF. He was a very friendly person and from that day on, we became close friends.

One night, I heard a lot of noise outside. A great many vehicles were speeding by, one after another, but it was too dark to see exactly what was going on. I could see trucks and artillery pieces. "What's happening?" I wondered aloud. I left late but was back before dawn. Then, when the sun rose, I saw what it was all about. There were about two hundred artillery pieces in a line. Then it all started. They opened up. The shells were hitting in the mountains that partly surrounded the base. What a sight! The mountains were coming down. The noise from the guns was fracturing to the ears and body. My body was constantly shaking and vibrating. So was the ground. Something was happening. No matter what it was, I had my work to do.

By the fifth day, almost all of the essential work had been completed. The FAA people left but I had to stay until everything was completed. The Flight Check aircraft soon arrived and were ready to go. Flight Check was finished very quickly and the TACAN passed with flying colors. The aircraft landed and I took a jeep over to the tarmac to say good bye and thank the Flight Check people for their work. It turned out to be a very bad mistake. As I left the aircraft and headed for the jeep, I heard a loud shout.

My nightmare had begun. I found myself standing in front of a machine gun nest. There was one machine gun and eight riflemen. They were shouting at me and all guns were pointing at me. They sounded angry and crazy. I couldn't understand what they were saying.

I shouted in Farsi, "I'm an American." That didn't seem to matter. Unknown to me at the time, they did not speak Farsi. They were less than fifty yards from me. I could see everything that was going on and it was not nice. They were ready to fire. My 9MM was strapped to my chest but that was of no use to me now. I was out in the open. It would be all over for me in a second if I had done something.

"Why does it have to end like this?" I asked myself. After all of the work that I had done for them, it didn't seem right. I started to pray and I had the feeling that my soul was rising out of my body. I guess I didn't want to feel the bullets hit my body. "My poor wife and kids," I thought, "They will lose their daddy."

A blue jeep was approaching. The gunners turned the guns towards the jeep. The jeep was driven by LC Rabii, the commander of the Air Force strike group. He must have been warned by the pilots. Most of them knew me and were constantly sitting in their planes near the runway, ready to go. When he reached me, he asked what was happening. I told him. He said "Stay where you are." I had no intention of moving. He started talking to them. After about 5 minutes of talking, I asked him what was happening.

He said that he couldn't understand what they were saying. Apparently they were speaking Turkish. LC Rabii said, "They want to shoot me too." Now what! I couldn't imagine them wanting to shoot a Lieutenant Colonel in a flight suit, but they were Conscripts and not too smart. After a few more minutes of talking to the soldiers, he said "Go like hell, Michael!" I asked "Are you sure?" He responded "Go now!" So I did.

When I was a safe distance from the machine gun nest, I stopped to see what was happening. LC Rabii was still talking to them. Finally he got into his jeep and drove off. After what happened on that day, things changed. We were never bothered after that. When I think back to that day and what might have happened, I shudder. If it wasn't for LC Rabii, I'm sure I would have been killed.

The Days After

The action went on daily but it didn't bother us. It was a routine by now and watching my people work, along with the military activities, became an entertainment for me. Training was tedious but it was essential that the IIAF personnel were able to keep the TACAN operating. I had to get them to the point where they could maintain the TACAN without my help. If some serious problem occurred, I could be brought in to solve it.

LC Rabii would drop by with the Base Commander to see what was happening. Grateful was not a word that was anywhere good enough to describe my feelings for Rabii. How can you repay someone for saving your life? He had told me how much good had come about because now this TACAN was available to IIAF pilots. They would not stray into Russian territory anymore. Planes were often lost because of that.

Now, it was a reverse situation for the Russians. They became the victims, but it was never made public. All pilots, no matter how green, were easily able to find the Tabriz airport. My efforts had saved lives and cost a few. TACAN's saved many lives all over the country.

Sometimes, the anti-aircraft guns would open up. The guns looked like Russian 39 MM.

They fired very rapidly. When they opened up, it looked like a steady stream of fire about 6 feet long coming out of the barrel. Very noisy, but not like artillery. It seemed as though they were using commercial aircraft for practice. They never shot at the aircraft itself; they would shoot just behind them. At times, the flak would come down on us.

The first time I saw the black puffs from the explosions in the sky, I knew that it might come down on top of us. I yelled at the men to take cover under the building counterpoise. They did and the flak came down on us. After that it became a standard practice to get under the counterpoise. They didn't perceive what flak was at first but learned immediately.

Even this routine got boring after a while, but at least I didn't have to work late anymore. That was a blessing. It took several days to recover from the first week of work. One day, I went into the city of Tabriz with an Iranian sergeant. My point of interest was the Bazaar. Kurdish men were in the city. They were very visible and identifiable. They all wore a one piece "jumpsuit" with a sash around their waist. An old percussion cap rifle was slung over their shoulder and they were always in small groups.

I couldn't understand them. I don't know what language they were speaking. It must have been Turkish. A lot of people in Tabriz spoke Turkish. Later on, in other parts of the country, I saw large concentrations of these

255

Kurds in isolated, fenced-off areas. They had
their own guards, posted at the entrance of
the camp. They had to be coming from Iraq
and the constant war along the borders had
something to do with it. Iran and Iraq were
not friends.

The Bazaar is always familiar. It's a giant
market. It has the distinct smell of a variety
of spices. How comforting it was to know
that I wouldn't have to think there. I had no
particular thing in mind to buy. Maybe I could
find something for my wife. While walking
around, I saw a picture of what looked like
Crusaders executing people. There were
people in different lines. Some were being
thrown off of a cliff, some being beheaded
and some being hit over the head. The
merchant was looking at me with hateful eyes.
I asked my friend to ask him how much he
wanted for the picture.

It was the wrong thing to do. The merchant
started screaming at the Sergeant and then at
me. People started gathering. The merchant
grabbed a club and started coming after me. I
had my 9MM but I couldn't shoot him. I
could have beaten him up pretty good if it had
come to that but that was a "no-no" also. The
Sergeant said for me to run, so I did. It was
sort of funny to me. I was laughing as I ran.

It was entertaining for me and for the people
watching. They couldn't understand why I
was laughing. I asked the Sergeant why the
man got so angry. He said that the man didn't

want a Christian to have that picture. He then
cursed the merchant.

An unusual thing happened while I was there.
Following an unusual heavy rain, the edge of a
gold casket made its appearance from the wet
earth. It was discovered by a peasant in the
area. Inside the casket were many jewels and
things of antiquity. To say it was worth a
fortune, is an understatement. Well, the
procedure that is to be followed in a case like
that was to report it to the authorities.
Instead, this peasant took the jewels one at a
time and sold them in the Bazaar. Needless to
say, he was caught and punished but a new
treasure of Persia appeared on the scene.
There are untold treasures still hidden in that
country.

LC Rabii and the Base Commander paid us a
visit the next day to check things out. He
asked me how I was. I told him I was fine but
I had to go home soon. He told me he needed
me there until things quieted down and the
crisis was over. He even offered to get a
helicopter and take me to an island not far
away to hunt wild sheep. He said there were
thousands of sheep there. I told him that I
didn't have a rifle to hunt with. He said it
didn't matter because the helicopter had
twenty millimeter cannons on board and I
would be able to use them. If that ever got
out, what would the Americans say about me?
I had to beg off.

Then, he started to talk to the men. He said that they must take care of me and keep me happy. They said that they didn't have any cars to take me places. They needed a car. Could he get one for them? I knew that they were talking about women. He said that he would take care of it.

The very next day, the men told me, we had a full sized bus with a driver assigned to us. It was for me. The driver could not go anywhere unless I was in the bus. They were all so happy. I wondered why, but I shouldn't have. The men told me we were going for a ride that night. Wouldn't you know it? They were looking for prostitutes.

I thought, "Oh well they need a morale boost too." They had a ball. I was sitting in the front of the bus and they were doing their thing in the rear of the bus. I felt as though I was running a whorehouse on wheels. I guess I was. They all loved me for their night of entertainment.

My scheduled home leave to the States was very near now and I was getting edgy. I would be going with my family to Germany, and from there to the States on the SS United States. It was a luxury ship and we were going in First Class. I couldn't miss that. I had to tell LC Rabii that I must leave soon. I met him and explained my situation.

He asked if I truly believed that the men could take care of the TACAN. I assured him that they could. "They have been trained extensively and I have a lot of confidence in them," I told him. He then said he believed me and I could go back to Teheran. What a relief! I must have been the happiest man in the world.

Back In Teheran

I cannot describe just how happy I was to be back at home. My family couldn't imagine the joy that I was experiencing. Lucretia embraced me and gave me a very passionate kiss. The kids gathered round me and jumped on my legs to get a "walk-ride" around the house. My neighbors were happy to see me also. This was an exciting thing for the MAAG people. All this action had happened. They weren't there but I was. My neighbor, R., was a Lieutenant Colonel in the U.S. Army and we had been very close for the past two years. He wanted to know everything that happened, so I went through it all. They had a small party for me. I was a hero to them, but I didn't think so.

I had to report to the office ASAP and I did just that. People weren't as happy as I thought they would be. I was told to go immediately to the USAF MAAG commander. I thought that I was going to get some kind of award. That wasn't the case. He asked me about Tabriz and what happened there. I went through it all. When I got to the part about the anti-aircraft guns and the commercial airplanes, he stopped me and said that the gunners weren't firing at the planes. I said that I know that they weren't shooting at the planes but they were firing in back of them. He said again that the gunners don't fire at commercial planes. Then it hit me. "Oh hell, what's happening?" I got it. I told him that I must have been seeing things and probably imagined it all. "I was under a lot of stress," I explained.

He told me that it's a good thing I hadn't seen any gunners firing at commercial planes because if I had, I would be sent home within forty-eight hours. It would have made the army look incompetent. I wisely repeated my statement that I'd been under a lot of stress and didn't know what I was saying.

The MAAG commander congratulated me on an excellent job. "You did a great thing," he said. I was dismissed and then went to my boss. He looked very concerned. He knew what was going on. I told him that everything is okay now. We were laughing. I asked him if I would be getting an award for the work that I did because I needed the money. He said that you really had to do something great to get an award. I wondered, "What the hell is something great? How great does it have to be?"

The Officer's Club was having a big party. They pulled out all of the stops. Planes flew in beer from Germany along with other foods that were hard to come by. If a person wore Lederhosen, which were short German leather trousers, they would get everything free. I was given a pair by my neighbor. They were very tight-fitting but money was money. I wore them.

My wife and our neighbors, R. and A., were with us as we went into the club. A man in the crowd said "Hi Michael!" I turned and saw that it was the leader of an archeological team that I had met somewhere earlier. I said "Hi," and shook his hand. We had a few words and then I proceeded to go on into the club but only after R.'s wife came over to us, slid her arm under mine and said, "Let's go Michael."

She then glared at the "queer." The LC's wife said to me "Just what do you do when you are in the boondocks, Michael?" It was obvious that the guy was queer. I said "I know that he's a queer but I can't control what kind of people that I run into in the boondocks." She sniped, "I always wondered about you Michael." I laughed at her. "Don't talk stupid."

The party began, and it was a blast. As we were sitting at our table, a USAF Lieutenant Colonel came to our table. He had already had a lot to drink. We knew each other fairly well. He then yelled at R. "You son of a bitch! You call yourself a friend! You know what you almost did to Mike?" There were more words and then I realized what had happened.

As soon as I told my neighbor what had happened in Tabriz, he went right to Intelligence. That's why I was nearly sent back to the U.S. I said this to him and then his wife said "How could you do a thing like that"? He said that it was his duty. That ruined the night. At least I was able to get my fill of real German beer.

As I was falling asleep that night, I pondered over the things that had happened. My boss told me that my reward would be the overtime that I made and my being able to stay in the country. There would be no award and no official recognition. I was learning. In the States, the awards came so much easier then here in Iran. They thought that if you were in a foreign country, you were on a vacation.

Mashad

Mashad is considered a holy city in Iran. Gold covers the great dome of the mosque in the heart of the city. There was also a U.S. Army attachment located there. The city is located close to what was then the USSR. It was a strategic location for the US and I was about to learn how strategic it really was.

The IIAF provided me with a vehicle and a driver who spoke English very well. The driver asked that I call him Johnny. I was able to find a room in a local hotel that was fairly nice. In one day, I was all set up to begin my venture there.

Americans who lived there soon found out that another American was among them. It's a wonderful feeling to have people seek you out, for no other reason than to share their life with you for a short time.

Some Christian missionaries who were stationed in Mashad invited me to visit them so they could show me where they lived. They were two women nurses. They had a small hospital where they trained young nurses. One thing that puzzled me was why Christians were allowed in this city. They explained the good and the bad that went along with the program.

"One thing that we dislike most is the final days of Ramazan. In Iran it is called Ramazan but in other counties it can be called Ramadan. The Arabic alphabet has no Z or P. Men especially come by the hospital in droves, because of stomach ulcers caused by extreme fasting," they said. "Many were so bad that they died from the ulcers." Fasting begins at sunrise and ends at sunset

263

Depending on the time of year that kind of fasting can be fatal.

The Missionaries were going to throw a party one night, and I was invited. There were no indications about what kind of party it would be, so I put on the nicest clothes I had. A party was a rare treat in places far from Teheran. American music was played. They had contests with prizes and dancing. The prizes were funny type prizes. One of them was an "*oftabeh*." That is a miniature sprinkling can that is used by the Iranians to wash their butts after defecating. Toilet paper was not used except by foreigners. I did not win anything.

Dancing began soon after dinner, which was a very nice spread. Someone put a lot of effort in making the food. Dancing was the usual thing. Iranian young men were dancing with each other but not with the nurses. The nurses just sat on their chairs but were not dancing. I danced a few dances with the Lady Missionaries and while I was dancing with them, I asked why the young nurses were not dancing. They answered that nobody asked them.

"Should I ask them?" I inquired. "Why not?" was the reply.

As I approached one of the young nurses, many sets of eyes were looking at me. She answered my request with a smile and replied in perfect English, "Yes". As we danced, I asked her why none of the young men were dancing with the women. She answered "They are so stupid. They just dance with each other and tomorrow, they will tell the whole city that I am a whore." At that, I pushed her away very gently and said, "I am so sorry. Forgive me, for I did not know about your ways. If I did, I would never have asked you to dance with me." She responded, "to hell with them; I like dancing with you." The whole thing gave me a sick feeling. I wished that I had never asked her to dance. She had to live there. What did this innocent incident do to her life? I'll never know.

While the work went on, I found out that there was a beautiful mansion in the city where there was a USAF Master Sergeant. Nobody knew what he did there. Since I had military ID that said that I should be treated like a US Major, I decided to stop by and pay him a visit.

The Master Sergeant answered the door and I introduced myself. He invited me in and appeared to be very happy to see me. He offered me a drink of the finest Scotch and I accepted. Then the conversation began. This man was responsible for running the house and I wanted to know more about his situation.

It turned out to be a rest and relaxation place for a group of CIA men whose job it was to snoop on the Russians. They were stationed on the border of Iran and the USSR. They would come to the house to rest and rehabilitate after spending thirty days on the job. They would look forward to the fantastic foods, spirits and women. This place was really beautiful. It was something to look forward to, for them. At the time of my first visit none of them were there, but I would see them another time.

Pilot Gary Powers had been shot down over Russia in his U-2 not long before. I don't want to go into that. But, since we were not able to fly over Russia any more, the snooping had to be done from the ground. These men spent their time in a very undesirable environment and when they got to the Safe House they looked very "Ratty."

A few days in "Paradise" did a lot for their morale. They must have been doing a good job because in the near future, a new terrorist group appeared. Their main target was assassinating Americans who were associated with the Intelligence gathering group in Iran. They were funded by the Russians.

The Iranian Airmen that were assigned to me took me on a tour of the city. As I wandered around the city, I really couldn't find anything that I wanted so I ordered some very large alabaster cigarette ash trays to be made for me. The ones that they had for sale were very small. Needless to say, that after my order, in a month, the same type of ash tray appeared in Teheran and sold like hotcakes. This happened with everything that I had custom made to my specifications.

Now a repeat performance of Tabriz was about to happen. While walking with the Iranian Airmen, I was hit over the head from behind with something and I fell down, dazed. Danger was here and I immediately realized it. As I rolled over I saw a crazy man with a club in his hands yelling. The Airmen were shouting at him. Still half dazed, I got up and had every intention of beating the hell out of that guy. I had my gun but there was no need to use it. He would be easy I told myself but I have to be careful not to kill him.

The U.S. Army taught its young soldiers very well how to kill and that never leaves you. It wasn't that long ago for me. When he saw me get up, there was a very distinct, frightened look in his eyes. He knew that it was his turn for a beating. The Airmen begged me not to hit him. "This is a very religious city and you are a foreigner. They will put you in jail and treat you very badly."

I thought about it very quickly and realized they were right, so I said to the man, "your mother is a whore and your father is a dog." There is no greater insult than that. The man did nothing. He was still scared. In, fact, he was trembling. He never expected that I would get up. That would be the extent of my pay back. We left. The Airman thanked me for not hitting the man and started calling him names and cursing him. They were ashamed

267

of his behavior. He was a religious figure of some kind.

My hotel room turned out to be not so good. The room smelled all the time because the drains had no traps in them. All the sewage smell came into the room. All the rooms were like that so there was no other place to go.

Another nuisance was the cat. At night, it would get into the room somehow and keep me awake by crawling on the bed, and on me. I kept putting him out, but he would always get back in. As to where he got in, I couldn't find out. The hotel manager was no help, so one night I shot it with my hi-power pellet gun. I always kept that pellet gun with me, to kill giant spiders, snakes and wild dogs that used to chase our vehicle.

I wrapped it up and dumped it near the airport the next morning on my way to the site. My work was critical and the lack of sleep would affect the outcome. If I didn't get a good night's sleep, I would end up making more mistakes and the work would take much longer if I had to correct them. There was only so much time.

The Hotel manager kept asking me if I had seen his cat. So it was his cat! Now he tells me. I told him that I hadn't seen it.

The final good experience came in the form of an invitation from the Missionaries that I go with them to the best Kabob place in Iran. It was outside of town. There was a large herd of sheep outside of the place and lots of people. They did a lot of business. When we finally got our order, it was well worth the wait. I had never had anything like it before that and I never had anything as good since. I have no idea why it tasted so delicious. One clue was constantly getting up from sleep and drinking lots of water. I just couldn't get enough of it. Salt! It must have been salt, and something to cover the taste of it.

One other thing was the U.S. Army troops. They were stationed on the Iranian base and had something to do with mapping. I went to their barracks one day and noticed a strange thing. On one side of the building, all the windows were covered. When I asked about the coverings, the American officer told me that the American troops would watch the Iranian troops during their drills and laugh. They thought their drills were just so funny, and they were, to us. The music was strange and the maneuvers were just as funny. The Iranian officers insisted that the windows be covered so the Americans would not be a distraction.

Mashad was a unique experience but I wouldn't want to go through it again. Teheran was always awaiting me and my family. I loved Teheran and all that it had to offer. It was a world I thoroughly enjoyed and just couldn't get enough of it.

Chapter 13

Last Days in the FAA

SS United States

Entering New York Harbor, 1969

The projects at Tabriz were completed and I was exhausted. Fortunately for me, my R&R trip to the US was one of the things that helped me to get out of that place. Now we had First Class tickets on the fastest cruise ship in the world, the S.S. United States. It was the end of May, 1969. It was not a good idea to leave the house vacant, so we let a couple stay there for free while we were gone. We would be gone for about ninety days. Sixty days were home leave and thirty days were scheduled for Transistor school at the FAA Academy.

Mehrabad International Airport was our departure point in Teheran and from there we flew to Frankfurt, Germany. We spent several days enjoying Frankfort and the German beer, then went to the railroad terminal to get a train to Bremerhaven. That was the port from which the S.S. United States was to sail. At the station, we were in line waiting to get our seat assignments when, lo and behold, I spotted an old friend of mine from the Army. I used to call him Rooster. He was a Sergeant now. When we got to the head of the line, I shouted "Rooster; you old son of a gun." He recognized me right away and put his finger to his mouth to indicate, "Don't say that." Too late, all the other men there, who were also assigning seats, started to laugh. This operation was conducted by the U.S. Army. He ordered them to shut up and they were quiet. We talked for a minute, and Rooster gave us first class seats in the train. It was a military train.

In Bremerhaven, there was a large band playing at the boarding area. At that time, no one really noticed the couple with five kids. When we got into the First Class section of the ship, people began to take notice. Almost all the people were a lot older than we were. There weren't any children that I could see. This was the end of an era. Ocean cruising was becoming less popular as more people preferred to fly to their destinations. Besides that, cruising was very expensive. Well, not for us; we didn't pay a thing. It was part of the benefits. After a long time, the ship finally set sail.

We stopped once, in Southampton, England, then went on into the North Atlantic. The waters on our way to England were not rough, in fact, the ride was extra smooth. On board the S.S. United States, it was a world in itself. Everything was so immense. If you didn't go onto the deck or look out of the portholes, you wouldn't know that you were aboard a ship.

When we departed England, things changed. A storm came up and the waters became rough and choppy. You could feel it on board ship, and some people got seasick. We were located in the middle of the ship. Fred Hemp told us to get a cabin in that location because there we would enjoy the smoothest ride. He was right. I decided to walk the ship when we had very rough seas. In the hallways, there was vomit all over the place. It really stank; the crew had difficulty keeping up with the stench. On deck, the ship was going up and down. Fortunately, that only lasted for a day. Maybe it was turbulent after that, but you didn't notice it after being exposed to a very rough sea.

Our cabin was very big. There was a fruit basket on the table all the time. We had our own dining table with a private waiter. The meals were fabulous. Every morning the kids would order steak and eggs. Sometimes they would make flaming desserts at the table. Anything that we wanted, they would make for us. It was the life of luxury. We had lots of caviar.

There was afternoon tea with a concert and shooting clay pigeons from the fantail. There were also movies and we didn't have to worry about baby sitters. That service was also included in our package. We were able to sneak into Second Class through the theater at night. Their casual style of dancing was more to our liking than First Class. We were allowed to mingle with a "lower class," but it wasn't the same for the Second Class passengers. There was a guard at the gate. When the ship began to sail, the doors to Second Class were locked, just like in the movies. In Second Class, we noticed the floor was always vibrating from the engines. That must have been annoying to the passengers. Back in First Class, we were invited to the Captain's table for dinner, where we were introduced to him and his wife. It was a touch of High Society and we enjoyed it.

The ship went to New York Harbor under the new suspension bridge, passing through the

Verrazano Narrows, and the Statue of Liberty. Many people were waiting for us there. We could see them from the ship. Disembarking was strange. The dry land seemed as though it was moving all the time. That feeling lasted for a long time.

After hugging and kissing our friends and relatives, we headed for my parents' place in Pennsylvania. Home leave started when you touched the shore of the USA. Our ninety days had just begun. Due to the length of our stay, we rented a large house in a camp. It was from there that we did all of our visiting and it was the focal point of our activities.

To keep up with technology, I had to go to the USAF Academy. It was July 1969, and Commander Neil Armstrong and Pilot Buzz Aldrin had just walked on the moon. To celebrate, President Richard Nixon, gave us all a day off. It was a Friday, so I took advantage of it and went to visit my old boss, Fred Hemp, who lived in California. I booked a flight to San Francisco and they picked me up at the airport.

It was a very pleasant visit and I enjoyed myself immensely. On the day that I was to return to Oklahoma, to the Academy, they took me to visit a few California wineries. I sampled good wine at every place we visited. I was feeling pretty mellow by the time Fred took me to the airport in San Francisco. When I boarded the airplane, I felt like I was floating, very relaxed. On take-off, an engine blew up on the port side of the plane and was burning like hell. The aircraft lunged to the side on which the burning engine was located, but the pilot recovered the plane immediately. We had reached the point of no return on the runway, so we had to get airborne and come around again to land. I watched the burning engine and kept expecting the wing to burn off and crash. The people appeared to be very calm and undisturbed but you could sense the feeling of fatality. The things that must have been running through their minds!

We were able to land and a fire truck appeared and put out the fire. That's when it began. A woman started screaming and ran to the front of the plane followed by many other people. I don't remember being afraid, in fact I seemed to be enjoying it to a small extent. The effects of the wine tasting were still with me. I had survived many near air disasters so this was just another one.

We changed planes and took off again with no incident. I was studying my FAA books when a pilot sat down beside me. He saw the FAA book and asked me what I did in the FAA. I told him and in our discussion I found out that he was the pilot of the plane that had just caught on fire. Then he said that this incident was nothing and started telling me about many other incidents. The trip to Oklahoma went by very quickly due to our interesting conversation.

My wife and I had done so much shopping during our home leave that I couldn't imagine packing all of this stuff. We managed. The things about the U.S. that you don't find in other places are the sales and the interstate highway system. These were the things that Americans in Iran missed the most.

When we boarded the plane, we had to pay for the extra baggage. My wife made out the check for two hundred dollars but the woman behind the counter said that she had made a mistake. 'Cretia said that she didn't have any more checks, so the woman said that we would have to pay the cost in Teheran. We agreed. The mistake that the woman made was eight hundred dollars. That made the bill one thousand dollars.

Upon landing in Teheran, we went through Customs. I paid one of the retired guys who sat there to collect the bribes. He then signaled the Customs people that these people were okay. Customs asked us what was in one of the twelve packages and my wife explained we had been shopping in the States. Nobody ever asked for the overweight payment, so we had enjoyed a fabulous vacation with an extra savings of one thousand dollars. That was a bonus.

Vahdati was my home again for the last few months of my Iran tour with the FAA. The year was 1971. A new RAPCON (RADAR Approach Control) system was being installed on that base. It included ASR (Airport

Surveillance RADAR), PAR (Precision Approach RADAR) and all the communications and tie-ins necessary to control Air Traffic. The man in charge was what we called an installation man. He had not been at any major school at the FAA Academy. In fact, he flunked out. Why he was put in charge, I'll never know. He was able to do wiring and physical work but knew very little about electronics and engine generators, let alone RADAR.

For the last four and one half years, I had worked on different bases around Iran, doing all different types of electronic work and installations. The IIAF Airmen would work their hearts out and were very eager to learn. We had a very good relationship both on and off the job. This would be my last assignment. My time in Iran had come to an end, so I thought. I liked RADAR and decided to enjoy my last days working on it.

The FAA people stationed there stayed at a house in the town of Andemeshk. They had very little contact with the USAF people, who were at the base. Several years before, I had stayed at that house. It was very large, a nice, comfortable place. Actually, it was a home coming for me. All the neighbors knew me and so did many people in town. The children were very glad that I had come back. They all remembered me and I was greeted with great enthusiasm. In a way, the other FAA people seemed to be jealous of this outpouring of delight from the neighbors. When we got home from work each day, the kids were all waiting for me to say, "*Salome agah mohandez* (hello, honorable engineer)." My Farsi was pretty good, so we would carry on conversations and I would give things to them. Their parents would watch and talk with me. They didn't know any English.

The kids and adults told me what the other FAA guys were doing. One of the FAA men would get drunk every night while sitting on a chair on his porch. He would then take off all of his clothes and just sit there, drinking. The kids were on the roofs of their houses watching. They would laugh and yell things to him. He knew they were watching. All the roof tops in Iran were flat with walls around them. People, at night time would sleep on the roofs in the hot weather, so the roof was a definite asset for the people. They also told me that one of the guys, my new boss, asked one of the fathers if he could marry his young daughter. She was only fourteen years old. The father refused.

It gets better. One of the officers told me more of the things that the boss did. A girl friend of his asked the boss to go out on a date with her. She invited her friends along and he had to pay the bill. They went to some nice places, so the tab was a big one. The boss told the rest of the guys that he had lots of girls that he would go out with in Teheran. The girls turned out to be guys. Where did the

FAA get these people? He also made money from the Black Market. He would also give Scotch to Iranian airmen and officers in exchange for "favors." It got to the point that I couldn't stand being near him. I soon discovered there was a considerable amount of politics involved in his appointment anyway.

After a while, things between us went from bad to worse. An incident happened in Vahdati that changed my whole world around. One day the boss told me that I could no longer go home on weekends because I was not working hard enough. That got to me. I worked very hard every day. I explained that I was up at three o'clock that morning to align the RADAR antenna before the sun arose. He didn't know that, but it didn't make any difference to him. My train was leaving at 2:30 that afternoon, so it was time for me to get to the station. He really was incompetent; knew nothing about the work I did for the FAA, and ignored me. Without other, more intelligent people around him, nothing would get done. I was tired of his nonsense; I just couldn't take any more of it.

So, I lost it. I picked him up while he was still in his chair and threw him across the room. He weighed about 250 lbs. When he landed on the floor, he was in shock. I was on top of him and began to choke him. He shit in his pants and was pissing. The force was unbelievable. Adrenalin had taken over. The

Iranian soldiers tried to hold me back. There were seven of them, but it didn't matter. I threw the first one against the wall with one arm and he slid down the wall, hurt. He was my friend. "What have I done?" That's when I realized what I was doing, so I let the boss' neck go and drew back my fist to break his face. The rest of the soldiers were holding on to my arm and screaming for me not to do it. I stopped. He couldn't get up. His eyes showed panic. I literally beat the shit out of him. Now, that's funny.

I never even noticed that I was bleeding badly. The boss had had a long screwdriver in his back pocket with the blade pointing upward, and when I picked him up to throw him, I ran myself through. I never felt any pain. My right boot was filling up with blood very quickly. The blood was running down the inside of my leg and into my right boot. It's a good thing that the boots were very high.

There was a man there from Oklahoma City who was with the FAA. Oklahoma City was FAA headquarters. He had been assigned to Iran to do a logistics job. We were very good friends. He was a boxer and I had been a boxer too, when I was in the Army. We had so much in common. When he found out how badly I was hurt, he took me to the hospital. They patched me up and I left, even though the doctors insisted that I must stay. When they realized I was going to walk out of

281

the hospital, the doctors started screaming at me and trying to hold me back. I wasn't going to give the boss the satisfaction of knowing that I was hurt so I left anyway.

The manager in Teheran called me and told me to return to Teheran. The IIAF found out about it and tried to stop it but they were overruled by the MAAG. They didn't want to lose me and they hated the guy I had just beat up. They knew about him. He was in the Airman's conversations every day. The boss wanted to file attempted murder charges.

Before I left for Teheran, a Colonel of the IIAF, who was a pilot and a friend, came to me and asked me if I could design and make a new system for them. They wanted to be able to count the bullets from a fighter airplane that would hit a practice target while that plane was making its practice run. I said that it wouldn't be too hard because the bullets break the sound barrier and I could make a directional sound system that could detect the "cracks" of the bullets as they passed through the corridor on the way to the target. The crack would be converted to an electronic pulse and that system could be connected to a simple electronic counting system that would record the strikes. He thanked me and left. He appeared to be happy to hear what I said. Why he did this at this time was beyond me. Maybe it had something to do with what was about to happen. I never heard about it again.

Upon my arrival in Teheran, I was questioned by my manager. I explained everything that happened and told the manager that he had an incompetent man in charge back in Vahdati. Later, I found out how right I was. There was sympathy for me and the MAAG agreed with me. The FAA manager was the person who had been with me in Ab Garm, where I had saved his life and mine. He said that I would have to stay in Teheran. Now that was good news. My tour was almost up and it would be spent with my family. I wondered why this situation was resolved so easily, though. Later, I found out. The friend from Oklahoma had told the manager that he would report what was going on here if the manager tried to hurt me. He must have scared him. Now I had the best of both worlds.

A visitor came to my house to see me. He was the original FAA man who was in charge of the FAA/AID when I arrived in Teheran originally. He had gone to Pakistan to see the work that I had done there and congratulated me on my fine work. He said that they spoke very highly of me there. He was now in charge of the FAA in Vietnam. He wanted to know what was going on and he came to me because he thought that I was an honorable man.

I explained everything to him. He then said me, "If you want it, I will give you a promotion in Vietnam." Now, that possibility made me so happy. It would mean a raise in pay. I would have more than enough money to support my family which was now up to almost seven children. Christel would be born very soon. My work place would be Saigon. I couldn't wait to tell 'Cretia. The FAA had planned to send me to Dulles Airport in Washington D.C. as a Technician in Depth. That's the last place that I wanted to be. Before I went to Pakistan, I had spent some time in D.C., learning about the equipment that I was to commission in Karachi.

I told 'Cretia about the offer of promotion and transfer to Vietnam. My wife's reaction shocked me; she went into orbit. She screamed at me "You just love war. I can't stand this anymore!" She was also trying to beat me up. Can you imagine the sight -- a woman eight months pregnant, beating up her husband? I went along with it because I didn't want her to hurt herself. I said, "Cretia, we do need the money." She said, "We don't need it that much. You will be away from us for a long time and you may never come back." There was no question of the family going; that was not an option. So, she totally rebelled against it, and said it was not necessary. I was interested, because it was a lot more money and a promotion. But I wouldn't see my family for at least six months if I went to Vietnam. It was a difficult decision. My wife said "You've been out in the field too long, what are you thinking?" 'Cretia felt it was an insane decision; she started hitting and kicking me. I fell on the floor and just let her beat me up a bit. I was laughing. She did not like that. She started screaming, "You will not go to Vietnam!" Later, when she calmed down, 'Cretia explained she was horrified I would consider such a dangerous assignment.

I tried to reassure her. "We will be able to see each other in Hawaii every six months and I'm not the type that gets killed." That was the wrong thing to say. She just beat me up more. She was screaming and crying. Now I felt depressed. I thought, "I'll never understand women."

The news went around like a wildfire. The neighbors found out the same day. I had a lot of officers who were personal friends in Vietnam or going there soon and I was looking forward to seeing all of them over there. One of them, a Colonel, said that if I ever got to Saigon I should look him up; he would take care of me. That man could drink more Scotch than anyone that I ever knew and would be able to keep up a conversation. At one of my parties, he drank a whole bottle of "Johnny Walker Black Label," and drove home.

It must be remembered that I lived in a military world and we were one big happy family. My neighbor, a U.S. Army Lieutenant Colonel who had spent time in Vietnam, came to my house and talked with me. He said that Saigon was actually a nice place and that I would enjoy it there. That sounded good to me, but my beloved wife was not happy. She wouldn't hear of this new job.

The next day, an Iranian friend, a woman named R., came to visit 'Cretia and me. I don't know how she found out about the "fight with my wife." The Iranians were evidently keeping close track of what was going on. She said that my boss in Vahdati needed the beating and that they were happy that I gave it to him. R. also told 'Cretia, "The Imperial Iranian Air Force (IIAF) people just love your husband and they really want him to stay. "The Shah wants Mike to work directly for him." All of this because of beating up that incompetent boss in Vahdati! How did they all know about it? She turned to me and explained, "The Americans said that they couldn't ask you to go and work for the IIAF. You must write a letter and ask the IIAF to hire you." I asked her why I hadn't heard about this myself. She said that I was hearing about it now.

I worried. "That would make me a mercenary and I would lose my American citizenship." She explained that I would not lose my citizenship; everything would be taken care of. Of course, I didn't believe her. Then she told me that the generals and the Shah had discussed all this in a meeting. They would give me whatever I wanted. They needed me. This was too much. How could these people know me?

I thought about it. The next day I wrote a letter, just as she said. I went to an old friend who was with the Deputy Chief of Staff. I told him what I had heard and named the generals that 'Cretia's friend had mentioned. I didn't know who they were. The Colonel said that he didn't know them. So I took the letter back but he insisted that I leave it with him. Now I was puzzled. Why wouldn't he know these generals but 'Cretia's friend did know them? How highly was she connected? Who was she? Why does she know all these things? This Colonel must be lying. Why? Why does he want that letter? It was all so puzzling. So, I gave him the letter with no hopes of this supposed job. I left, thinking I could at least accept the position in Vietnam.

Two days later, I received my answer. I had a new job. 'Cretia's friend came to our house and said, "Congratulations Mike! You are now a Major General in the IIAF." She was so happy. That was too much. "Why would they give me such a high rank?" I asked. "Because they didn't want to have any other American higher than you," she explained simply. She said that the generals were celebrating at her house. Then I realized that I didn't know anything. This woman knew what was going on and I didn't, but I was happy.

I immediately went to my friend, the Deputy Chief of Staff. Would you believe that he congratulated me also and asked me when I could begin working in my new position? "I

287

can't start now," I said. "I must first go back to the States for a little vacation". What an elation this was! Was all this real? It appeared to be so. They were all just waiting for that letter. All it took was a beating for my boss.

My next step was to go to my manager and break the news to him. He was not very happy. "I have an official letter here from the IIAF," I said. Then I handed it to him. The rest of the day was spent resigning and filling out paperwork. The news spread all over the MAAG in no time at all. Most people who knew me didn't believe it. It was just too incredible. A lot of them told me not to do it. It was too risky. Why should I care? 'Cretia was happy that I didn't have to go to Vietnam and we would have more money than we ever dreamed of. It was a risk, but how else do you make it big?

'Cretia's friend was back at the house, telling what we would have to get and do to fit into the new upper crust of Iranian society. I said that I didn't want to get involved in that and that we would live the way we always had. Why should we spend all the money that we were going to make and go home with nothing? That made no sense. 'Cretia agreed. We would be high ranking peasants. That was good enough for us.

The next thing that we had to do was to plan our trip back home and prepare for a new life. We waited for the new baby, Christel, to arrive. A few weeks later, we headed back for the States. We were two very happy people. We were both in a state of elation. This was a new Paradise for us and our family.

Chapter 14: A New Era

Mike, Mr. & Mrs. Ed Mc Cullough
(Livvy's boss)

Teheran, 1972

I had been offered an assignment in Vietnam, in Communications. As I mentioned earlier I turned it down, despite the promotion and the extra money I would have earned, because Lucretia was so adamantly opposed to separating the family. We both agreed we spent too much time apart as it was.

So, in 1972, after spending five years installing navigational aids, RADAR and

Communications, engine generators, whatever was needed in Iran for the U.S. Government, I accepted a position as advisor to the deputy Chief of Staff in charge of Communications, Electronics and Meteorology for the Imperial Iranian Air Force (DCS/CEM/IIAF). Influential Iranian friends informed me no other American held a higher rank than me, as a major general the highest-ranking position of any American in Iran. There was another American two-star general in Iran, in charge of the Military Assistance Advisory Group (MAAG). Now I was an employee of the Imperial Iranian Air Force (IIAF). A new and very different life had been handed to us. It is so difficult to describe the feelings that came along with our new life with the IIAF. I felt so alone. The FAA/US Government had always handled everything for us. Any problem had a very quick solution. In the past we needed that help often.

Now that was all gone. We had the rights of a tourist as far as the Embassy was concerned, and rightly so. For the previous five years we were with the US Government, but now we were with the IIAF. As strong as these feelings were, I didn't show them. Many people warned me not to take this new job, so I couldn't give them the satisfaction of saying "I told you so."

It was done, and now we had to start our new life. Cretia made her feelings known to everyone. This was a new life for us and we were very happy with it. We were in a foreign land but we, as a family, would be together. I'm sure that she was thinking this was a lot better for us than letting me go off to a dangerous assignment in Vietnam.

What held very strong in my mind was sitting down at the table with the family and looking at them. Now we were on our own. The most sickening feeling came over me. "What have I done?" came into my mind. I stared at my wife. Maybe she was thinking the same thing. It was too late. We were in it for the long haul. We didn't say anything.

My new position was very different from the job that I had in the FAA. On the first day, I moved into my new office. The new organization was called DCS/CEM (Deputy Chief of Staff/ Communication Electronics and Meteorology). The office was in a separate building that was away from the ones that I was used to. In fact, I don't ever remember being in that building except when I talked with an officer about my job application for this position.

The people were so nice to me. They were very polite and respectful. I really didn't know what I was supposed to be doing. They just assumed that I knew everything that must be done. What would this be like? The Iranian military was a big part of my life in Iran but I was an outside advisor. Now I was in that group and a part of it. I was a Mercenary and

I realized it. This was indeed a new type of life.

My first surprise was the appearance in my office of a soldier who snapped to attention and asked what I wanted for breakfast. I answered, "*Tauk ma morg vah chie.*" That means eggs and tea. He snapped to attention again and quickly departed. In a few minutes he was back with the breakfast. This was great! Now I knew that everyone had breakfast while on duty or maybe just certain people. What a pleasant surprise.

An officer that I had known for a long time came into my office with the usual Iranian greeting, "*Salam Alaikom.*" Then we started talking. "Zehbel, it's so nice to have you here. We can do so much now," the major said. My reply was simple. "What is it that you want to do?" He said that he wanted me take over all of the activities that were now done by other foreign entities. That was not entirely possible, but we could do a lot of it. Then I began to think of just how much I would have to do. It was overwhelming. How could one man do all of that?

The first thought that ran through my mind was losing my job. That would be a catastrophe. Our discussion was about what it would take to provide the entire country of Iran with an all-weather air force. They thought that I was able to do anything. Just learning management would take a long time. My thought was that I would make a lot of visits to the MAAG and observe more closely how and what they were doing. That was one of the smartest things that I did. In six months I felt very comfortable in my job.

They immediately gave me a secretary. My secretary couldn't type my letters very well so I took them to one of the US Military secretaries and explained the problem to her. She was more than happy to type my letters. I didn't have a typewriter at the time so I couldn't do it. Later on, I got one and did the typing myself. The IIAF replaced my secretary with a female Master Sergeant. She was a follower of Ba'hai, a modified form of Islam. They didn't like her. From that time on, the old secretary didn't like me either.

I had them bring a large map of Iran to my new office. I would have to calculate all the coverage of the various electronic facilities, including RADAR. That in itself was a very big job, so I got started. After each day, the map would be covered and the room secured. My slide rule and I worked hard. It was a big project and I had many areas to cover. There was a staff of engineers that were attached to DCS but most of them had no post graduate training in the things that we were doing. They were not helpful to me.

Many of my old friends in the IIAF who worked in other offices came to congratulate me. One of them, who had spent a lot of time in the field with me, just couldn't get over it. He kept reminding me about times we spent together. He also spent a lot of times with the Americans.

"Do you know what some people are saying about you?" he asked.

"No I don't. Is it good?" I responded.

"Some of them are happy for you and some are saying that you don't deserve it. They are saying, 'We are the professionals. His wife is a brood sow.'" "Who said that about my wife?" I asked.

"I can't tell you, sir," he said.

"Why?" I asked.

"You will kill them," he responded.

Now I could have some fun and I just couldn't help myself. "Of course I will. They need it!" I came back.

"Yes they do but something bad will happen to you if you do that," he answered.

"Maybe you're right. Thank you for telling me."

"My pleasure," was his response.

When he left, a smile came over me. I knew who the ones were who didn't like me. Now they would punish themselves with more hatred for me

The IIAF had to officially introduce me to the USAF and the FAA. I was given an officer to introduce me at an official meeting. The meeting was headed by a USAF Colonel in the USAF MAAG Headquarters. I had no uniform, just a three piece suit. As the meeting got started, there was an outburst from my old boss. He spoke in a very insolent manner and refused to talk to me about his program. My accompanying officer immediately stood up and said that the IIAF would not tolerate insults to one of its officers. The American Colonel stood up and said that the man would immediately apologize or be removed from the country within forty eight hours. After that exchange, everything went smoothly. My status in the IIAF had been established. All of the business at hand was then discussed. All ended in a very friendly air. From that time on, I was recognized as the liaison to the USAF. The extent of my technical skills was already known to the MAAG and the IIAF. Now it was demonstrated that the powers of the IIAF and the MAAG recognized the authority of my office.

When I was in Teheran at the Headquarters, I developed a routine. In the confines of Doshen Toppeh, security was excellent. At lunchtime, I went to the restaurant of the MAAG. It was run by a nice French lady who provided good meals. Now that I was in my new position, no one would sit at the table that I occupied, so I had a lot of "privacy."

One day, as I was eating lunch there, a man I had never seen before sat down at the table. He knew my name and addressed me as Mr.

Zehbel. He introduced himself as the man in charge of CIA operations in the Middle East and Southeast Asia, including Viet Nam. He showed me his ID and explained that he approved targets there. He congratulated me on my new job. As he spoke, he verified everything that 'Cretia's Iranian woman friend had told us about the circumstances and reasons why I was selected for this position.

Everything that she had told us was true and many people knew about it. It made me feel so good to really know that I was living in a very real new life. The CIA representative confirmed that the US Government approved everything I was doing and I was in no danger of losing my citizenship by working for the IIAF in this capacity. Ordinarily, if an American citizen accepted a sensitive, high-ranking position like mine, with a foreign government, they would lose their American citizenship.

The CIA representative stressed my continued allegiance to America. I was to be sure and show favor to American contracts. We had a very nice conversation. As he got up to leave he said, "Don't ever forget who you are." Then, he left.

For me, it was a very nice experience. "What does that mean exactly?" I asked myself. I decided he meant "Don't ever become a traitor." Some people thought I was just that. They didn't count. I knew who and what I was.

My dreams of a peaceful, fulfilling life came to a stunning halt five days after I had begun my new life in the IIAF. In addition to setting up navigational devices all over the country of Iran, I was responsible for approving multi-million dollar contracts. This was an incredibly powerful position for any man. My "thumbs down," on a contract was of great concern to those involved in the deal. After just five days in this highly demanding position, I learned that my name had been placed on a hit list. A major, who was a friend of mine came into my office and broke the news to me. "Zehbel, I hate to tell you this but you are now on the terrorists' list. A list has been compiled, of the most important people in the IIAF and it is now in the hands of the terrorists," he told me.

"How did this happen?" I asked, surprised.

He told me that the Americans made up the list and a copy of it was mysteriously found downtown in a tailor's shop. Nobody knew how it happened, but my name was at the top of the list. I thanked him for the information and he left. Now I was sick. My personal vehicle was an IIAF Land Rover which was well marked with IIAF insignias and very identifiable. My only consolation was my .357 Magnum. It was always with me. Now I knew that I needed it. One thing was for sure -- I was an easy target. Although this was much more than I had bargained for, I actually found the job very exciting for the first few years.

My everyday life changed drastically as I had to practice evasive measures, often changing my destination at the last minute, etc. Basic security now became a way of life. I checked my vehicle every morning, looking for bombs, before I got into it. I varied my routes to and from work. Fortunately, I was always going to different locations as part of my work. Vigilance was a must. My .357 was always near my hand.

Shortly after I discovered my name on the terrorists' list, a strange thing happened. While I was walking from the USAF MAAG, a car blew up near me in the parking lot. The car was blown into the air and then came back down very near the place where it had been parked. In fact, it landed right on the tires. Nice sight! The bomb was attached to the gas tank of the car. The trunk of the car had been blown off. Oddly, it did not catch fire even though gasoline was all over the place. That would have been a mess.

The car belonged to one of my old bosses. He had just filled the tank. Some people theorized that was what prevented it from catching fire, along with the type of explosive that was used. When he came out to see his car, I told him that there must be a lot of people who don't like him. He didn't laugh. We weren't really good friends. He used to take credit for my inventions.

Not long after that, while I was traveling in my Land Rover in Teheran, a jeep pulled alongside mine. The plastic window on the door of the jeep was zipped down. There was no way to see into the vehicle because the plastic had been tinted brown from the hot sun. A hand poked out of the plastic wing with a gun in the person's hand. The gun was pointed at me. My .357 was in my hand and I was about to fire through the door of the Land Rover into the jeep to kill the person who was pointing the gun at me but something didn't appear to be right.

I didn't fire. It was a young boy's hand and the gun was a toy. That was a shocker. I had almost shot a young boy. Thank God I didn't fire. There was only a split second to make the decision. When you are that close to doing something like that, the after-shock is indescribable. It makes you more vulnerable when a real situation occurs. I decided the time had come to get a motorcycle. A motorcycle was much more maneuverable in traffic -- and Teheran had lots of traffic.

Imperial Iranian Air Force

When I worked for the FAA/USAF I would install heavy electronic equipment, teach others how to use it, have it Flight Checked and work out difficult problems. The guys I worked with told those in charge I could do anything. I could weld things, fix engine generators. So they wanted me to be in charge of everything. I was a manager, high up in the company. It was a big change; I went from being a technician to running the entire company.

Now my job was to determine what we needed and who to get it from. I was to contact the factories and order equipment. I'd have to analyze the people they'd hired, and choose those who were qualified, (tell them to get rid of the others) and check on how things were running all over the country. I was awestruck; how was I going to do all this?

I went to the MAAG and studied their management procedures. They didn't know why I was there. I copied their management techniques. Even though they were military, management was basically the same. Everything was so vague. I was told by a friend that the IIAF wanted to incorporate everything that had to do with electronics. That included RADAR, Communications, Navigational Aids, Automation and Air Traffic Control. That was an ambitious undertaking, since there were advisors and contractors everywhere. The USAF was the largest component of this structure so I was to be the liaison to the USAF.

The IIAF had to be brought up to modern standards. It had to happen very quickly.

Their planes were being replaced with F4s, F5s, a training fighter plane and the F14s. Pilots had to be warned about enemy planes intruding on Iranian air-space. They needed equipment to guide them to their mission and safely back to their bases. In addition, we were expected to provide facilities for landing in all kinds of weather. Monitoring activities over Iraq was essential. It was equally important to keep that equipment in great shape, to make sure it was reliable. All of this required equipment, manpower, training and proficiency in the English language. Various offices were already in place but the people were young and lacked experience.

To say that this was an awesome responsibility is an understatement. How was I going to do all of this? My first reaction was that I couldn't do all of it. That's easy to say, but the people who selected me for this position thought that I could do anything, and I had accepted the job. My family was depending on me. My choice was very simple: I told myself I would do it.

Soon, I learned that I was expected to provide requirements for contracts that would be given to companies around the world. The IIAF would put out the requirements based on what the IIAF wanted. Then the company would put in bids. For example: "The ____ is pleased to comply with the requirements of the IIAF…" They would list everything they would provide. Sometimes, they would lie like hell. If the IIAF accepted their proposal, they would sign off on it. The chief bidders were England and the US. Smaller bids came in from Israel, Denmark, even Canada, though the Canadian company was controlled by a company from the U.S.

When the bids came in, I would review them and advise the IIAF on which company could do the best job and if the equipment would be supportable. Equipment usually has a lifespan of 20 years, sometimes more. The navigational equipment especially was important. We were in a transition from vacuum tubes to transistors, so integration on a large scale was a big concern. I had to consider whether the equipment might still be usable in twenty years. Even then, technology was changing. In addition, thorough training was essential.

It didn't take long for people to figure out I was the one in charge of approving contracts. If everything was on the up and up, it would not have been that bad but it wasn't.

Soon my office was filled with salesmen representing various companies. Some of them knew about the "agents" and were "great friends" with them. Some did not. I had to tell them, not officially, that in order to get anywhere, they had to have an agent. First, you have the companies who are selling things, the salesmen representing them, and the contracts. You had to pay off the agents.

Their job was to insulate the powerful ones for whom they worked.

Iranian agents were the most visible in the process but they spoke on behalf of powerful people in high positions. The agents were expected to do everything to get the money for themselves and those powerful ones they represented. These "unknown" people were not unknown to me; in time, I found out exactly who they were. Of course, the agents did not openly identify themselves as agents; that was illegal. They pretended to be the ones actually making the deal. Everyone knew, no one spoke.

It was an elaborate game with specific rules: If this was a contract from a company, thirty percent of the money in a contract went to the agent. If the contract was associated with the US Government, the Iranian agent would somehow manage to get seven percent of it for themselves. I never found out how that was done. On one of the smaller contracts, for just one million dollars, a young officer I knew got three hundred thousand dollars.

He didn't know that I knew about the kickbacks. I asked him, in a roundabout way, "Don't these people know what they are doing?" He said, "The Americans have a lot of money so what does it matter?"

I explained to him that the salesmen knew about the kickbacks, so they raised the price by at least thirty percent, to make up for the money that goes to these Iranian agents. So, agents like that were really stealing from the Iranian people. He was silent and then walked away.

On another occasion, a General was holding up a contract because he wanted thirty million dollars. This shocked me because I knew that he already had eleven million dollars. Now I had to find out about this. I asked a confidante who knew almost everything about the corruption "Why is he doing this, he already has eleven million dollars." His answer was very simple; "Because he knows someone who has fifty million dollars." He added "You Americans don't seem to know anything." I guess he was right, but I was learning.

One of the stories going around was about a Navy Admiral. It seems that an Italian jewelry salesman was displaying jewelry to the Empress. One of the pieces that he showed caught the Empress's eye, but she said that it was too expensive, ninety thousand dollars. At a party, she saw the same piece around the neck of an Admiral's wife. As the story goes, she asked the Shah how an Admiral could afford that much money. An investigation followed and they found a room filled with money in his house. We are talking millions of dollars. He was put under house arrest but nothing came of it that we heard about. At least, we never found out about what happened to him.

One unpleasant consequence of my job was that some people were unhappy when they didn't get a contract. These people would seek some form of revenge against me because they wanted to make a lot of money and I was preventing them from doing so. On a very big contract, I explained why we should not buy an obsolete piece of equipment that this particular company was selling. The company could not give me a good reason why we should buy it. This company was a favored one, but I nixed the deal. A few days later, I met with an "accident." Fortunately for me, I survived.

U.S. government employees were not allowed to have motorcycles in Iran. I needed one now -- and I was no longer with the U.S. Government. The time had arrived when I needed extreme flexibility. Terrorists were in Teheran and I was on their list. In Teheran, traffic was horrendous. It was very commonplace to get trapped in traffic. A motorcycle was both an advantage and a disadvantage. It was easy to get killed on a cycle in traffic, but it was also possible to escape from danger as well. A cycle could weave through the cars and travel on the sidewalks if need be. With a motorcycle, I had the option of going off-road as well. Skill was very important, to capitalize on the advantages and minimize the disadvantages.

I already had that skill. In my U.S. Army days, I had owned a cycle. There really wasn't much of a choice; pay was so low that not too many soldiers could afford a car. Many days were spent riding on the deserts in Texas and New Mexico and also on the roads. I had developed my skills to the point of being able to ride with no hands on the handle bars, stand on the seat while riding, scrambling, jumping, etc. I could even shoot while riding. These skills would be a godsend in my present situation in Iran.

The cycle that I selected was a Yamaha 360. It had an aluminum engine and encasement. That was just made for the desert. If you went through water in the heat of the desert, nothing would crack because of extreme temperature change. A cast iron engine would break. The Yamaha 360 was also light; it could be used in the mountains as well as the desert. The Yamaha would bring me great adventure and fun, besides its strategic value. This motorcycle was a compromise between a street bike and a scrambler.

The cycle was never parked in front of my house. It was always inside the foyer of the house. You couldn't see it from the street. People I worked with didn't even know I had a motorcycle. The neighborhood where I lived had a few Americans but mostly middle class Iranians.

You should know that all the homes there had a very high wall around them. The wall was at least ten foot high, so no one knew exactly what was happening in the street. In order to

308

find out, they would have to leave their house, walk through the garden to the gate and open it. I really didn't know what most of my neighbors looked like and they didn't know what I looked like, so I thought.

After my first year in the IIAF, 'Cretia and four of the children were able to go to the States for a long vacation. I didn't go with them because I had to be back in one month. That was the extent of my leave. Three of the children were staying with friends, so I was alone in my house. The reason for this situation was due to my being away from Teheran a lot of the time. At this particular time, a very big contract was signed. The favored contractor was not selected, mostly because of my objections and the information that I had provided as to why we should not buy that equipment.

Unknown to me at the time, I was in extreme danger. I was warned by a friend to be very careful and leave for the States right away. I didn't follow that advice. I thought since my wife and the four younger children were already in the States, and the older ones were staying with friends, I could take care of myself.

That night, I got away from the house and was going to a hideaway in Teheran. I was on my cycle. As I was traveling on one of the main streets, I notice a car following very closely behind me. I was near Imperial Iranian Army Headquarters. A bus turned right in front of me, which was not very unusual, the car behind me came up close and pushed me under the bus. It all happened very quickly. It was a double decker bus. As I was going under, I saw a woman inside the bus. She put a hand to her mouth and began to scream very loudly. I could hear her. She was watching me; she saw it all. The bus stopped immediately. The back wheels were about to crush me. I was down on the ground, under the bus.

I moved very quickly to get out of the death trap. The car was there and the three men inside were watching me. They had evil eyes. They made a left turn and sped down the road. Adrenalin had taken over once again. I took off after them, pulled alongside, ripped off the mirror and smashed the passenger side window. The driver turned into me and I went off the road. In a split second, I was in the air. I had hit an up-turn along one side of the road. It was dark, because this was a side road with no lights. All I could see was dark empty space in front of me. I could only hope that when I landed, I would not fall over or hit something.

When I hit the ground, I skidded and made a soft landing. Both I and the cycle were on the ground. Not even a scratch! How lucky can you get? The lights of their car hit me. My .357 was out, and I was aiming at them. They slammed on the brakes and did a fast turn-around. There was a lot of dust and squealing of tires. Should I fire? A vengeful mind would decide yes. A senseless shooting was very illogical. You must know where the bullets would hit before you fired.

I couldn't fire. A .357 bullet goes pretty far. I couldn't be sure that I would hit them. The bullets might go through the windows and keep on going, to the crowded main street nearby. There was a risk that bullets might hit innocent people. I did not shoot. It was a very close call. That was not an accident. Today, I can still see that woman in the bus, screaming. Thank God for that woman.

Now they knew I had a cycle. In addition, I realized someone was keeping track of me. The next day, I told my friend, who had warned me of the danger, about the incident. He checked with someone else and the reply was "Get out of Teheran now!" I didn't have to be told again, so I called in a few special favors and left Teheran that day. I flew back to the States.

My wife was surprised to see me. Something kept me from telling her that I was out of a job. After all, I had abandoned my position; I left my job. The big problem for me was that I wasn't sure who was responsible for my misfortune. I had my suspicions, though.

As soon as I could, I called my friend in Iran and asked him what I should do. At this point, I must leave out some details. A company's name was given to me and I was to go to them and apply for a job. This I did, and was promised a good job in a foreign country other than Iran, as soon as I was ready. All was not lost. My mind was busy: I had to arrange for my three older girls, still in Teheran, to be brought back to the States. I would get a friend to liquidate our belongings, everything we had left behind in our house. Now, I needed to take a break. I decided to visit a friend, an army officer from Teheran who was now stationed in the US.

Everything was going just fine. Two of my younger kids went with me on the visit. It was so nice to see my friend and his family again. Everyone was enjoying themselves, until I got a phone call from the company that was supposed to hire me. The man apologized and told me that he was informed by someone in Iran, whose name he could not mention, that they could not hire me. That was all he could tell me. What a shock! I had no job again.

I called my friend in Iran. Another surprise -- he told me that things had been taken care of with the people who were after me. I could come back, and the IIAF would give me a raise in pay. What choice did I have? It was my duty to take care of my family. We still needed money to live. My friend who gave me all this information was completely trustworthy so I decided to return to Iran, to my "old" position.

I flew back to Iran. When I checked in for duty at IIAF Headquarters, I reported to a new person. Nothing was said about anything, so I didn't ask questions. I was thankful that I had my job back. Someone told me that the Shah had been informed of my situation and as a result, things changed. That ended a mysterious episode, but others followed. It was a strange way to live!

There were some small contracts that other people pushed through without my knowledge. Problems came along with these deals such as the installation of the equipment. Whoever arranged the deal knew nothing about state of the art equipment. This time, the deal was very close to home, and I figured out who was responsible. Of course, I made my feelings known but the response was, "It's here, we have it and it must be installed."

"How am I to do that, with no people available?" I asked. "You'll have to find the people and do it," was the response. So it did; I found the people, bought things that were needed and went with the team to put the equipment in. They had never done that. It was a great success and went very quickly. All the men were very proud of themselves and their leader.

One particular assignment comes to my mind. We had to go to a place that was famous for the ambushes along the way. The usual procedure was to provide the team with an armed escort. We did not get one. My concern was for the men's safety, so I picked the ones that were not married or had no children.

With this thought in mind, I bypassed an old friend, D., I had known for years, since I first arrived in Iran. A few years earlier, D. had been in a bad situation. He was dying and the doctors were just giving him aspirin. His appendix had burst and he was full of poison. I got him into the hospital and saved his life. From that moment, D. insisted his life belonged to me.

I said to D. "You cannot go." He angrily fired back "Why do you deprive me of this honor?" My reply was, "It is no honor to have your brains blown out. You have a wife and three children. They need you to take care of them." D. responded, "you have a wife and seven children." I replied, "I must do this, you don't have to." He answered, "we would all follow you to hell because we know that you would lead us back."

I was shocked! All the men shouted "Yes Sir! It's true!" That was the most humbling experience that I had ever had in my life. They actually believed that if I was with them, nothing would happen to them. That was unbelievable because they knew that I was a Christian.

I then said to the Airman "You can go but do not get more than three meters away from me."

This made him very happy and he shouted, "you are a great man, a very great man." All the men shouted the same thing. That was my day of humility. I just could not get over the confidence that they had in me. Nothing too exciting happed on our way to and from the site. These terrorist were bad shots. All they did was make a lot of noise.

Naturally, in the American tradition, I recommended them all for awards for service above and beyond the call of duty. To my surprise, all the men were called in to their commanding officer and interrogated. In fact, they were beaten. The officer demanded, "How much did you pay him to write you up for the awards?" It was not a nice interrogation. When the men came back to me, they begged me not to do that again.

My question was, "Just why did they do this?" I went to their commander and was very nasty to him. I even grabbed him by the throat and called him a no-good son of a bitch. That was the wrong thing to do. Assaulting an officer was a crime, so I was forced to go to a high-ranking officer friend to ask him to stop the bastard from reporting me for my behavior. While we were talking, I inquired as to why anyone would question what I had done for my people. The answer was a shock: "Iranians are expected to do good all the time. They were not rewarded for doing things well. They were punished for doing things not so well." This was their mindset. He then told me that everything would be taken care of. I thought it was settled.

I had become a pain in the ass for many people and they wanted me to "Go away." Of this I was sure. There was always something hot going on at the Iraqi border. It seemed to be the right time to send me there, so that's what happened. I was called in and told that an Iranian pilot had defected to Iraq and now we must change all our communication frequencies. My answer was that the people assigned there should be able to do that. Their response was that it needed to be done right so I must do it. Was there any job in the world like this one? A C-130 and a helicopter were assigned to me and were waiting for me and in a very short time, I was on my way.

Soon, I was at Vahdati. From there, I was off to the border in a helicopter. The pilot knew me and we went straight to a hot place – it was under fire. Something was happening on the ground. It looked like a shelling. There were lots of fires. I asked him what we were doing here, since we were supposed to be going to a RADAR site. He asked me if I was afraid. I said that we were wasting time. He then did something dumb. He gave me control of the ship and said, "I was under the impression that you could do anything. Here, take over the controls." That pissed me off, and I ordered him to leave immediately, as we were now drawing fire. Someone was certainly trying to get rid of me.

316

When we got to the site, I found out that I could not change the frequencies without waiting a long time for new crystals that had to be made in the States. It was old equipment. This had to be done right away, so I ordered new equipment from Teheran and had it flown along with a team of my choosing to help with the work. There was so much to do, including a great deal of travel, in an area known for ambushes. It was an exciting trip. There were no casualties but lots of dumb driving and shooting. Imagine, guys with camels who had submachine guns and didn't know how to aim. Somehow, we completed the job. Some people were happy and some weren't. This time, I didn't recommend anyone for recognition.

Twenty Five Centimeter Team

I chose the best people in the IIAF to form the Inspection Team that I needed. Something had to be done to get the system working better. After all of the time I had spent with the people at the various bases, I knew who the best ones were. If they needed something to facilitate their work, we would see that they got it. If there was incompetence involved, we had to address that also. Our main purpose was to inspire the people at the various bases to do the best possible job and make them proud. Those people who could not be encouraged to do their best, would work well for fear of punishment. Either way, I would get my best work from them.

The official name of the team was the CEM/SEP (Communications, Electronic and Meteorology Supervisory Evaluation Program). The USAF was a part of that Team. It also provided experts to work with the IIAF people who would perform the inspections.

A meeting was called to brief the people as to what they were required to do. This was only for the IIAF people. The USAF people already knew what they had to do. As a form of jest, it was suggested that we call ourselves "The Twenty Five Centimeter Team." That is metric for ten inches. The word would be leaked into the "grapevine" that each of the men had been selected because they had a twenty five centimeter penis. This would instill fear into the minds of the men that were to be inspected as to why they had that requirement to be on the team. Their minds would take over from there. Extreme measures bring swift results. The men insisted that we should do this and we would get good results quickly.

The results of the first inspection were brutal. When the results were revealed to the Commanding Officers, officers were replaced on the spot. This news ran through the IIAF like wildfire. At a closed meeting, after the

318

conclusion of the inspection, one of my men told the group a story. This is what he said; "One of the people at the base that was inspected asked if it was true that everyone on the Inspection Team had a twenty five centimeter penis."

The reply was swift; "Are you calling Mr. Zehbel a liar?" "No, no," was the response. "Okay" he said. "I guess that I'll have to show it to you but our orders are that if we take it out, we must use it. The man went into a frenzy. "No, please don't do that. I believe you." "Okay! Now, don't call Mr. Zehbel a liar again," he said. The Airman was terror-stricken and swore that he would never call Mr. Zehbel a liar.

After that incident, the whole atmosphere of the inspections changed. Discipline and respect were changed forever. Things really improved. The USAF people found out about our other name. They couldn't stop laughing. "If it works, great!" they said. The program was a great success.

Chapter 15

Our New Life in the IIAF

Mike, Livvy, Dave Bernstein

At a party in Teheran, Iran 1974

Our social life changed drastically when I began working in the Imperial Iranian Air Force (IIAF). When I was with the FAA/USAF, parties and get-togethers centered on the circle of friends we knew and met at the Officer's Club. Now, we experienced a gradual transition from the Officers Club to the Iranian business and International set. Instead of the Officer's Club, our social life was set in the finest hotels and entertainment centers. Someone was always inviting us somewhere, often to places we never knew existed. Many people knew us, but we didn't know them. Cretia and I were both thirty two years old and we seemed to fit into any social circle. We now had a life that we never dreamed we could have. My wife loved it. She was now a "Queen Bee." All of our old friends were still with us and we made a lot of new friends.

The kids really didn't see any difference. They still went to the same Teheran American School. They had their same friends and went to the same places that they always did. The only problem was the people at school. There, someone was always asking, "who does your dad work for?" They answered, "The Iranian Air Force." That was not good enough. People wanted to know what the name of the company was. Finally, they gave up.

Dave

Who was this guy? Dave Bernstein showed up a month or so after I started working with the IIAF. Cretia had an Iranian friend she worked with in the IIAF Language School. I didn't really know her, but she approached me while I was at a party in the US Officers club. I was sitting with a couple of Colonels. She wanted me to get her husband a job in the IIAF. He was out of work and they needed money. She walked right up to us, sat down and began to talk with me. She had guts, doing that. Her name was S. and she had an interesting story. S. had been a sixteen-year-old Iranian woman, on her way to her wedding to a much-older man. She didn't want to get married, and ran away just before the ceremony. Her parents had arranged the marriage and they were annoyed when she didn't follow through. S.'s father, to save face, packed her off to California to stay with her brother. There, she met Dave. They married and had a couple of daughters. Then her parents asked her to come back to Iran. The parents were getting older and wanted her to run their farm for them. They lived in Teheran and had a farm in the country. Some local villagers worked on the farm, but the parents wanted S. and her husband to run it for them. So she came back, with a husband who needed a job.

I asked her to arrange a meeting between her husband and myself, so we could talk about it. Also, I wanted to see a resume. He made one up very quickly and gave it to me. It was sort of cute, but I gave it to some IIAF Colonels.

They hired him right away, to help with fixing engines. His job was in a part of the compound that I didn't even know existed.

Dave had blonde hair and sort of looked like me, in a way. Some people actually mistook him for me. One day General Rabii (who later became the commander of the IIAF) talked to him while he was walking around IIAF headquarters. The general and I were good friends. He was the one who saved my life in Tabriz when I was trapped in front of a machine gun nest. Dave spoke perfect Farsi and while he was talking to the General, he gave no indication that he wasn't me. So the General thought he was having a conversation with me. I had to find the general to tell him that he had not been talking to me. At that time, General Rabii was commander of the Strategic Air Command (SAC) which was headquartered in Shiraz.

Dave felt at home in the IIAF immediately. He would come to my office around lunch time and sit in my chair with his feet up on the desk. The people would walk by the office door and wonder who this was. When I arrived at the office we would go to lunch at the USAF/MAAG restaurant. He was the only person who would sit with me. Dave went with me on a lot of my adventures, both on and off duty. He was with me when I was poisoned in Esfahan. That was a godsend, in my mind.

Gambling

Shortly after we started in the IIAF, we were invited to dinner at a gambling casino north of Teheran. We never knew it was there. After dinner, during which a lot of alcohol was served, Cretia and I hit the craps table. In no time at all, we were winning and winning and winning. Everyone was betting on us. Piles and piles of chips stacked up on the edge of the table.

It seems as though we couldn't lose. They changed the dice; sometimes they even hit the dice in mid-air with their sticks. She was on one end of the table and I was on the other. Finally it came to an end. They shut the table down. Some people were betting very heavily and won a lot of money. We won a lot too, but our chips were small ones. If we had changed to larger ones, we would have made a fortune. It was the first time that we had gambled.

Money was no longer a problem for us. Cretia was working at the IIAF Language School teaching Pilot Cadets. All that money was paid to her in *rials*. It didn't matter to us; *rials* were the only currency we could use in Iran anyway. Half of my money was to be deposited in a New York bank in dollars, and the other half was supposed to be paid to me in *rials*. So far, I hadn't got paid.

When I needed money, I went to a Lieutenant in Finance. I signed my name and he gave me a bunch of money. After three months of that routine, they notified me to come to the Finance Office. The Lieutenant and I were to go to the Central Bank and get all of the money that was owed to me. Future payments would be issued on a normal schedule. So off we went.

Inside the bank, we were taken to a room that was full of money and full of uniformed men with sub machine guns. The dollars were stacked in piles that went high into the room. There were hundreds of millions of dollars there. Never had I seen so much money in my life. The Lt. and I signed some papers and they got out a large amount of *rials*. Not all of it was for me. The Lt. asked me to open my briefcase and put the money into it. I didn't expect that, and I was worried; I kept my Smith & Wesson .357 Magnum in the briefcase.

What would happen when the guards saw my gun? I whispered in the Lieutenant's ear and explained the problem. He laughed, and told everyone one that I had a gun. They all laughed too, so I opened the briefcase and they moved in closer to see the gun. There was so much money that I had to take the gun out of the briefcase and put it in my belt. They were impressed when they saw the gun.

Everyone was used to seeing automatic pistols. Revolvers reminded them of Cowboys and Iranians loved Cowboys. Now everyone was happy and talking about the revolver. An unusual payday! Now I had a briefcase full of money, so I asked the Lieutenant, "What happens if someone tries to rob us?" He said "Sir, you now have your gun in your belt. Just shoot them". Easy enough -- a license to kill! Fortunately, I didn't have to send anyone to the "Happy Hunting Grounds" that day.

My next month's paycheck was a different story. Now I had to go to the Teller part of the Central Bank with my check. When the Teller gave me my cash, he gave me all two hundred *rial* bills. That was about two dollars and fifty cents per note. There were too many bills to carry, so I had to go through the same routine of putting my .357 inside my jacket and stuffing the bills into my briefcase. When I got home, I poured all the money on the table. The kids went bananas. They started counting it. My question was "Why did they give me such small currency?" It wasn't very convenient to transport.

When I went to the office the next day, I told an officer about it. He laughed and said, "You must give him a tip before he pays you." Can you imagine having to tip the Bank Teller? This was Iran!

'Cretia had another friend who was British. Her name was Monica. She taught English at the same place where 'Cretia worked. Her

327

husband, Jim, and I became good friends. He was Scottish. They invited us to celebrate the Queen's Birthday with them. To our surprise, it was a spectacular event, and a formal occasion. Tuxedos only! All the British people in Teheran must have been there.

Back in the States

While we were on our vacation, before I started working for the IIAF, I had bought a new type of tuxedo that was made of a polyester-type cloth. The black was really black and the strips that were on the pant legs and collar were even blacker and very shiny. It looked like woven rope that was flattened. Very outstanding! That's what I wore to the celebration. 'Cretia looked so beautiful in her new custom -made gown. Of course, she had her hair done by Ingaborg at the salon. We stood out like sore thumbs. Everyone came over to see my handsome new tuxedo. Among them was a very elegant Lady in a beautiful gown. I had never seen her before. We talked and I told her jokes. She laughed and laughed in a lady-like way.

When we sat down to eat, I saw her again. She was sitting beside the Ambassador. That's when I asked Monica who she was. "Why she's the wife of the British Ambassador, Lady___," she answered, "Why do you ask"?

"Oh, well, I was talking with her and telling her jokes," was my reply.

"Oh my God, Zehbel, you didn't!" she squeaked. Then she slid down in her chair so as not to be seen. Some of my jokes weren't very nice, and Monica knew that. Lady _____ then waved to me and smiled. I waved back. Monica seemed to be terror-stricken. "That's the last time that I'll ever take you to one of these celebrations," she mumbled.

She didn't know the circles I had been put into. They knew me but I didn't know them at this time. Oh well, I was an invited guest -- I wouldn't have been there if they didn't want me. It turned out to be a wonderful evening. Lots of people introduced themselves to us. After the joking, I put on my best diplomatic-behavior hat.

Salesmen are an unusual type of people. Once you are in a position such as mine, approving contracts for the IIAF, you are targeted. To the salesman, you are the source of money for him and his company. I was able to avoid most of them but some were just too nice. Most of them were knowledgeable as to how things were done in Iran but some were not. A very few of them became my friends and they would ask me for advice as to exactly what we needed. Becoming friends did not happen quickly.

I noticed that one of the companies was doing dumb things that would cost them money. I pointed this out to them, and advised them what to do, and what not to do. They got a big contract and they wanted to know things that I knew so that they would not make any costly mistakes. That would take up a lot of my time. I ended up having to hide from them, to get things done.

Even when I was on vacation in the States, they would find me and send an airplane for me to make a "quick" visit to a factory they owned or that was making equipment for them. I seldom spent much money on these visits and was treated to the finest hotels, entertainment, food and drink.

They knew that I loved lobster. At one occasion, I was served the largest lobster that I had ever seen along with elaborate food and old wine. What a life! The tab for me only was one hundred and thirty dollars. That was in 1973. Who knows what it would cost today?

During the day, I would go through the factory to check on the system that they were making and tell them the changes that I wanted. In the end, it saved me a lot of time and frustration. At night, it was entertainment. We would get into places that were filled with surprises of all kinds.

I couldn't get over how rich people lived in the States. One time, in Hollywood, I saw all kinds of stars in a special nightclub. Charlie, my escort, got a table that must have cost a fortune. Dancers, who worked there, danced on the tables. They were all so different except for the fact that they were all strikingly beautiful, had perfect bodies and did different types of dances to the same music at the same time. After doing a few dances, they would rotate to a different table. We were drinking the finest Scotch and I had just ordered a very fine, rare cooked steak. When I began to eat the steak, an acrobatic dancer came to my table and began her dance. She had black hair, black eyes and had a Mid-Eastern look. As she was dancing, she began to shed her costume. She was always looking at me and smiling. Near the end of the dance, she did a split right in front of me and stayed in that position smiling at me. This was a sight! Very different! She had no clothing on at all. My appetite totally left me and there was that expensive steak that I had just started, going to waste. Charlie was laughing his ass off. He must have paid dearly for that exhibition.

While we were in Washington, DC, I met Bob Hope and his wife. What a world this was for me -- and I was doing it as a favor! There was no money involved. They were taking my vacation time and making it as comfortable for me as possible. They benefited from it by the money it saved them and I was able to keep my electronics time-table on schedule in Iran. Slipping on schedules was a no-no.

Washington, DC seemed to be where everything happened. Now I began to see what the real world was like. Everything was money, money and more money. Just sitting in the office of the president of the company made me aware of things. People heard about me and the work I was doing in Iran, approving contracts. They would just sit down by me and start talking. Name dropping was a big thing. I guess it made people feel important. I learned a lot of interesting things about very important people. In the end I understood much better how the Government works. It didn't make me feel good at all. I realized just how dumb I was about how things worked in Washington, DC.

I was having a conversation with the president of the company, explaining why a contract with a certain United States government agency was desirable. I explained that they were able to support everything and were able to do it for a long time. Their equipment was very supportable, which presented a problem in selecting a contract bidder. That issue was settled in a few days with a Congressional investigation. As a result of this well-timed (for me) investigation, a certain government agency was banned from competing with private industry. Easy!!

At that time, in Iran, money was no obstacle. There was no limit as to the type of electronic equipment that I got. It was the best in the world at that time. Sometimes, after seeing the finished product, I couldn't believe it. Our people were going to have to become much more skillful in electronics to take care of this sophisticated equipment. That gave me another responsibility.

Most of my time was spent monitoring programs, making sure that mistakes were caught very early and providing trained people to keep the entire system reliable.

The threat to my life was always there when I didn't expect it. As I mentioned earlier, our neighbor, Sweet Livvy didn't like my gun. Lucretia and I spent a lot of time at her house. On one occasion, I got a phone call from her. She was panic-stricken. Someone was trying to break into her house. I told her that I would be there in one minute and to open the back gate. Her house was on the corner of the street. The entrance to her house was on one street, and the gate to the compound was on another street. I was at the gate in what seemed no time at all. She was there waiting for me.

We went into the bedroom, and opened the front door of it, so I could see the entrance door of the house. It was a translucent glass door and it was possible to see someone at the door but not possible to see who it was. I cocked the hammer of the Smith & Wesson and waited there. When she saw the person's shadow by the door, she said, "Oh, my God". Someone <u>was</u> trying to get in. Whoever it was stopped and moved away. In a minute, the door opened. I took aim, but and it turned out to be her daughter, Beverly. She must have scared off whoever was trying to get in. I immediately ran to the door to see if I could spot the person. No one was to be seen. He was fast.

Assassination Attempt

On another occasion, we were playing bridge at Livvy's house. When the game was over, 'Cretia and I started to walk home. I was not armed, of course, because Livvy was afraid of guns. As we went around the corner, there were two men with sub-machine guns waiting for me. Our house was only about 70 feet away. I immediately told 'Cretia to get away from me. She wouldn't. I pushed her away and shouted, "Someone has to take care of the kids!"

I have never felt so naked. No gun! I can still see so clearly, what happened next; I've never forgotten it to this day. My wife ran towards me and wrapped herself around me. The two men looked at me and then at each other. I tried to get her off me and kept telling her to get away. She wouldn't; she had super-human strength in her. She kept wrapped around me. I was walking toward the front door of our house. The men kept looking at us with their guns raised. They did not shoot.

I was in shock. Was this some kind of act of God? She had acted so bravely and her actions saved my life. Apparently, the men didn't want to shoot a woman. When I got in the house, I grabbed my Smith & Wesson. 'Cretia yelled, "What are you doing?"

I said, "They didn't shoot me because of you. Now I must give them their chance again, because of their honor." Honor was very important to me even though it might seem dumb. I ran out with my S&W cocked. I would do everything I could to kill them, but I thought that I owed them this chance for not shooting my wife.

They were gone. I don't know how they got away so fast but they did. We are talking about a half a minute. It must have been well planned. I had never seen such bravery on the part of 'Cretia and such honor of the assassins. It all happened so fast. Going after them was a dumb thing for me to do but for some reason I thought that it had to be done. When I came back into the house, we hugged very tightly. That was true love on her part. She is a very brave woman and a credit to her sex. How could two people be so close? The mother of seven children, living in a foreign country. My wife is an amazing person.

The Wedding

A very close Iranian associate and friend told me that he was getting married soon. "I would like to have you there at the wedding," he said to me. "Yes! I'll be there with my sweet wife," I responded happily.

'Cretia and I had attended many weddings together but nothing came close to this one. The invitation was verbal, so we thought the wedding would be somewhat casual. It wasn't like that at all. I wore the finest clothes that I had and of course, my wife had to have a new gown made. As we arrived in my IIAF Land Rover, I knew right away that we were out of place. This was a huge mansion, like a palace. Everything was done in the grandest style, impressive and so beautiful. A valet took the car and we were escorted into the mansion.

The gowns and jewelry that the women were wearing must have cost thousands and tens of thousands of dollars. No necklaces were small. This was big money and the upper crust of Iranian society. We didn't fit in at all. My friend met me and escorted us to a place right beside him and his bride. It was a place of honor. From a verbal invitation to a place of honor was sort of shocking, but we were easily able to fit in. Just keep a glass of wine in one hand and chit chat with the people as they approached you. They all seemed to want to talk with us. Everyone spoke English to us, so it was easy. That was one thing about Iran that made it hard to perfect the language.

As the ceremony began, I was sitting just behind the groom. A woman was standing behind them with two bars of sugar, rubbing them together over the bride and groom's head. Sugar was falling on them. It was very different and very nice. We had never seen anything like this before. The groom was whispering to me as this was happening. He was giving me instructions as to who I must call about a deal that was going on. An interesting topic to discuss while a wedding was taking place! The thing was, it all seemed so natural at the time. Strange when you think about it!

All the music was Persian and the orchestra was fabulous. The young men were dancing a Russian-type dance. This type of dance required a man to be in excellent physical condition to perform. Was this dancing Russian? Maybe it began in Persia as many western and eastern traditions did. As the dancing was going on, I heard a friend, who was a high ranking general, say "Where has our youth gone?"

In a conversation with a young officer, he told me that the terrorists were no longer after me. They had learned I was doing work that was for the good of Iran. Isn't it strange that I learned this here rather than from the IIAF? Then it struck me! There was nobody here that I recognized from the IIAF. So many people were eager to talk to me, but I didn't know any of them. They were speaking Farsi, but as soon as they knew that I was near, they would change to English. We were engaged in many conversations.

I was told that I was liked, not so much for being American but because of my Slavic heritage. Both my wife and I were one hundred percent Slavic, so they considered us the same as them. I wondered how they found that out. They must have known a lot about me. A lot of the upper crust people in Iran were from the Slavic areas north of Iran and they were proud of it. There were two types of names in Iran that I knew of. One was Muslim and one was Persian. At times in Persian history, Persia was a vast empire. I remember at one time, when I was discussing this with an Iranian friend, I asked why the Persians never conquered Russia. His answer was, "In those times, who the hell would want it?" I think that they considered the areas north of Iran to be Persian, even now. Never associate Iranians with Arabs. They hate that.

When the Arab Muslims conquered Persia, they tried to destroy all Persian history, culture, religion and language. At one time, anyone caught speaking Farsi had their tongues cut out. Every one of those things survived, except the religion. There are places in Iran where the Zoroastrian religion still exists and is permitted to do so. The Shiite Muslims still consider them "People of The

Book." The Sunnis do not. They believe only Christians and Jews are people of the Book.

In one night, we learned quite a bit more than we had already known about the Iranian people and their culture. It was an impressive experience.

Chapter 16: Bandar Abbas

South Iranian Desert, near Kerman, Iran

A new assignment was about to transpire, and I didn't want to go. The place was a port on the Persian Gulf called Bandar Abbas. It was always hot and very humid there and I was not looking forward to it at all. Unfortunately, there wasn't anyone else who could do it.

'Cretia knew how I felt about staying away for such a long period of time, and there was no way for me to get back to Teheran until the project was completed. She didn't want to be alone either. It was the night before I was scheduled to leave. The neighbors wanted to give me a send-off so 'Cretia and I went along with it.

They took us to a famous nightclub to have dinner and dance for a while. As I downed the first drink, I called the waiter over and told him that the drink was too weak. "Put more vodka in it," I told him. He looked very angry. The drink that he brought back was pure vodka, and it must have been the strongest stuff that they had. It didn't take me long to get started. I remember knocking people into the band while I was dancing. I turned over the table behind us. They wanted us out of there. Then I did a really dumb thing; I actually lit the bill on fire. Lucretia paid the bill so we could leave. I made it to the first set of steps before my legs gave out.

Our LC (Lieutenant Colonel) neighbor sped through town at eighty miles an hour, so the cops couldn't catch us. What a performance! When we arrived at home, the night watchman helped get me in the house. We found the front window was shattered. There was blood all over the place and we never found out whose blood it was. It must have been the night watchman's. He denied it later.

The next day, I was not in good shape. The neighbors came over, and the LC brought me a Bloody Mary. Just looking at it made me sick. My wife took me to the C-130. It was a sad good-bye. Boy, was I a mess!

All the equipment was being loaded aboard the cargo plane, along with my jeep. My favorite Iranian officer was there, so that made me happy. He was going to accompany me on the trip. There were two IIAF Airman there, begging to go along to help me. One was okay but the other one was a bum. I'd had run-ins with him before. He didn't seem "right" to me, but I said he could come with us. What was the attraction to Bandar Abbas? I found out later he was interested in buying smuggled goods there; that's what he was after. I should have known better. I never should have taken him with me.

I remember the take-off and conversations with the Iranian officer, F. He couldn't understand why I took the "bum" along. Neither did I. Before I knew it, we were landing. I had slept all the way and it was a long trip.

Bandar Abbas was different. The heat and humidity hit me as soon as the aircraft doors opened. After supervising the unloading, we went to our rooms. They gave me the red carpet treatment. It was a Naval/Marine Base. The ID that I carried said I was to be treated like a major in the American military, and that they did. My jeep was brought along on the C-130, so I had my own transportation. This wouldn't be too bad a tour.

Next morning, the work began. My plan was to work long days and get the project completed as quickly as possible. It was one

343

of those projects in which everything had to be done from the ground up. That's a lot of work. How would I get them to work late? These guys didn't want to work at all. There had to be an incentive. What would that be?

The officer who was with me told me everything about the place. Then he said it: there was a whore village near the base. It wasn't that close, but I had my jeep with me. That was the answer, the whore village. There were literally hundreds of whores. No one else lived there except for the whores. Now it was easy: if the men agreed to work late, I would take them to the village. If they didn't I wouldn't. How simple could it get?

Work progressed at an astonishing rate. The plan was working beautifully.

The promise of recreation at the end of the day was a powerful incentive to the men. A usual day was something like this: work, work, and more work. After the work was finished for the day, the men went to their rooms to get washed up.

Bandar Abbas was hot and humid, so sweat was on you all day long and it had to be gotten rid, of along with the smell that went with it. Then it was off to the whore village.

This is what an average day at the whore village was like: everyone jumped into the jeep and the short ride began. They were all very happy and told funny stories and made jokes. These guys were boiling over with joy and anticipation. This was their reward for a long day of work. When we got there, it was like going shopping. The name of the village was Shazho. Garbage was piled everywhere and there was an aroma that went along with it. It wasn't an inviting place.

The men went from compound to compound, looking for the prettiest women and haggling about prices. A lot of the establishments had walls around them. Some had the doors open and others didn't. The men would go in and look around. One day in particular stands out. We went into a compound and the guys started looking. Mr. Peston, as we called him (we all thought he looked like Charleton Heston), found a whore sleeping on a blanket underneath a hanging shade made of wooden circular strips they called *hasirs*. He gave her a slight kick in the butt and she woke up. Mr. Peston told her what he wanted and negotiated the price. After a short period of haggling, they scooted off to a small shack. The door closed. The door opened again and a chicken ran out. The ladies had given me a chair to sit in and brought me a Coke. I told them that I was just the driver so they didn't bother me, but were very polite in everything that they did and said. My Farsi was fair, so I could talk with them. I was still watching the little shack, when I saw a rat run out of it. "Must be a nice place that they are making love in," I thought.

Then another one ran out. This was getting interesting. "What were they doing in there?"

Another one of the men, Mr. Sneezer, selected another girl. They went through the same ritual: first a chicken, then the rats. I had fun watching all of this. Meanwhile, I was sitting there in the shade just enjoying myself. One of the women, who seemed to be in charge, kept bringing girls near me and they would do exotic movements. She knew I was a foreigner and they charged them more money. The usual cost was from a dollar and twenty five cents to four dollars, depending on the girl. She just wouldn't stop. The girls who were near me, serving me Coca Cola, smiled at me when I said no to the wares that were being displayed. The madam finally got disgusted and quit the parade.

The guys stayed in quite a while so that they were all getting their fill. I assumed that they were very happy.

Sitting in the shade, talking to the girls, and being served Coke was doing something to me. I had the feeling that I was with normal people. Why were they here and doing this kind of work?

At this point in time, I had been in Iran long enough to know about people of various origins. My mind wandered. Girls in Iran couldn't marry if they were not virgin. The mother of the groom would examine a prospective bride to make sure that she was,

346

in fact, virgin. At that time, a girl could have an operation to "restore" virginity. When that became known to the public, some people had a doctor check the girl out to make sure. Other women couldn't get married for various other reasons, so they had to get some kind of job. Wages were very low and it was hard for them to make a living.

That made the door of prostitution look more inviting, but once a girl entered that door she was finished socially and looked down upon. Thinking about this showed these women in a different light. They were, in fact, victims, I thought.

I began to feel ashamed of myself because of the harsh thoughts I had about them. Most of these women were genuine people who were condemned to this way of life. Now I had a sick feeling in my stomach. Being in the midst of these women and being treated so nicely changed my perspective on this type of prostitution. That little bit of time spent with them made me a changed person.

When the men finished their entertainment, they came over to me. They asked why I didn't find a girl. I said "Not today." They couldn't understand me.

We walked back to the jeep on a different route. This village was a very big place. There were hundreds and hundreds of ladies working and living there. It was their workplace and home. As we walked past one house that had a compound with the door open, I saw these dark women. Their features were not African except for the very dark skin. They were squatting, cooking over an open fire, while small children ran around nearby.

The women were very close to us and we could see everything, since they were squatting. They weren't wearing underclothes. This was a very strange sight. Then I asked the guys why their private parts were so different. It looked like a budding flower. They told me that these women were "circumcised." The outer lips of the vagina were cut off. Just think of that -- and the pain involved. I'd been told that was done in some Muslim cultures. Now I saw it first hand, so I realized it was true. The women were very gracious and invited us in. We begged off very politely and continued on our way.

That was what a normal workday was like in Bandar Abbas, though each day was a little different. To me it was entertaining, but for the men it was paradise. It looked as though I would get back to Teheran much sooner than I anticipated.

One very dark night, I was late getting back to the Base. Something was different. There wasn't enough lighting at the gate. Very soon I found out why. There were hundreds of rifles pointed at me. At the time I was wearing a Pith Helmet, so that didn't help. To them, it must have looked like a foreign soldier in a foreign jeep. That was not good. As my eyes adjusted to the light, I could see that some of them were just a couple of feet from the jeep. I could see their faces. No smiles. They had American-made M-1 rifles.

That's the same rifle that I had when I was in the US Army. Somehow the muzzle looks so much bigger when you're on the other end of the rifle, and the power of the bullet is massive. My mind went back to one time when I set a truck on fire at eight hundred yards with tracer bullets and blew up a tank with a white phosphorus rifle grenade. An M-1 is a real weapon, and a whole collection of them were pointed right at me. The best thing that I could do was nothing. I was extremely uncomfortable. These were Iranian Marines and at the time, I was the target.

After about five minutes, an officer approached me. He asked me who I was and what I was doing here. I told him that I was an American and that I was working at the Air Base. Then I told him the name of the Naval Officer who was my liaison. After showing him my ID, he let me pass. I found out later that there was an alert this night but no one told me anything else. A few drinks melted everything away.

The next morning, I thought the time had come to take a break from work. We were almost finished. The Naval Officer who was attached to me came to visit. He must have been contacted about the incident last night. It seemed as though he wanted to make amends. "How would you like to go hunting in the mountains?" he said to me.

"Right now, I think that is just what I need," I replied.

"Good, I'll get everything ready," he said. "I'll be right back." The men had to be notified. When I told them that they had a few days off, they went into orbit. Such joy! I knew where they were going.

In an hour, he was back with another officer, a Marine and a soldier. My jeep was packed and ready to go. In a very short time, we were on top of the mountain. I expected to start hunting. That wasn't the case.

The Officer said that we must walk for a while to get to the village. The soldier had a goat skin over his shoulder and headed for a big rock. A part of the rock was indented and was full of water. The water was covered with a green slime, and yellow jackets were buzzing around it. Many years later, I saw that very same sight on Superstition Mountain in Arizona. He washed away the slime and filled the goat skin. There was no way that I was going to drink that water. I had a canteen with me and I had filled it at the Base. "That should hold me," I thought. We weren't going very far.

It was high noon and the sun was very hot. The humidity from the coast was gone, here

350

in the mountains but it was hotter. By four o'clock, my water was all gone.

My decision was, do I die now of dehydration or later from the water in the goatskin? No contest! The soldier filled my canteen and I drank the water. It had a strange taste. Every time I asked the Naval Officer how much further we had to go, he answered with "Not far, just a short time more." This was not rest. "Where are we going?" I asked myself.

At six o'clock, we still weren't there. For six long hours, we were walking in mountainous country. We finally came upon a small house, the first one we had seen. The officer went to the door and called a greeting. A woman came out, and they talked. He returned and said that we would be spending the night in the stable where the sheep stayed. The sheep weren't there right now. It was like a cavern in a cave, in fact, that's what it was. Sheep droppings were all over the place.

I told the officer we couldn't stay in this place. He said we could clean it up. That's what we had to do. What a mess! The officer gave the woman some money. She appeared to be very happy about it even though it was a small amount. The woman provided blankets for us and we prepared to spend the night there. The place didn't smell very nice but we had to stay somewhere.

Early in the morning, before the sun rose, we were on our way again. At six o'clock, we arrived at the village. The officer told me that this was a village of bastards. The young Iranian Marine who was with us had been born and raised here. That sounded different. It was a very isolated place. Roosters were crowing, but there were no people awake. And, there weren't any dogs. That was unusual.

The officer told me to wake them up. I fired my .357 three times in slow succession. Everything came alive. People began to come out of the huts to find out what was happening. When they saw me, they appeared to be frightened. After all, they had never seen an American and this one had guns. My first reaction was to smile and say "*sobor kay*," which means "good morning." It appeared to work; at least they calmed down, and some of them smiled. They had no idea what was happening. The young Marine who lived in this village shouted to the people and they responded with shouts of joy and words and affection. He was very happy for the opportunity to visit his home.

We all sat on the walls of a small dam. I noticed a big plug on the bottom of the wall. It was there for the irrigation of the quince trees that were growing all over the place. There was a small building with a spring feeding into it. The water then came out of the stone building into the pool that was formed by the dam. This was the village refrigeration, drinking water and an irrigation system all in one.

On one side of the dam there was an outlet to water the sheep. The Marine showed us a .22 rifle. They would put ewes that were in heat in a special pen at night. Then wild rams from the mountain would come down at night to try to mate with the ewes. One of the men in the village would be posted there to shoot the wild rams in the head. That was the meat supply for the village.

Quince was the money crop for the village. There were a lot of trees growing there. Life here was very primitive. They sold the quince to buy what they could not produce for themselves. The one thing that everyone needed was kerosene for their lamps. There must have been other things but I can't recall what they were. It was a glimpse of the very ancient past.

The Naval Officer began to arrange a hunt. We didn't need any guides since the Marine knew the mountains very well. Once again it was climbing and climbing. "Will this ever end?" went through my brain. This trip was meant to be a rest but what it turned out to be was lots of exercise in the art of climbing. Off we went into the high mountains.

While we were hunting, I noticed that the Marine was looking for wild sheep through a very old brass, naval telescope. It was so attractive to me that I just couldn't take my eyes off it. This piece I just had to see. It was really something and I wanted it so badly. I asked him if he wanted to sell it. He didn't want to, but he saw an opportunity to make some quick money. He asked for forty dollars, and I gave him the money. It turned out to be a British naval telescope from the early 1800's. I still have that telescope today; it is one of my treasured possessions.

We went to the top of a mountain. While we were there, I shot a ram. They had to take care of it, since I had no facilities to deal with a large piece of game. The village was very happy about it; after all, it was fresh meat.

Now we had to deal with going down the mountain. I was very tired, and dreaded the long trek back. To my surprise, the Marine showed us a very quick way to go down the mountain. This was a steep side of the mountain and it was a long way down. There were many remnants of landslides there, a lot of loose rocks and stones.

I watched the Marine and copied his movements, jumping from one rock to another as he did. Essentially it was a controlled fall. It didn't seem too difficult, but it was dangerous and strenuous. While I was falling, I twisted and turned to prepare my body angle for when I hit the ground or stones I was aiming for. It was tricky. You tried to aim for softer dirt so it would absorb the jump. Even so, there were little pebbles in the dirt which would tear the hell out of you.

Then I would quickly determine the next target. When I reached solid rock, I would have to leap up, down, left or right and run slowly on the rock. The thing was, you never stopped moving, bouncing fast as if you were doing jumping jacks. Sometimes you had to stop and get to another spot. The technique was a strain on every part of your lower body. Fortunately for me, I had bought a new pair of boots before I left for Bandar Abbas. The boots saved my legs from getting torn up, but the stones also ruined the boots.

We reached the village very quickly. The villagers were very gracious and served us roasted sheep. Everyone enjoyed it, except me. The meat had a rotten smell to it. The refrigerator was only about 55 degrees and that doesn't keep meat from spoiling. They were used to it but I was not. I couldn't eat it.

We paid the villagers, which made them very happy. In order to return the hospitality, I was offered a donkey to ride back on. Now, instead of walking back to the jeep, I was able to ride a donkey. They go fairly fast, though I was bouncing up and down; the animal was always at a trot. It was a new and exciting experience. While I was riding the donkey, my wallet fell out of my pocket. There was no way to absorb the shock of the bounces, without stirrups.

I did not know I had lost my wallet until a young boy came running up to me, holding the wallet. First I was shocked, then immediately overjoyed to see it. All of my important things were in that little bill fold. Of course I offered the boy a reward but he would not take it. That really impressed me.

When I got to the jeep, I waited for the rest of the party to arrive. My thoughts were about the nice people that I had met and the way that they treated me. It was impressive to say the least, and to think that it was a village of bastards. That didn't show itself in any way. No one ever explained why it was a village of bastards and who gave the village that name, but it wasn't hard to figure it out.

Finally, some pleasant news: my wife was going to visit me. I had not been expecting a visit, since she had just given birth to our baby boy, Mark, not long before. She was not the usual woman. They were both coming. I can't express to you just how I felt about my wife, 'Cretia. She was my life. Her visit meant the world to me. This visit had to be a very special experience for her and I had to do all that I could to make that happen.

Her airplane landed. It was an old DC-3. They were noisy aircraft and it seems that all of them leaked oil. I had spent many hours on C-47's which was the cargo version of the DC-3. What sticks in my mind the most about that aircraft was the coal dust that was still in the indentations that held down cargo. The coal dust was the remains of the Berlin Airlift. 'Cretia had recently won a free trip to Beirut at the Officer's Club in Teheran but the trip had a time limit. She would not go there by herself and since I could not leave my assignment, she decided to visit me instead. Good thing for me.

She was carrying baby Mark in a carrying sack which was made for babies. We hugged and kissed and then hopped into my jeep. We put baby Mark in the back part of the jeep and headed off to my room. Mark never cried even though this was very new for him. A jeep is very bouncy ride.

'Cretia was fascinated with the new setting. She had never been to Bander Abbas. We toured the waterfront and the city. Then we went to the desert and the shore to see the way people lived. The shore was strange with the layers of petroleum residue that had leaked from somewhere. There was a lot of it. It wasn't a very pretty sight.

The tribal women at the shore area were different. Instead of the traditional face covering, they wore black masks with sort of a beak on them. They looked like giant black birds. Actually, it looked like a Halloween mask. The men had a mean look on their faces. 'Cretia really didn't like the place, so we left in short order.

Next was the fishing. The streams had rock dams built across them. These were not permanent dams. They were put together with various sized stones. Several spots in the dam had outlets and in the outlet was a wooden basket. It was really was a net. The fish that went over the dam were trapped in the basket net. It was an easy way to catch fish.

At another place, I had got friendly with the men. They used dynamite to fish. The way they did it was sort of ingenious. They cut the dynamite sticks into small sections and then rewrapped them and put fuses into each piece. Now each piece was a small bomb. They would light individual pieces and throw them into different parts of a large body of water. The fish would float to the top. Some were stunned and some were dead. They then selected the fish that they wanted and then went on their way. It was interesting.

The civilian engineer that I worked with asked me if I wanted to take Lucretia and the baby to an island. My wife said she would love it, so we rented a thirty foot long fishing boat and started our sea trip to the island. Stench was a word that isn't good enough to describe the smell in the boat. It smelled like well-rotted fish. That, along with the waves, made it hard to keep our breakfast down. The water was full of jellyfish. Some were Portuguese Men of War. Not a good place to swim. As we approached the island, the first thing we saw was an old Portuguese castle. It must have been there for hundreds of years. It was in an advanced state of ruination, but very recognizable. Other sites in Iran had been there for thousands of years so this castle was relatively new.

Our boat landed on a stony beach. It was different. The civil engineer immediately smashed open some oysters growing on a rock and began eating them. He offered one to me. One was enough; it didn't set too well with me. I asked him why he was eating them because Muslims were not allowed to eat that kind of food. He replied, "I'm not a Muslim."

There really wasn't much to see but it was different and that in itself is interesting. It reminded me of Pakistan. There were little islands in Karachi Bay, crawling with tens of thousands of crabs. You could see a movement in the island. This was a desolate island except for the sea life crawling around. We studied the strange little creatures for a while, then started on our way back. Baby Mark seemed to enjoy it. He was always so quiet.

Time passed very quickly. Too soon, 'Cretia had to leave. Great despair filled me and it was such a sad day when she left. Now, all the more, I wanted to finish this assignment up and leave. At least now I could re-live the time that we had spent together. In very little time, at least that's the way that it seemed to me, I was on my way home again.

Chapter 17

The Sniper at Alamut

Alborz Mountains, northern Iran

There was a door to which I found no key.

There was a veil through which I could not see

Some little talk awhile of me and thee.

There seemed – and then no more of thee and me.

-Omar Khayyam,

11th century philosopher

Alamut was a beautiful place up in the mountains that my friend Dave and I discovered. We first heard of Alamut because of a story related to me by one of my Iranian friends and another story we saw in the English Iranian newspaper. They said the mountains were beautiful and it was good hunting.

Assassins was the name of a group of people who lived in the mountains that run from Turkey to Afghanistan. The English word assassinate originated with these people, because of legends told about them. Their principal city was Alamut which means Eagles Nest.

West of Mashad was Neyshapur where Omar Khayyam was buried. The mullahs used to visit there, to piss on his grave. The mullahs hated Omar Khayyam because his idea of Islam wasn't fatalistic. Khayyam felt you should enjoy life now. You couldn't have more than four wives at one time. They don't really know how many wives Mohammed had. Pardis, "beautiful garden," was something to look forward to. That's where they got the word "Paradise."

Many centuries before Osama bin Laden, around 1200, there was the legendary Hassan Sabah, leader of a tribe of Ismaili Muslims who retreated to these mountains to get away from the authorities. He formed a band to get back at those in power, to assassinate them. Sabah was a friend of Omar Khayyam. They had agreed to help one another. Hassan Sabah created the Assassins. Sabah had some kind of psychic control over his men; they would jump off a cliff and kill themselves if Sabah ordered it. Here, the Assassins built beautiful castles, grew crops and demonstrated feats of water engineering that astound people to this day. Back in Europe, people made up stories about these people, calling Hassan the "Old Man of the Mountains." Most of the castles were destroyed by the Mongols who took over this area in the 13th century, but there are a few left, and some ruins.

So, Dave and I went to Alamut to hunt. Hunting meant getting away from the problems that come along with being in a foreign country. We had such freedom as

Americans. The mountains were so beautiful and there were so many exciting things waiting for us to experience. I don't know what I would have done without being able to hunt.

An interesting incident happened while I was on a hunting trip with a very high ranking person. Hunting had stopped in the middle of the afternoon because of heavy rain. We were seated on an elevated area that looked like a stage. The servants served us dinner and after the food was eaten, the pipe came out. All the equipment was very elaborate. I was offered the pipe first and I couldn't refuse it. That would be an insult. So I smoked it. Then it happened. A man came in running and announced there was a bear after the mules. I was told "Take care of it Michael."

I took my .308 and .357 and went out. The visibility was nil. I couldn't feel my body too much, but my senses appeared to be better than normal. The mules were going crazy. I saw movement but nothing that I could shoot at. I followed the sound of the bear. At times he was in front of me and then he would be in back of me. It went on and on. I was soaking wet. The water was running down my legs. The hair on my neck was standing up. This went on for quite a while I was in a deep ravine now. There was a very large tree in front of me on top of the ravine so I climbed up to the tree and placed my back against it. I then began to make noise. Finally the bear came up the ravine to me. He was huge. It was a Russian bear. I shot him in the top of his neck, angled towards his heart.

I immediately tried to reload but the rifle was jammed. All the rain had swelled the wood. I could not reload. It took just a second for me to draw the .357 and fire six shots into the bear's head. That was it, but things could have been much worse. Opium is not the thing to smoke in a dangerous situation

My IIAF Land Rover was my principal mode of transportation and I was able to use it for anything I wanted. This all happened while I was with the IIAF. I visited Alamut with the Land Rover many times; each was a new experience. This chapter integrates some of those experiences into one journey. Dave was usually with me when I went to Alamut, but not always.

Our journey from Teheran to Alamut started by traveling towards the city of Gazvien, (The IIAF guys joked about Gazvien, calling it the City of the Queers). Before we got there, we would have to turn north into the mountains. The roads to the mountains were rocky, no more than rough dirt paths. In some places it was difficult to travel over the rocks. There were always interesting events that happened on that road. On one trip we came across a man who was very hungry and thirsty. We gave him some water and bread; we offered to transport him out of there. He refused because he was going to some place high in the mountains. There were no roads to his destination.

Further on, down the road, we ran into four people who were stuck on the road in a Volkswagen. Two young Englishmen and two women waved us down. I asked them what the hell they were doing this far out. They said they wanted to explore. We had an interesting conversation, pulled them out of their predicament and wished them farewell.

We arrived at a village where all of the people were very polite and friendly. They invited us to join them in a dinner that they put together for us. The people had sort of an orange tint to their skin and had an oriental look about them. They might have been descendants of Genghis Khan who conquered the Assassins. We enjoyed their hospitality and then went on our way, but not until they directed us to a man who they assured was honest and honorable. We had to leave my vehicle with them and go the rest of the way on foot. We could see by their faces that they were honorable people, so my vehicle would be safe with them.

My very young son, Michael was with us on this trip. He was always very close to me. I didn't see any danger in this place and I wanted to make him familiar with the wild. I had my .308 with me, but it was slung casually over one shoulder. We walked along the side of one mountain for a fairly long way until we finally approached the house of this shepherd/farmer. Suddenly, we were attacked by a pack of dogs. I didn't expect that. My .308 was in my hands, ready to shoot the dogs. The farmer was near the dogs and shouted something to them. The dogs looked back at the farmer and when they did, the farmer threw his walking staff in the air. The dogs immediately stopped running and barking. I realized the dogs had been well-trained to follow his commands.

We set up our tent so we had a place to sleep. In the morning we would take to the mountains. The dogs were always out there and would growl when anyone of us went outside to relieve ourselves. The lead dog had something against me. I think that he thought that I was the lead dog of our group and he wanted to beat me up. It kept going through my mind that he would try this if no one else was around. Early morning came and we were up before sunrise. Our breakfast was a meager pack of survival rations. It was not a very good breakfast but much better than nothing. Then, it was off to the high ground.

Little Michael slowed us down, but that wasn't a problem. There was lots of time. The farmer was now a shepherd and a guide. A young boy, along with some of the dogs, was tending the farmer's mixed herd of sheep and goats. The farmer was supervising the young shepherd, and guiding us at the same time. The guide would go back to them periodically and check on things. While he was gone at one time, I saw the lead dog far down the mountain. I decided that this was a good time to get rid of my problem. I got in the prone position and rested the rifle on a rock. As I was about to squeeze off, a voice in back of me said, "Sir, please don't shoot my dog". I replied, "I'm sorry, I thought that was a bear." It was our farmer guide. I felt so embarrassed. He knew I was lying.

It was a successful hunting trip, that day. I shot an Ibex through the neck, at a distance of four hundred yards. He was leading the herd, running towards us. We were pretty high up and the Ibex was on the other mountain. The farmer took care of everything. Mountains to him were like flatlands to us. Looking down on his house was like looking from an airplane. The house looked very tiny.

At one point during the hunt, little Michael was with Dave and I was running on a part of the mountain that was much higher than they were. My foot hit what seemed to be a soft spot on a rock. Fortunately, my other foot was on solid rock, because I had just started an avalanche. A good portion of the mountain started heading downward. The noise and rocks got larger and more devastating as the landslide progressed. What a spectacular sight! It's a good thing that Dave and Michael were far away from that spot.

It took a while, but when we were back down the mountain, we began to make preparations to leave. While waiting for the farmer and the young boy to bring the Ibex to the house, we were watching one of the wives doing her daily chores. She had a baby tied onto her back and had a sort of bag hanging round her waist. In her hand, she had something that looked like a child's top. There was wool in the bag and, with fast movements, she spun the top with her right hand and fed wool into the top with her left hand. She was spinning yarn. This she did during the daylight hours. In the evening and late into the night, she would weave the wool into fabric to make things out of it, including carpets. During the winter they wove carpets. In the spring they would sell the carpets at the market, further down the mountain.

I noticed something very peculiar while I was walking by a stream: there were large holes on the banks of the stream. At first, I thought that some type of muskrat inhabited the hole. It was a big surprise to see very large crabs coming out of some of those holes. What a surprise! Large Crabs lived up here in the mountains. There was no end to the surprises in that country.

The farmer sold us some pinto beans and we paid him much more than he could get in that area. He was very happy. A donkey took the Ibex and the beans to the village where my Land Rover was parked. We then left for Teheran. The result of the hunt was a dinner party where the Ibex was served, along with other dishes. People raved about the Ibex; it had such an exotic flavor. I've never tasted anything like that since.

We decided to use the other side of the river as a base and looked for a village we had seen earlier, from the high ground. We found it. Fortunately, I was able to drive right up to the village. The people were surprised to see us. They began to bring the sick people to treat. Not having much, we did the best that we could with the large first aid kit that we had in the Land Rover. Then we were taken to the village chief. After telling him that we wanted to hunt, he got a happy look on his face. All would begin very early in the morning. The nice thing was that we also had a room to sleep in and we were able to lock the door.

The awakening came very early. It was very dark when we started with the village chief, two mules and a midget. I don't know where the midget came from. The mules were very neat and clean and looked like good looking horses. Mules are very expensive in Iran. A donkey costs fifty dollars. A horse costs seventy-five dollars and a mule costs five hundred dollars. In the mountains, a donkey is good but too small. Horses aren't as sure footed, don't know when to stop walking and could kill themselves. A mule stops when the exertion on him is too much.

Riding one of those mules is not at all like riding a horse. First of all, there is only one rein. There was no way for me to control that mule. The mule kept turning his head, to try

370

and bite my leg. The chief gave me a small piece of a tree branch. I had to show the mule the switch when he turned his head to bite me. When he saw the switch, he would immediately turn his head forward. After a while, I learned how to get some control over the mule.

We left the chief's home, went to the edge of the village and stopped at a house. Almost immediately, the door opened and another midget came out. There was a woman with him and they bid each other good bye. She was not a midget. It was an unusual sight but nice. Not a mile from the house, the mules went crazy. It was hard to stay in the saddle. The chief began yelling "curse," which means "bear." The Russian bears there were quite big. We couldn't see him, but we heard him crashing around. They covered the eyes of the mules and they calmed down. Soon, we were moving again, with the guides holding the reins.

The morning sun began to rise and the mountains and sky began to show beautiful colors. Blues, reds and purples lit up the mountains. The colors made a progressive change to orange and yellow, until the sun came up and everything dissolved into its natural color. Eagles were soaring beneath us. This was something I had never seen before and it was breath-taking. We soon came to the end of the journey for the mules. Now we had to climb, and climb we did.

It wasn't long before we saw the mountain sheep. There was a big herd of them. They were very far away. I took some range readings and came up with 600 yards. I dialed 600 into my scope. I had reloaded all of my bullets myself, as usual. The bullets were very accurate. When the herd stopped, I took a shot at the biggest one. A cloud of dust appeared on the opposite side of him and I knew that he was hit. The sheep didn't fall, because at that range the bullet doesn't expand and has no knock-down power. It just goes right through them.

They all started running, but they didn't know where we were. The herd went to the top of the mountain then turned left and ran along the mountain top. They turned left again and ran a diagonal path nearer and nearer to us. About four hundred yards from us one of them dropped. I took another shot and another one dropped. This one fell down the mountain. Two was enough for me. Dave began shooting with my .357. He had fun and insisted that he got one, but I didn't see any fall.

Now the midgets went to work. The Chief just lay there, giving orders to the midgets. I couldn't see how they were going to bring the sheep back. Watching them was sort of pitiful. The shoes that they wore were made of auto tires with thongs tied around their toes. We wore boots. After a long while, they did get the sheep to us. They immediately gutted the

372

sheep and made a fire. They took out the intestines and put them in the running water so that the water flowed through the intestines. At first, the water was very dirty and after a short while, it became clear. Afterwards they built a fire and began roasting the innards. It smelled very good. The midgets began eating along with the Chief. I took a bite so as not to insult them. A villager showed up to take one of the sheep, the big one, back to the village. I don't know how he got there.

A good part of the day was gone now, so we started back to the village. On the way back, I saw movement far away. I looked with my field glasses at the movement and saw a man in camouflage. I wondered what he was doing there by himself.

We did not pick up the mules where we were left off. We were far from that place. It was a long day and I could feel the fatigue from all of that climbing, walking and running. We met up with the rest of the party, and the mules, further down the mountain. What a welcome sight they were– and what a relief it was to climb on one of the mules.

Our path hugged the side of a steep mountain and it was very narrow. My left shoulder was touching the rough rock. On my right, it was a sheer drop to the valley below. Then the mule began to run, on that rough, narrow path. I closed my eyes. There was nothing I could do, except pray. My life was in the hands of God and the mule. It was a scary ride, to say the least. The mule finally stopped when he had passed the steep drop-off. It seemed like an eternity.

We arrived at the village. As Dave and I looked around, we noticed that the tires were flat on the Land Rover. Everything that had been in the vehicle was gone. As we walked to the Chief's house, we saw the sheep. The "backstraps," or loins, were gone. That is the best part of the animal. I grew angry as questions raced through my mind: Who let the air out of the tires? Why? They stole everything. Do they have plans for us? Are we in serious danger?

I could feel the adrenalin coursing through my veins as my body prepared to go on high alert and get nasty. Dave told me not to get excited. "Why not? We paid for the hunt and now we find out that they stole everything from us," I answered. We walked into the house. "Well, I'm not talking to that son of a bitch. You do the talking." That would be an insult to the Chief.

Dave sat down and started talking to the Chief and explained everything that we saw to him. I was glad my friend could speak Farsi fluently. I remained standing, with my hand on my .357. The Chief managed to look surprised and then called for the man who carried the sheep back. When he arrived, the man came in the house. He was confronted by the Chief. He explained that while he was

374

walking back to the village he was attacked by dogs. They must have eaten the back straps. The chief started to smile and said, "You see?" That made me angry. It was obvious that the back straps were ripped out by a man. I said to Dave, "Tell him, if he doesn't bring back everything that was stolen and doesn't pump up the tires, I'm going to blow his fucking brains out." Dave responded, "I can't say that." Then I yelled back at him "Say it!" So he did.

As my friend was talking, I gave the Chief the meanest and angriest look that I could. I was sure now that he had plans for us. Next I took my .357 out. The Chief's face fell. He was frightened. Then he called for someone. When the other man arrived, he shouted instructions to him. Off he ran. In five minutes everything was brought back to the house and laid on the floor. Outside, the tires were being pumped up. No back straps though. I put the gun into my holster and the Chief smiled. I didn't.

We left quickly, before anyone else could do something stupid. Our pace to the vehicle was very fast, so no crowd could gather around us. That would make us extremely vulnerable. We sped out of the village. It was dark now and we were still in the mountains.

There was a woman walking along the dirt road. Since it was dark, we stopped and ask her where she was going and could we help her. A mistake! She was a prostitute selling her wares. Once a woman is divorced by her husband, there isn't too much else she can do to support herself. Dave was laughing and I was about to. Can you imagine, she's out here in the wilderness conducting her business in darkness? Where are the customers? Every time it's something new.

The Land Rover took us home to the comforts of my dear wife and the rest of my wonderful children. I never told them about my escapades. If I did, they would just worry every time that I was away.

By the time I made my last trip to Alamut, my life had changed dramatically. My family had returned to the States to begin a new life. I had stayed behind to finish out my contract. People warned me that my life was in danger. They never said exactly who was trying to get rid of me. I had made many friends, which was a plus for me; otherwise I wouldn't have been warned. It had happened many times in the last five years. I had to get away from my house as much as I could. Alamut was calling me; I thought I would be safe up there, surrounded by mountains.

This time I went to the friendly village. While talking with the village Chieftain, I casually mentioned the incident of the theft in a previous trip. He was shocked. He explained that where I had been was a village of thieves. It was a dangerous place. Of course he told me to go to the farmer/shepherd. That's what I decided to do.

376

In the morning, I went to the farmer's home and told him that I wanted to spend some time in the mountains. If I shot anything, he could keep it. What was I going to do with it? He took me up to the mountains but I really didn't need him. All was familiar to me and I didn't need a mule. The farmer left me there, as I requested. All was peaceful and quiet. That day, I didn't shoot anything. Game was the last thing on my mind. As the day faded, the colors started to set in. I had no tent with me but I wanted to stay in the mountains that night.

When the stars began to appear, I found myself looking at the sky. As daylight disappeared, the sky was white. Never before had I seen something like this. At that altitude, it was so clear. The stars lit up the mountains and valleys. I could see everything. My mind wondered off to the beautiful times in my life. I thought of my family and wondered how the new life set with them. After hours of staring and dreaming, I fell asleep. I awoke many times from the animal sounds but I did get some rest.

The sun arose and colored the mountains in breath-taking hues. Around noon time, I saw a man in camouflage, on the other mountain. I had seen this man, before so I watched him intently. He was coming in my direction, but was still on the other mountain. I moved to a large rock that provided some cover. I could see over the top and the sides. There was a solid wall of rock in back of me. As I watched him from the top of the rock, he laid down. What the hell was this all about? As I put my head down behind the big rock to think about this, a bullet smashed into the rocks behind my head. He was trying to kill me.

I had no idea how far away he was. The time between when I brought my head down and the bullet hit was milliseconds. He couldn't know that he hadn't hit me. The recoil of the rifle makes the rifle go up in the air and you can't really see the exact hit. It was a shock to me, but I was alone. I must do things right, if I was to get out of this. My advantage was that he wasn't sure if he had hit me or not. I felt sure he thought he had. I quickly took some range readings off to the left side of the rock, to a point that I thought was the same range as he was. It was 1000 yards. That's a long shot for a .308. I dialed the range into the scope as best I could. It was beyond the scope-marking calibrations, so it estimated where it should be. There was no place for me to go. I took a quick peek from the left side of the rock.

He was there, looking to get another shot. I waited for a minute and very slowly moved to the right. I got a perfect sight picture and squeezed off a round. I didn't see any dust kick up but I saw the man jerk a little. At least I thought I did. "I couldn't have gotten him at that range," I thought. There was no wind that I could feel. Usually at that range, wind will carry the bullet, and you will miss.

I waited. After about five minutes, I looked around the left side of the rock. I saw something through the field glasses, but couldn't tell what it was. I got the rifle – I had set the scope on maximum power -- and looked. I thought it was him. Was he faking, to get me out in the open? He was partially hidden by a rock. There wasn't much exposed to take another shot.

I wondered. I took another shot and nothing moved. He would have moved if he heard the bullet go over him. Just hearing the shot would have made him do something. Was it a set up to get me in the open? How could I know?

I waited for about two hours and then ventured into the open. There was no movement anywhere. Were there any more of them? I went back to the rock and scanned the mountain from the rock for another hour. Nothing! Now was the time to make a run for it I thought, so I did. For two hundred yards I would run like hell, come to a halt and run again until I got to another rock. Then, I scanned again. Once again I ran for a longer distance. Now I was out of range. My routine kept up until I got to a place that I could get off of the mountain. Instead of going to the farmer's house, I went to the village.

Since I couldn't be sure what happened and why, and who was in on it, I waited outside the village until dark. Then I ran to my vehicle and took off. There was no need to explain; I would never come back there again.

Once I was on the road, the sick feeling set in, along with the "happy to be alive" feeling. When I got to Teheran, I went to a friend's house and said nothing about what happened. We had many drinks and I began to feel normal again. I slept there that night. That was the end of my visits to the mountains. Alamut was lost to me forever. There was no safe place to hide at Alamut, since they knew it was a place of refuge for me. No longer. Teheran was now my only place to hide. Could I keep this up until I was able to get out of Iran? Only God knew.

Chapter 18

Getting My Wife and Kids

Out of Iran

Bazaar at Esfahan, Iran

Lucretia:

After Christel was born in 1971, I taught
English at the Imperial Iranian Air Force Pilot

Cadet School at Doshen Toppeh (Rabbit Hill). That was Iranian headquarters. S., an Iranian girlfriend taught there, and our friend, Teymor. Wives of American military personnel and foreign girls married to pilots also taught there. American Military officers were not permitted to teach.

I attended college at the Teheran American School. My friends and I walked up there twice a week for classes. I took history, Russian politics, English and Math, as well as required courses towards my B.S. in Nursing. Eventually, I planned to use all my credits toward a degree in nursing.

Then, Lloyd Jones' car was blown up in 1972. He wasn't a close friend; Lloyd had been Mike's immediate boss when he worked in the FAA. We didn't know why that happened. He wasn't military. They may have wanted to start a fire in the parking lot.

I first became aware that things were not so good around 1975. I heard stories of more terrorist activity. It seemed to be on the increase all over the country. I wondered if we would have to leave Iran, if things got worse. Military personnel were being ambushed; many of them were our friends. It was happening more frequently; you never knew where they would strike next. Mike used to look under his jeep to see if there were any bombs planted there. I wasn't experiencing any of the hostility Mike knew at work. The danger had not directly touched me or the children yet.

I didn't want to leave our friends, and a life that we had known for nearly ten years. I thought of all the hard work involved in moving our children, possessions and ourselves back to the States. Mike had bought property in Pennsylvania early in 1976. He had gone home to visit his mom and saw an ad, land for sale. We had talked about it more in the past year, on those rare occasions when he was home with us in Kuche Zarrine. I knew we would have to move back at some point. We didn't say anything in front of the children. I guess we tried to keep things as normal as possible for as long as we could.

It seemed easiest to plan the move in three stages. So, one morning, when the older girls came down for breakfast, I told them our plans. They were to say nothing to their friends yet, just start packing. It was August 1976. Sharon, Shelley and Lucretia Ann would go first. We arranged for them to stay with relatives in Pennsylvania until Carolyn and I brought the younger ones home. It would be hard on Carolyn – she'd have less time to adjust to the States, and this would be her junior year in high school – but I felt I needed her help with the younger ones and the rest of the packing.   Christel was only five years old. Mark was seven and Michael was nine. We planned to leave a week or so after the older girls. All the children were unhappy when we told them our plans. It was a shock, to think of leaving Iran. I looked around the living room, at the beautiful, custom-built furniture we had brought with us from Pennsylvania. That would have to be sold. It would be too difficult to move everything. We had been sending pictures, rugs and little tchotchkes back to the States with friends who were transferred home. Now I had to pull out the suitcases and trunks, and get organized.

Mike:

There were only four months left until the end of my contract with the IIAF. Three of my older girls, Sharon, Michelle and Lucretia Ann, were already in the States. School was to begin in September so my wife had to get back too, and organize our new life back in the States. What a responsibility she had! She had seven kids to care for, with no place to call home. I had bought a car for her when I was home in July. Work for her would be 24/7. We already had the tickets and we thought that our visas were also good. It was not the case. We were told at the last minute that the three younger children could not leave the country until they had all the proper documents completed.

Why should this be a problem? It's complicated. These three kids, Michael, Mark and Christel were born in Iran. Under the laws at the time, they were American citizens because they were born while I was under the jurisdiction of the United States Government. We all had official passports, so there should have been no problem. Iran also considered them Iranian citizens because they were born in that country. As such, the boys would be expected to serve in the Iranian military. Normally, when you leave a foreign country after an official tour of duty, there isn't a problem. Someone made it a problem.

My first idea was to go to the US Embassy to get some help. They provided us with papers affirming that these three children were born with official US Passports. The papers were very impressive; they were elaborate with gold seals. Unfortunately, it didn't help us at all. The Iranian government officials gave us a stack of papers with which it seemed to impossible to comply.

How depressing it all was! We had the airplane tickets, but they would not be able to board the aircraft. It was Wednesday and the airplane was to leave on Saturday. It looked like the Iranian government officials had won -- but a miracle was in the making.

An officer friend offered to help me get this thing fixed. He got a vehicle with a driver and guided me through the process. We raced from one government official to another. If he hadn't been with me we would never have got it done but he was a real friend. We got everything signed except for the last document. That had to be signed by a General

385

in the Imperial Iranian Army at the Central Army Headquarters. I had been to that building a few times but I didn't know anyone there. We just couldn't get the last signature. The officer with me had a conversation with another officer there who knew him. His fellow officer promised to be there early the next morning. The officer assured us that he would be there on Thursday morning. My heart sank. Why could they not get it signed now? Nobody worked on Thursday; it was like our Saturday. They reassured me that the General would be there and the papers would be signed.

Nothing that I said changed anything. Tomorrow it would have to be. Early the next morning I was there, waiting. The officer was not there. I waited and waited. Two hours later I spotted an old friend. I was so glad to see him. He asked me what I was doing there and I explained to him what had to be done. He took the papers into the General's office and came out in five minutes. The papers were signed. Everything was all set now I hoped. Now, I was all smiles.

"How did you get those papers signed so quickly?" I asked.

"He just signed all the papers I put in front of him. He never looked at them," he replied.

"Why are you here today? You don't work here," I observed.

He was evasive, "I come here every few months to get some things signed."

"But you don't work on Thursday," I pressed him.

"Today, I decided to get this work finished," was all he would say. I thanked him profusely and left. My heart was pounding. My thought was that there was someone looking out for me.

I prayed hard that nothing else would happen to screw this up for us. I was scared; it wasn't safe in Iran any more. I wanted my family out of there as quickly as possible. It was hard to sleep. I was still worried about any last minute snafus. What would I do if some official refused to let them board the plane? What could I do? Besides, once they left, I would not see them for a long time, if ever. My life would be a very dismal existence. The important thing was that they would be gone from Iran and safe. That outweighed everything else. When I got home later that day, Lucretia was elated.

Saturday morning came. We left for the airport early to make sure that any problems that might occur could be taken care of. Nobody at the office knew I was at the airport. I just didn't show up that morning. Everything went like clockwork. This was unbelievable and I was ecstatic. My heart was broken as they left me. There were tears in my eyes as my dear wife, our eldest daughter and the three little ones walked out of my life. Would I ever see them again? Fear weighed me down, like a stone on my heart.

The plane took off and I watched in silent sadness as it flew out of sight. Now they were gone and I had to finish out my contract. I focused on what I had to do, to keep myself alive so I could see my family again. The Land Rover, my .357 and I drove over to Headquarters. I had to be extra careful from this moment on. Very shortly, everyone would know that my family had left Iran. It took me a half-hour to get to Headquarters.

I had no idea what had just happened there. As I came into the office, one of the secretaries saw me and screamed. She ran to me, hugged me tight and started crying. "Oh," she exclaimed. "We thought you were dead! There was an ambush near the gate you use to enter the office compound. Three Americans were killed by terrorists. Nobody saw you this morning. We thought you were one of the ones who were killed."

It all happened at the time I would have been at that gate. I was soon surrounded by nice people. Some of the other people were not so happy to see me. I could see it in their eyes. It appeared to be so logical to them. First, I did not show up at work. Second, there was an ambush in which three Americans were killed, so one of those Americans had to be me. That made two miracles in two days. My family was gone from Iran and I was still alive. All of it was very humbling to me. I was very grateful and happy.

The Americans at the MAAG told me just how brutal the assassination was. After the Americans were down, the terrorists shot them in the face with a flood of bullets. One of them took seventy bullets. An over whelming feeling of sheer rage came over me. All I wanted to do was to kill the bastards. That time would come very shortly. They were sending a message to Americans and I got it, but not in the way that they wanted.

My first impulse was to call my family, so they would know I was alive. An assassination would be big news in the U.S., I thought, and the news would travel very fast. My mother was upset and wanted to know when I was coming home. I assured her that I'd come home as soon as I could and that everything would be all right. She didn't believe me. That I could feel. I asked her to let Lucretia and the kids know I was fine.

Iran was no longer my home. All the family who had surrounded me these past ten years were gone. It was an eerie feeling and I had to live with it for four more months. I felt so empty inside. It was like being dead.

Chapter 19: Final Getting Out

Radar tower, FAA facility

Philadelphia Airport, Tinicum Township,
Pennsylvania, USA

Thing weren't going well. The time had come for me to make all of this come to an end. I had been moved to another branch of the Imperial Iranian Air Force (IIAF) to keep me out of company selections for contracts. In January 1976, I had decided that it would be my last year in Iran. At that time, my intention was to get out of Iran alive with my family. At the very least, I was determined to get my wife and children out safely.

From the very beginning of my employment by the IIAF I had declined to mix in the elite upper levels of Iranian society. In my mind, I had done the right thing but maybe it wasn't. Maybe I could have got more useful information from the "Upper Crust," but I didn't know that then. It was too late to think about that now. I had learned at an Iranian wedding that the terrorists were no longer after me. My safety was not guaranteed, nor did I know if that bit of information was true. It might have been said to throw me off guard. The real threat came from the Shah's crackdown on corruption and my knowing the corrupt people involved.

At one point, the Shah said that if he were to arrest everyone involved in the corruption, he would not have anyone left to run the country. I took that to mean he was picking off people one at a time and hoping that the others would stop their criminal activities. The Shah had a lot to deal with. At parties, I know that I was being shunned by the people on the take. Some would be artificially nice to me but I could feel the contempt in their phony smiles and false words.

The CIA had advised me in the very beginning of my IIAF tour to favor American companies and I had done that as much as possible. Money attracts people with evil intent. The big problem was that once people get into it, they only wanted more and more of it and didn't care about repercussions to the country. My biggest concern was to get my family back home to the US. This mad world was not for us anymore.

By January 1976, it was time to make a trip back to the States and get some real rest. I needed to set things up for my family when we got home. My savings had grown quite a bit, so I was ready to invest in our future home. While I was there, I tried to buy a house in the town of my birth. It was so refreshing to be there, surrounded by the friends with whom I grew up. It was like going back in time and being a kid again. What a difference from Iran and the IIAF!

Unfortunately, the guy who was selling the house decided to renege. I didn't know him and he pissed me off because I didn't have enough time to get another deal going. I was so angry that I told a close friend to beat him up. As my friend was beating him up, the guy kept saying "I ain't right." It was easy for me to have this done because at that time, I was hard as a rock. Afterwards, I was sorry. I was glad he wasn't beaten up too badly.

I had so little time to find a place to live. What could I do now? Everything was screwed up. Then, something amazing did happen. I ran into a deal I liked very much. Another man was selling eleven acres of land in a wooded area. I snatched it up immediately. That, to me, was a godsend. After the transaction, I returned to Iran. Now we had something to look forward to when we got home.

It was spring time now and the winter was gone. *Nowruz*, March 21, was here. That's the New Year in Iran. They celebrate the solar New Year. There must have been talk going around about me. Some people are just plain good and you can recognize them. One of these people told me to be very careful and watch everyone. That said something to me; "People who seem to be your friends, aren't". One friend, who was with me from the very beginning, paid a visit to my home. His words to me were, "Zehbel, try to do what they want. Don't get them angry."

My response was simple and to the point. We were outside. There was a raven flying in front of us. I picked up my powerful pellet gun from a nearby table. One shot and the raven crashed to the ground.

"I know who sent you. If he sends someone to finish me off, and he misses, I will pay him a visit and blow his brains out." He was shocked, after seeing how swiftly the raven plummeted to earth.

We ended our conversation as friends and he departed. My friend and I genuinely liked each other and I was sad to see the path he had chosen. My intent had not been to make a lot of money, but to progress in my mission. It would have been nice to make more money, but not that way. Some of the shit that they bought was pathetic. I did understand the lust for money in Iran. Without it, you would have a miserable life. It was especially true for Iranians who had spent time in the States. They had become aware of what life could be and they wanted to live that kind of life back in Iran.

There was a lot of travel in my schedule. I was a busy bee. For the sake of the country, I wanted finish as many projects as I could before I left. I did not tell people that I was leaving. Everywhere I went, from one corner of Iran to another, I saw the projects I had completed and how they were making people's lives better. It made me very proud.

Finding a new job was an essential part of my exit plan. I had to get one set up before returning to the U.S. permanently. My focus was to get back to the States, find a job, and get building started on my new property. I got there just before the Bicentennial. When I arrived in Washington, D.C., in late June 1976, my negotiations were short and turned out to be sweet. I was placed in charge of bringing Indonesia's airports into the twentieth century, with navigational aids, TACANs and more.

I'd given the company, International Technical Products, a list of specifications to ensure my safety, including a powerful sailboat with back-up motor. Part of its ballast is diesel fuel so you can go a long way without any wind. With this kind of boat, one man could adjust the sails in and out, tack and operate the boat by himself. It's what they call a motor-sail. I wanted one with high-tech communications on board. My plan had been to live on the boat while I worked to bring Indonesia into the 20th century, as the Shah had done for Iran.

Pennsylvania and my newly acquired land were awaiting me so I drove up to Bucks County. It was so refreshing to see all that beautiful, untouched land, teeming with wild game, large and small. Right away, I sketched out plans for building my family a beautiful house. Trees had to be removed and I needed a bulldozer for all the heavy work, so I bought one. I was having trouble with the township building permit. I got that all straightened out with a good lawyer. That same night I went with my lawyer to see the Wagon Train that had travelled all the way across the country from California to celebrate the Bicentennial Celebration. It had stopped at Quakertown for the night, not far from my new home-site. It was nice to feel a part of an American celebration, after being away for so many years. Work on the land was started. What a feeling! We would have a home in the U.S. once more. All I had to do now was finish things up in Iran and complete my contract with the IIAF.

I went back to Iran. Shortly after my return, I found out the Indonesian deal fell through. Unfortunately, someone stole all the petroleum money from the Indonesian government and it turned out that was the money they planned to use for this ambitious project. Then this group offered me another job, travelling around the world, fixing equipment. But that fell through, because the group, International Technical Products (ITP), based in Washington DC, lost a tremendous amount of money during the Iranian Revolution. They'd had a lot of contracts in Iran. The money was held in a Boston bank. I think the United States froze Iranian assets held in the U.S. Other job offers were coming through, but things were unstable. I needed to find a job as quickly as possible, but I was frustrated at every turn.

Soon after my return to Teheran, my family left for the US in two separate departures. Now I was alone to face the rest of my tour. Most of my projects were completed, equipment tested and personnel trained to operate and maintain it. My focus was to survive the next few months. There were numerous attempts on my life during this period, but I managed to evade most of them before they started. I had to be on full alert at all times, and that was very tiring. Almost all of my time was spent away from Teheran. It was around this time that I was poisoned in Esfahan. Thank God that I had Dave with me. Without him, I would not have made it. No place was safe for me. The poisoning affirmed that.

The Poisoning

Esfahan was the last major project on my schedule. It was a big air base just outside the city. Esfahan Air Base was re-named Khatami Base after the Commander of the Imperial Iranian Air Force. General Khatami had been killed in an Air Kite accident at the Dez Dam near Vahdati a few years earlier. I had to get this project completed on time, because my contract was running out. The control tower/IFR room was flawed in its design, so I insisted it be modified and so it was. It turned out to be an unusual and beautiful tower. The city was 280 miles from Teheran; it would take five or six hours to get there by car. Everything at the base was state of the art. Even the fighter planes were F-14's. The American technicians were housed near the Base. The Techs, along with their families who were assigned there, lived in American-style homes surrounded by green lawns. Most

Iranians lived behind high walls for protection, but this development was really like a small town back in the States.

I asked one of the men why he chose to come here. He answered, "It was either here or get fired." Interesting! I lived in a hotel in the city, but spent my whole day on the base. Esfahan was a relatively safe place for me, or so I thought.

Seeing these F-14's on the taxi ways and on the runways was a thrill for me. These were the latest American fighters. There was a very different look about it. Esfahan was the only place in the country that had F-14's.

A story went around the base that one of the pilots had just shot down a MIG Fox Bat. The Russians would fly over the place at a very high altitude, seventy thousand feet, to snoop. We knew this was going on. The Fox Bat was put together quickly by the Russians to counter the B-70 bomber. It could fly very high. The F-14's were equipped with Phoenix missiles, but the F-14 itself couldn't reach the Fox Bat. However, it could get close enough to fire the Phoenix missiles and those long-range air-to-air missiles were able to reach the target. One day, an Iranian pilot shot one down. This story originated with the Americans there, so it was probably true. After that, no more Russian planes flew over Iran.

My job was to make sure that all of the electronic equipment needed to support an all-weather Imperial Iranian Air Force was installed and working. That responsibility kept me a very busy man. At this point in my career, these things had become routine for me. Trips from Teheran to Esfahan were frequent. I would stay for a week or so and then get back to my other duties.

While I was there, I picked up some new habits. Changing my breakfast habits was one of them. *Kallepache* was a breakfast made up of the head and feet of a sheep. It wasn't served in most of the places I had lived in Iran. Here in Esfahan, there was a place close by, the Feed House, that served excellent *Kallepache*.

There was a group of very strong men in Esfahan called "Danger Men," by the people of Esfahan. These guys swung objects that looked like giant bowling pins around with their hands and they did it as a group, combining slow, artistic movements with ancient Iranian music. It was like a dance. I had seen them on television, performing for the Shah. They would practice in the very early hours of the morning. What does this have to do with me and my breakfast? It turned out that they regularly had breakfast at this new place I had discovered.

The first day I went there for breakfast, they all stared at me, but no one spoke. The second day, they were much more friendly. On the third day, it was like old home week.

400

Suddenly, it was like I was an old friend. They all stood up and insisted that I be served the best part of the head of the sheep. The server complied. Actually, it was very good. From that time on, they all stood up when I came in. Now I was their buddy. It was a very good feeling. There was no danger for me at that place. No one ever saw my gun, even though it was always with me. If they knew that, people would have stayed away from me and I would have missed out on this beautiful experience. Iranian people are very friendly and respectful to people who they think deserve it. These strong men thought that I deserved respect.

Now, the story gets more involved. The Iranian people that worked with me at the various electronic equipment stations knew I was having breakfast at the Feed House. Something had changed. Now, when I came near them, they would move towards a wall and put their backs to the wall. I noticed it and after a while, I asked a close friend why they were doing this. Reluctantly he explained: it was well-known that people who ate *Kallepache* for breakfast would become oversexed and feel compelled to give it to people in the butt. Oh well! I just laughed. It was funny. Another bit of info to add to the cultural differences all around me.

I had also heard eating sheep testicles had the same effect. In the Officers Club at Vahdati, I had sheep testicles for dinner one night. As I was leaving, there was a table where a group of pilots were sitting having dinner. They all knew me, so they greeted me. I replied in the proper way. Then they asked me what I had had for dinner. I was ready for a laugh and I decided to pull their tails. "Koss Kabob," was my reply to the question.

One of them had just spooned in a mouthful of soup when I answered. He exploded and noodles spurted out of his nose when he heard what I said. The rest started roaring. There is a dish called Toss Kabob which is sort of a beef stew. "Koss Kabob" means "Roast Pussy". They thought that I mispronounced the word Toss. They then explained what I had just said. I apologized for the "mistake", even though it was no mistake. The expression spread around the country. They also explained what eating sheep testicles can do to a person. It makes them oversexed -- so they thought! Life was so interesting over there.

On this particular trip, we were staying at a hotel that was outside of the city. A group of Americans checked into the hotel. They were travelers and were now spending some time in Esfahan. They reminded me of some of the hippies that I had run into in the past. We got to know them and during some of the conversations, they found out that I did handwriting analysis. My friend must have told them. There was no other way they could

402

have found that out. I had studied Handwriting Analysis under an American in Teheran for two years and had got pretty good at it. Now I had a new job. They all wanted to have their handwriting analyzed. It was a good way to pass time. What else did I have to do in my non-working hours? This went on for a couple of days. We would sit out in the patio area, drink beer and go over their handwriting.

Did you ever get a strange feeling that came over you in which you thought that something wasn't right? I sensed it now. Quickly I scanned the people in the patio area. Nobody looked like a threat. I had just ordered a beer and had taken one sip. The particular writing before me was interesting. After about twenty minutes, I began to feel sick. It became painful and I began to feel strange. Remember, I had only taken one sip of the beer. I had never experienced this sort of thing.

I looked at the beer and then over to the bartender. It was not the same man who was there before. This one had a mean evil look about him and he was glaring at me. I immediately told my friend that we must leave now. We headed for the Land Rover. I told him I thought I had been poisoned. Too weak to sit upright, I flopped into the back of the vehicle and gave the .357 to him. He had learned to shoot with the .357 on our hunting trips. I also told him to watch out for other cars that were suspicious-looking in their movements.

He understood the gravity of the situation, so he sped home for Teheran. The agony started. It was extreme pain, sickness, dizziness along with an indescribable feeling. I passed out for a while and awoke soon after, in great pain. There was nothing I could do, but endure it. I began to pray and hoped that I would not die. When we reached Teheran, five or six hours later, I was in pathetic shape. My friend wanted to take me to a hospital to which I replied, "how could I defend myself in a hospital?"

I drank some milk at my house and went to sleep. My friend stayed with me. It wasn't a nice kind of sleep, but by the next day, I felt much better. There was something wrong with my vision; my sight was blurry and I was seeing double. I prayed that it would not last. In a few days, everything cleared up. "Just let your guard down one time," I thought, "and see what happens."

I had never experienced someone trying to poison me, but now it had happened. Now I had to suspect anything and everything. My mind pondered over all the things that had already happened to me and I wondered, 'How long can I survive this? What's next?' There was no one to tell, or ask for help. About this time, in 1976, the Shah was trying to find out who was involved in all the corruption spreading through Iran. But corruption was pervasive throughout the entire country! There were so many terrorist groups and individual assassins. I could not tell which group was behind this attempted poisoning. I'll never know.

I had arranged for people I knew and trusted to stay at my house while I was away from Teheran. That served two purposes. People thought that I had left. Someone else was living in the house and there was always someone there to take care of things. When I was home in Teheran, which wasn't very often, I stayed in a special room with a covering on the windows. That was for grenades. There was also a dog in the room to warn me if anyone was coming. Bullets were on the bed, a lot of them.

The *Savak* had let the Terrorists steal some boxes of hand grenades but had cut the fuses off so when they let loose of the handles, the grenade would blow up in their hands. It took the Terrorists a while to figure it out, but every little bit helps.

Jack was a Master Sergeant in the USAF who had been assigned to work with me. He was a very definite asset because of his acquired skills in RADAR. He was also a good shot with a side arm. It made me feel safer, when he was with me. He didn't have a gun but I gave him my wife's P38 to carry. An extra pair of eyes, along with an extra gun, was a comforting feeling and while he was there, I felt at ease. We became very close friends and

we are still in touch to this day. After he left
Iran, I was alone.

December had now come. I had to get out. It
was now common knowledge that no new
contract had been drawn up for me. I didn't
talk about it, but I knew people were
wondering. The final confrontation was about
to happen.

The great blessing that I had going for me was
my special visa. Nobody around me knew I
carried that visa. With it, I could just go to the
airport and leave. With a regular visa I would
have had to go through all kinds of exit
procedures, but for some reason, this young
friend who worked in the IIAF happened to
issue me an unlimited visa. It was better than
a diplomatic one. That was a godsend. I made
reservations on planes to Egypt, Greece and
Germany, to try to throw people off, just in
case anyone was checking up on my travel
plans. The fact that I had that visa and
nobody knew about it was a life saver.
Applying for a visa is a big tip off, and I didn't
want anyone to know what I would do next.

The motorcycle that I had was gone. I needed
something different. A strange looking
American from California came to my house.
He said he heard I was looking for a fast
cycle. He had it with him, so I took it for a
ride. I could hardly keep the front wheel on
the ground. I fell in love with it. Nobody
would be able to catch me on this machine, I
thought, so I bought it. This was a new

experience for me and I spent lots of time getting used to it.

This machine was something else, light and easily maneuverable. It was easy to go along the right side of traffic and even onto the sidewalks. I made a leather sling for the .357 so I could quickly attach it to my left hand. The left side of the handle bar was the clutch. That was much more practical than the right side which was the throttle. Actually, it was a diversion from my routine. In a way, I liked it. Some of the things I did with it were like scenes in a movie. The Iranian drivers probably thought I was crazy. They weren't far from the truth. Facing death on a daily basis had probably altered my perspective on life, along with changing my habits. Who lives this kind of life voluntarily? I was getting a little tired of living with danger as a constant companion.

My favorite hideaway was a little bar in the center of Teheran, and the Inter Continental Hotel. The Inter Continental was part of the world-wide Pan American chain. (There was one in Karachi, Pakistan, that I stayed in for a while on my assignment there.) Fortunately there was a lot of shrubbery there, so I was able to hide the cycle. The Inter Continental Hotel was a fancy place. I didn't fit in very well because of the way that I dressed, but people didn't seem to care. It was a way to pass the time and keep myself hidden to some extent. The bar was comfortable, not at all like the luxury of the Inter Continental, and the people there were very friendly.

My last few weeks in Iran were packed with finishing projects and mentally saying goodbye to places and people I would carry with me all my days. Here's where events become somewhat jumbled in my mind. Some things are very vivid and some have seemed to grow dim. What I'm about to tell you comes from my mind as best as I can recollect.

My mind and body were very run down. Each day was a strain on me. Escaping from people in the traffic of Teheran was routine. At this point in time, I had turned my Land Rover in to the IIAF and mostly relied on my new cycle. Now, I didn't have to constantly check for bombs. My contract would be over in January and it was early December. Somehow, I just had to get out of the country. That was my number one priority. Nothing else mattered except staying alive to make that happen.

I went to my office. My old secretary, Romy, saw me and came running towards me. She wrapped her arms around me in a quick hug. Then, she took off her gold chain with a crucifix attached to it and put it around my neck. She kissed me, turned away and ran down the hall crying. She was an Armenian Christian. It was a very touching scene, but I sensed that she knew something. Everyone who was watching wondered what was going on. I wear that same crucifix to this very day. (Romy died recently. She had been in the States since 1977 and lived in California. I mourned her passing.)

On that very same day, a good friend, someone I'd been close to for a decade, since I first arrived in Iran, came up to me and began to speak. Many officers and men gathered round. He said to me, "While you were not home one day, I went to your house and screwed your maid on your best Persian carpet."

He was grinning from ear to ear. Everyone who heard him had a sad look on their face. He was trying to humiliate me. You must remember that most of the people in the IIAF were very good people. Now I knew he was a "plant." He had been reporting my activities to the Intelligence people. I answered, "You have just dragged the reputation of Iran through the mud." Everyone started laughing. I had said the right thing and he was humiliated in front of everyone. He turned away and walked away with his very angry face. That meant that almost everyone knew that I was leaving Iran. Too bad for me!

My reservations were all ready and I just had to wait. It was two days before my plane would leave. I was not myself anymore. My memory has failed me to an extent and I can't really remember what happened to me on that almost fatal night. Where I was, I can't remember. How I got there, I don't know. I was standing and then I threw my gun on the ground. There was a feeling that it was all over and there was no need for me to keep going. My world was gone and all that I wanted was peace and rest. No more running and fighting! I think I was crying. That's when it happened. Someone was speaking to me. "All right Michael, it's over for you. You will find your rest, but who will take care of your wife and children as you would?" That was it. Something came over me. It was a strange feeling and a rush that is hard to explain. They were out there somewhere and I could feel them even though I could not see them. As I write, a strange feeling has settled upon me and it's hard to keep writing.

My .357 was back in my hand. I had the most terrible feeling in me. I dropped down and it began. There were flashes and noises from submachine guns and bullets. I was not hit. That's where it ends. The flashes and noise started to go away and then there was nothing. I remember the shadowy figures and they disappeared one by one. In no time at all, in my perception, it was all over. All was quiet. A wonderful feeling came over me. That's the end of it. I don't know how I got there and I don't know how I left. To this day, I don't know what happened to my motorcycle. It seemed as though I was in a different world. The .357 was hot so it must have been at work. My hand was clenched around it very tightly. It stayed there.

The next day was my last in Iran. I stayed at home since there was no sense going out. Not after last night. All my bags were packed and I had arranged for a close Iranian friend to take me to the airport. He brought a friend of his along. We made it look like there was a party going on but kept watching outside. It was dark and there was a guard standing outside of the front door on the other side of the street. He just wouldn't move. After a long time, he walked up the street and all of us ran to my friend's car. It was one quick sweep. My luggage was in the car and I was on the floor. Next stop was Mehrabad airport.

Home To The USA

At the last minute, I changed my ticket to the USA. Now, here I was standing in line to check in. My .357 was still with me and loaded. There were now four people in front of me. I had to get rid of the gun so I went to the rest room and threw the bullets into the toilet. Then I hurried back to my place in line and put the .357 into my baggage. I paid the baggage attendant for my excess weight. I was way overweight. I bargained with him, paid him forty dollars and he was satisfied. It would have cost me about a thousand dollars.

Without my gun, I felt so naked. Take-off was perfect and I was feeling much safer. I could

411

see the different facilities pass by us as we were taking off. It was a strange feeling – I had put in so much time and effort into setting up these installations – somehow it felt as if I was leaving a part of myself behind. Because of my efforts, and the teams of men I had trained, an entire country was ready to repel air attacks, to detect and shoot down enemy planes. Iranian people, Iranian borders were safer now. That was something to be proud of. My men and I had done good work. As the plane pulled away from Iranian soil, I was experiencing strong flashbacks of each project, the challenges, achievements, the people I'd worked with so closely. My feet were pushed against the carpeting, willing the plane to keep going. Hoping nothing would go wrong. I was praying we wouldn't be asked to return to the airport. When we crossed the Turkish border, I felt so relieved. The pilot informed us we were flying over Mount Ararat, where Noah's Ark is said to have landed. Assured, I fell asleep.

We landed in London where I bought some things. The British pound was very low at that time, so everything was cheap. Next stop, JFK airport. It's hard to explain the feelings that were going through me as we approached the United States. My home was calling me. Oh my God, my God! It was real and I was almost home. There were so many times that I thought that I would never see it again. Now, instead of going home in a pine box, I was sitting in a comfortable seat, looking out at the beautiful blue sky, scattered with clouds. My family was waiting. We broke through the clouds. I saw the Atlantic Ocean, a familiar coastline, and New York harbor.

They took me to a special place in Customs because I told them I had guns. A woman was taking care of me and seemed to be a little edgy. Then another woman came. I told them that I had led a very dangerous life in Iran and explained the guns. They looked at each other angrily and began hurling verbal insults at one another. A Major came to stop it. He told them to leave. They were both looking at me and smiling. How nice! We went through it again and he finally said, "Welcome home, Michael." That was it; the tears began to flow. It was real. I had made it.

My dear wife was waiting for me. When we saw each other, we embraced, kissed and wouldn't let go. Our happiness was overwhelming. We could feel it in each other. To this day, I can go back and feel that love. I never told her so many things that happened but somehow she knew. Our life in Iran was over, but now we had a new life and I couldn't wait to get into it.

I was unemployed, for one thing, and had to find work quickly. I arranged with a company to set up a Radio Frequency Interference (RFI) testing ground on my property in Quakertown. That fell through because the American company went bankrupt. So I took

413

as job as a sewing machine mechanic for six months until a position opened up with the FAA. They agreed to employ me as a relief technician, the same job I'd had when I started with them years ago. It was a way to utilize all my skills, once again filling in for anyone else in the organization. Only now I knew a great deal more.

Meanwhile, our new land was sitting there, waiting for me to get to work. I'd bought the 11 acre parcel of land, and a good tractor, on my trip back to the States in January of 1976. While still in Iran, I had arranged for my wife's uncle to dig the foundation and pour the walls. I planned to live in the basement and work on the house. Dave was back in the States and I asked him to help me with some arrangements as well. Unfortunately, he did nothing.

Lucretia's uncle dug a hole that fall. It filled up with water and froze like a skating rink. I came back in December of 1976 to a hole in the ground, filled with ice. In the springtime her uncle poured the foundation. I took over from there. I was wasting time, because I had no job. There were some additional difficulties with zoning laws, but I could deal with that. After what I'd gone through in Iran, I felt I could handle anything. I was home!

Chapter 20: Carolyn and Sharon

Shelly, Cretie, Carolyn, Sharon,

Quakertown, Pennsylvania, 2011

Carolyn

I contracted staph meningitis right after I was born. I wasn't expected to live.

Lucretia & Mike: We were in the hospital in Pennsylvania for about 4 days, then home for six weeks. Then, we left for Oklahoma because Mike's next assignment was there. That was the incubation period. We didn't know she had meningitis at first. Once we moved to Oklahoma, I started seeing signs: her head was swelling – actually the fontanel was bulging – and she had an unusual, high-pitched cry. I called Mike saying, "I think something's wrong with Carolyn." A nurse caring for her evidently had the staph virus and Carolyn was infected in the nursery. They thought it may have happened while they were cleaning her umbilical cord.

We took her to the Catholic Hospital. They wouldn't look at her. Staph meningitis was considered fatal, that's probably why the hospital didn't want to touch it. The staff made us wait quite a long time before telling us they couldn't do anything for her. Being a nurse, my wife was upset, because she knew Carolyn was very sick. They put us in a private room, because Lucretia was making so much noise. An intern talked to us. He told us he knew a good pediatrician. Then he went and found Dr. Buckner. That was how we met this wonderful doctor. Dr. Buckner came in to see us, and explained he could take Carolyn to a Baptist hospital where he worked. We followed him right then, to the little Baptist hospital. They used experimental drugs on my newborn. Lucretia got a job in that hospital while Carolyn was there.

The Jewish doctor was dedicated. He was so hard-working; he had a heart attack while caring for Carolyn. My wife took care of him after his heart attack, and I took Carolyn to visit him at his house. He was touching Carolyn's hair, so happy to see her recovered. The hospital billed us for $1800, but they reduced the bill quite a bit. My wife thought it was because she had nursed Dr. Buckner. We paid them a much smaller amount, don't remember exactly how much, but they accepted it.

Carolyn had to be on phenobarbital for an entire year. Meningitis irritates the brain, so Carolyn had a lot of seizures. She didn't have any problems after that. She was a very active baby; she would bounce up and down in the crib, and put the cat in the dryer. Carolyn was walking at nine months. She would go over to the dog and step on him; she thought that was fun. The dog was very patient, a German Shepherd. I think she had been spoiled in the hospital.

I was taking a course there in Oklahoma City, a review of electronics, navigational and landing equipment. It was very hard. I told them I couldn't concentrate. They said I would have to leave. I couldn't, because I would have lost my job and Carolyn was in the hospital there; we couldn't move her. So I had to work hard, to get through that.

Carolyn: I was there for about six weeks, and my mom was pregnant with my younger sister. The doctor wrote a journal piece on my illness and how I had survived. It was published in a medical journal. Sharon and I are 9 months apart. She was born 3 months early. The doctors said she wouldn't survive either, but she did. Sharon is also very strong-willed, like me, but more intellectual; she's very bright.

One of my fondest memories from my childhood was The Circle. Just a block from our house in Teheran, The Circle was really a half-circle of stores that sold fresh-baked bread, chickens, candy and ice cream. We would go to The Circle to buy *Barbari* bread and goat cheese. In the morning before school, we would buy candy and after school we bought snacks like ice cream, cinnamon or peppermint gum and Cheetos. Orange ice cream was the best. Once in a while my mom would send me to The Circle to get a chicken. The chickens were alive when you picked one out. The shopkeeper took it in the back room, killed it, and then stuffed the chicken in a bag so we could take it home. We were used to

418

seeing animals being slaughtered right before being prepared for dinner. From noon until about 4:00 pm it was nap time for the store owners and nothing would be open. Stores would re-open at 4:00 p.m. and stay open until at least 7:00 p.m. or later. Today when I think about The Circle, I feel a sense of comfort. It was a huge part of our childhood life for ten years.

My dad had a friend called "Dave." He had a nickname from the Air Force, the Mashed Potato, but no one remembered why. Anyway, Dave and his wife owned a farm outside Teheran. I remember it took a long time to get there. I spent my time at the farm eating pomegranates and riding on the motorcycle with my dad. I was not too fond of the farm, I guess, because it was boring to me. The younger kids enjoyed it more.

I remember my school, The Teheran American School (TAS). It was a "once in a lifetime" experience on so many different levels. I remember my first grade teacher, Mrs. Hill, and how shy I was as a child in her class. I joined the Brownies and Girl Scouts and went to Girl Scout camp every spring. We used to sit around a campfire and sing songs. We had fireworks the last night and I recall how beautiful they looked against the sky.

The Middle School was at the beautiful new campus in Lavizan. The Shah of Iran had built us a new school. In the background were the breath-taking Alborz Mountains. You could see it snowing up there and know it would be snowing in town a few hours later. It snowed quite often in the winter months causing the schools to be closed for days at a time.

We had eight football teams at the Teheran American School. It seemed like all the boys played football and all the girls were cheerleaders. Sports were really a big deal at TAS and everyone participated in them. In the summer we all played softball at the Gulf District Club where the Non-Commissioned Officers (NCOs) and their families lived. In the evenings, there were great bands: we had four bands that used to play at the Teen Club. Everybody went to the Teen Club on weekends to play cards, chat or just hang out. This is where a lot of young people would start dating each other -- or break up with each other. We spent most of our free time at the Gulf District because it was a safe place, and all our friends were there.

High School was the most memorable time for me. My best friend, Bev, was two years older than me, so this meant that I could be with the cooler kids. During my last two years in Iran, I hung out with a lot of older friends. My first boyfriend was a junior and I was a freshman. He was the drummer for the band Watermelon Jam and was very popular with the ladies. I felt very cool dating him. I am still in contact with him today.

A friend of mine lived next door to us in Teheran. We went up to the beach one time, when our families were vacationing at the Caspian Sea. We weren't supposed to go to the beach by ourselves. He got caught in a whirlpool. I dove in there and got him out. It was scary; I thought we were both going to drown. I was about ten years old then.

We had spontaneous student body assemblies at TAS. I particularly remember one of those assemblies: a bunch of seniors lined up along a balcony and mooned everyone in the compound. We laughed for days after that. They got away with it because the Principal thought it was hysterical. I could go on and on with great memories about TAS. We still talk about it at the reunions, held every three years. One thing we all agree on is that the bond we have as TAS kids is probably the strongest bond that exists. The education we received was the best there was to offer in a foreign third world country. The ties that bind us cannot ever be broken

By the early 1970s terrorist action was on the rise. I remember hearing about military personnel being ambushed on their way to work and in buses. My dad moved around so much, we didn't usually know where he was. I knew he could take care of himself, but I was scared for my dad.

We left the States to go to Iran when I was about six years old. It seemed our life over there was full of excitement, danger, and crises. There was something new and unexpected around every corner. Once, when I was 15 years old, some guys tried to kidnap me. A few months later, there was another attempt. Everything was starting to heat up in the area. Terrorism was becoming a real problem for Americans in Iran. The attempted kidnappings happened in 1976, shortly before we left the country for good. I would go to school in the morning and hear stories about terrorists killing American military personnel. But they weren't just stories; these were our friends and people we'd grown close to. Dad carried his guns in the car, loaded and ready to go. You just thought all Americans were at risk. I didn't realize my Dad was a target, nor that I might be a target because of him.

I remember walking down the street one day with my friend Debbie, and her brothers Mike and Mark Patterson. They lived down the street from me, and we often got into trouble together. They were fluent in Farsi and knew all the best places to hang out. We were going to raid a hotel that weekend. A car pulled up and some guys got out. They started following behind us.

We had mace. Debbie whispered, "Get your mace ready." I said, "You get yours ready." She and her brothers were American Indian, and pretty tough. We sprayed the guys, but it didn't seem to do much. "Run!" We ran as fast as we could. These guys were chasing us, and they were fast too. Debbie's brothers turned around; they were further up the street. "What's going on?" The men let Debbie go; they were after me. They were trying to put me in their car.

Mike and Mark came back and went after the men. "Carolyn, go with Debbie," so we ran. Later, Mike and Mark came back and said "Don't worry, they'll never bother you again." They were Karate experts, but also wanted to be mercenaries. Their goal was to be assassins. They were highly trained. Years later, Debbie told me they killed those men. Again, I didn't tell my parents. It was just part of my life. I didn't know people were after my dad. I think these men had a picture of me; at any rate they seemed to be after me.

Another time, Debbie and I were near a pizza place, leaning up against a fence. Suddenly, I felt a gun at my back. "Debbie." "I know," she said. She didn't say anything else. "We're going to run back into the restaurant and call Steve." I told her. Steve was a friend of my dads who owned a taxi service in town. He often helped us out with rides, whatever we needed. We ran across the street, crouched down under the bar, motioned to the bartender for the phone, and called Steve.

When I got home, I just went to bed, didn't tell my parents. Both times, I just ran, and managed to get away. I probably had about three attempted rapes in different situations, in addition to the attempted kidnappings. All this happened in Teheran. Somehow I got out of every situation. It never occurred to me that I wouldn't.

Why did those guys try to kidnap me? I was a competitive swimmer and swam against other schools. My name and picture was in the paper almost every week, for winning medals. I was out in the community more than my sisters. My little brothers and baby sister Christel were mostly at home with my mom, and Dad was always away, working. I guess I was just an easy target. I could speak Farsi pretty well and I hung out with older, more affluent kids who knew the language very well.

Still, I had a great life over there, I felt safe about every situation. My personality was a lot like my father's; I thought I could get out of anything. We kids were aware of the tension all around us; it was just something we accepted. My dad would ask me to check underneath his car, to see if anyone had planted a bomb there, when he got home. We knew things were getting worse, but that became normal too.

Now, when I deploy to Afghanistan, I am fearful, because I know things can happen. But then, I always had faith that I would survive everything I went through. My life parallels my father, on a lesser scale. Things happened to me over there and I survived them. Dad was never home, so I didn't know a lot of the things that happened to him at the time.

I felt like I was always in turmoil. My sisters did well in school. In swimming, I had to be the best, because my dad expected me to. I was constantly swimming. I trained so hard, I ended up getting Osgood-Schlatter disease, which caused inflammation all through my body. The Iranian doctors were puzzled by my condition. They had to bring in a specialist from the States, from New York. I had to be hospitalized and spent two weeks in an Iranian hospital, getting daily penicillin shots. The disease basically ended my swimming career for a while.

At first, couldn't walk. Later, I was on bed rest for months. I was eleven, I think. I was growing so fast. In just a few months I went from 5'2" to 5'6". I eventually stopped at 5'8". One leg is shorter than the other. I think that may have been from having Osgood-Schlatter disease. I eventually went back to swimming and kept it up until I was 16, when we went back to the States. There, I went through one more year of high school. It was a difficult transition. I tried working with the high school swim team, but couldn't adjust to a new coach and a new country. The Iranian coach knew me for years and we worked well together. This American coach didn't know me at all. I gave up swimming, graduated and went into the Air Force.

The experiences I went through shaped me. Some people think I'm guarded, but I'm happy with my life. I like my job in Probation, enjoy my work with the Air Force and am close to my family, and my children.

My friends and I have been part of the Overseas Brat Conference reunions since 1984. We used to have them every three years; now they are talking about having them every other year, as the get-togethers are so popular. About 300 people show up, both students and teachers. Like other schools in Teheran, the Teheran American School alumni like to stay in touch. There is a TAS chat line on Facebook, blogs, etc. At the last Conference, about half of the 300 participants were kids and teachers who had been in Iran.

Sharon

I often look back on my years growing up in Teheran when I need to dissect why I am who I am and why I choose to do certain things in my life. Those were unbelievable experiences; I don't want to forget the memories. My childhood playground experiences in Iran would have been unfathomable to an average child growing up in the United States. At gatherings I can talk about boar hunting with my father at the Caspian Sea. He'd tell me to look for a tree to climb, in case a boar should come chasing me. I remember I was scared to death the whole time, always looking for that tree. What about motorcycle riding in the desert, clinging onto the front of the jeep as we sped through dusty terrain -- only to stop just in time before going over the small cliff. I have a picture of me, mesmerized, as my sisters and I watched a sheep being gutted. Its intestines were ceremonially removed and used for one of the many Iranian celebrations we knew so well.

'What did you do as a child growing up in Teheran?' I am asked frequently. I lived with my mom and dad along with six other brothers and sisters and we played, invented and experimented like all kids, but in a different culture. I loved going to school and strived to get perfect attendance and straight A's. Army brats would come and go every two years but the Roman family was one of the icons. In the middle school I knew all the ropes and being at TAS (Teheran American School) was fun. The Shah donated money to build the Elementary and Middle School on the outskirts of the city and it was beautiful, with wall to wall carpeting and open football fields. Believe it or not, I was a cheerleader. Go Broncos!! Softball was another one of my sports and I was the pitcher for the "Ladybugs." Mom was always in the stands,

427

cheering with her distinct voice, even though she usually didn't know when to clap, cheer or when to say "Boo." You gotta love her!

There were so many things that we did to entertain ourselves at and around our house. Our home was our fortress. Roofs were flat, so we climbed and explored from rooftops to rooftops trying not to topple over sun-baked tea jars lined up like soldiers. Nothing was better than iced tea made with dark loose tea leaves baking in 100 degree heat. We weren't popular running across strangers' roofs and many times found ourselves scrambling to get away from screaming old ladies with brooms. The walls and ledges were narrow, so good balance was a necessity. Draping from the second floor of the house to the downstairs backyard were awnings that rolled down wobbly metal bars. We girls would hang from these bars with our hands and slowly make our way across to the opposite side of the porch without falling. We hung about 12 feet in the air. How one of us didn't break our neck, I don't know. Mom must have prayed every night.

The back yards in Teheran were like gardens. We had cherry trees, a pear tree, a big weeping willow and a heart-shaped swimming pool. We swam, played kickball, SPUD, Red-Rover and course shot frogs in the back yard, from the back porch, with dad. Dad always made sure that our aim was accurate and still. I always wanted to please dad. "Yea!" I hit the frog. It was bleeding and dragging its bloodied body across the pavement, but my aim was dead on. I had to make Dad proud of me.

Through my eyes, the inside of the house was huge. The kitchen and dining rooms were large enough to ride our bikes around the tables. With seven children running around I am sure our maid could not keep anything clean long enough to show that she even tried. Therefore, she frequently locked us out of the house. To sneak back into the air-conditioned house, we would climb up to the second floor and sneak in the window above the steps. The latch would be left unlocked.

I will always remember toilet paper fights in the bathtub , sleeping out in the front room by the only air-conditioner (because it was too hot in our bedroom), avoiding the small bathroom upstairs because I thought it was haunted, having beauty contests with made-up interviews, switching bedrooms with my sisters depending on who I wasn't getting along with at the time, and so on. I miss my childhood home and neighborhood and I won't ever see them again. Where are all the sheep and camels passing through the streets? I loved riding the camels.

My sisters and I frequently visited The Circle, a couple of blocks away. Stores occupied half of the circle, which was simply a conversion of roads and a market area. As we approached The Circle I could smell the *nanni taftoon* baking in the open oven. It was the best bread I have tasted. I have never had bread as mouth-watering since I left Iran.

At times, but not often, I would ease my way into the poultry butcher shop and watch. A live chicken would be grabbed from its wire cage and slaughtered, shoved head-first upside down into the grinder. I don't know why I watched; I was always grossed out. A bit messy, but effective. Seeing the death of animals was not unusual for us kids. We were used to seeing dead dogs in the street, poisoned by order of the city to control the over-population of stray dogs. Sheep were regularly cut up and sacrificed in the streets for all types of celebrations, from the birth of a new child to getting a new job. Dad would often shoot a pet cat or dog if it posed a threat to one of the younger kids. One of our cats got trapped in the air conditioner on the roof. By the time we noticed and got it out, the cat was a bit crazy and had to be "snuffed." I would be sad but understood Dad's reasoning. This is probably why I don't get very close to pets and if they get sick I feel no remorse in having Dad shoot them, to end their misery. I feel that injecting a drug into a pet is costly and a prolonged experience.

Outside the front gates of the house was the city of Teheran, another playground for us.

430

My mother never seemed to worry about our safety. As young teenagers we would jump into a taxi and go out into the city alone. Sure there were scary times where we ran from trouble or danger, but we always had each other's back. I didn't like to walk down to "the dump" by myself. Groups of young boys were trouble and I always looked for a way out when I saw them walking towards me. This is kind of similar to out-running a boar if I was attacked. Dad somehow taught me survival strategies.

I loved going out to "the farm" in the dessert. I was stupid, fearless or naïve enough to taunt wild pigs locked up in dilapidated mud barns. I was sure that the door would always hold each time they charged us. If they got out I could quickly climb up to the window ledge or roof. One day a well was being dug at the farm and I had the brave notion that I wanted to be lowered on the black leather pouch that was used to extricate dirt. As I was lowered the air became thick and the circle of light above me darkened. What was I thinking? What if the sides caved in? I made it to the bottom because I didn't want to be a coward. I must have been ten or eleven. No wonder I am claustrophobic. Motorcycles and mini bikes were always a thrill. I loved to ride with dad, he was invincible. Dad almost laid his bike down, with me on it but I wanted to still keep going. "Do it again!" I knew he would protect me. My dad was so cool and he was my hero.

The Caspian Sea vacations were less dangerous but further away. The drive was long and we must have sung "when Buick went over the mountain" and "ninety-nine bottles of beer" a thousand times. I personally don't remember a lot about the sea, except that it was a time that we were all together and the cottages were peaceful and safe.

How did Mom do it? She was forever the matriarch of the family. Mom was always there with unlimited energy and love. She helped us with our homework, drove us everywhere, supported us through our booster shots that I didn't want in the butt, and lovingly de-wormed us with medicine in our food. I loved to shop with her and learn how to cook. We made great cherry pies with the fruit from our trees. The one thing that I remember and was a little embarrassed was how Mom would use the collection basket in church to break her large *rial* bills. She also pinched us a lot in church when we misbehaved. How can you keep seven children occupied?

I never really knew what Dad did for a living while growing up. I remember counting his money from the briefcase and if the count was off by one bill we had to start all over again. He made us say our prayers every night and ask to be excused from the table when we

432

were done with dinner. I was petrified to do this. For some reason it was very scary to me. We were disciplined by getting the choice of the strap or sitting in the corner. Sitting in the corner was for a very long time so often I chose the belt. I remember him waking us all up one night after he went on a duck hunting trip and he made us pluck all of the ducks so that they could be gutted and put away in the freezer. This pissed me off but what Dad wanted, his girls had to do. Another learning experience I suppose. I loved to make Dad proud. We girls were the only ones who were allowed to make his bullets. I distinctly remember placing the small round primer under the shell, measuring the gun powder, placing the head of the bullet and then lining it up perfectly to press them together. This was very important to Dad and I made sure that each one was defect less.

I did not want to leave Teheran! How dare my parents change my life! I had to leave my friends, home, and school to come back to what? I had nightmares for a couple of years. In my dreams the Iranians were capturing Americans and beheading them. My mom and dad were not around and I had the responsibility of caring for my three younger siblings. Surviving and making my way to the airport was the only way out. I always woke up before I knew the ending to my dream. One day the repetitive nightmare just stopped. My life in Iran was permanently gone. I was

433

proud to have grown up in Iran. My childhood was incomparable to most American teenagers. I viewed life through cultured eyes. The majority of the kids I met grew up in one town and had never been out of the United States. Most people don't even know where Iran is on the map. The American way of life was all that they knew and I found out quickly that Americans were materialistic and spoiled. It is hard not to be judgmental to those who don't know or care about other cultures. I always had friends in high school and college but they seemed to just occupy that time of my life and none ever became a best friend. Inside my thoughts I was a loner but with goals to succeed.

I was married for twenty-two years and had two children, Sean and Jennifer, of whom I am very proud. They seem to have caught the travel bug from me and have experienced many cultures in the world from Thailand, Europe, Central and South America and more. They appreciate my childhood and their grandfather's stories and advice. Their interest to travel the world grows with each year. I have been reaching out to other countries for years by volunteering my anesthesia skills to the under-privileged children in other countries. I am an anesthetist and have been to India, Thailand, Ecuador and recently Vietnam. My experience as a child in Iran has molded me into who I am and I could not imagine it any other way. I would like to just go back one day to Iran but I don't see that ever happening.

Chapter 21: Shelly and Cretie

Shelly

I hold the honor of being the first child to ever grace my father's arms. Not that he didn't love my two older sisters. Each of us seven children knew we were deeply loved and cherished by our parents. It was just that I was the first infant my mother successfully carried full-term. I was strong and healthy; my father had no hesitation in picking me up.

Although I was born in the United States, Teheran is where my story, and memory, begin. I was born in 1963. Three years later, I was an American toddler in Iran. It would be my home for the next 10 years. As Iranian housing goes, ours was moderately upscale. A fairly large two-story building, it was neatly tucked between two neighboring homes on a long, curved street. Each house was surrounded by a high partitioning wall. Naturally, we kids would walk along the walls to get from one house to another. Ironically, the walls gave the impression that the houses were connected. The same walls built to separate our homes became the literal bridges that connected us with our neighbors.

437

Iran was hot, a dry, oppressive heat that lasted from sun up to sunset every day during the summer months. Our outdoor escape from the 110-degree heat came in the form of a quaint, heart-shaped swimming pool. We'd have a pool party, order *Chelo Kabob*, the Iranian national dish, and have it put on Dad's tab. Inside, we went without the luxury of air conditioning, instead relying on industrial cooling fans. Our neighborhood was predominantly Iranian, but we weren't the only Americans.

Growing up, we never wanted for a place to play. Our yard had it all: there were apricot, pear and cherry trees scattered across the back yard. Rather than a neighborhood ice cream truck playing its jovial fanfare, our ears were tuned to pick up the telltale bells that meant a camel was on its way down the adjacent alley. The camel driver knew to look for us and would always stop to offer us a ride. We'd pay him some coins; he'd have the camels lie down on the ground so we could climb up for a quick journey down the street.

That same area was frequented by a number of street merchants. It was from them that we discovered our taste for unripe apricots (what our juvenile selves referred to as "green things"). Other vendors offered us sealed envelopes. It was sort of like gambling; you paid for an envelope and if your luck held, there would be money inside.

438

Another element of the city that commanded our attention was the stray dogs who wandered the streets. We got to know one, Lady, particularly well. Of her many talents, Lady was especially good at getting pregnant. When the city of Teheran sent men out with poisoned meat to attract the strays (an annual springtime routine), my sisters and I would coax Lady inside to keep her safe. We wouldn't let her out until the danger was past. The Iranians didn't like dogs, thought they were dirty or something. We learned to get some *mast* (yogurt), and feed it to the dogs, to get rid of the poison.

We didn't have TV for the first few years. When it finally did arrive in the home, it was for no more than an hour or so each day. The grownups spent what leisure time they had playing bridge at each other's houses. While they were ensconced in their card games, we kids would make up shows or skits, practice gymnastics, and organize games of kick ball.

Growing up in Teheran certainly had no negative effect on my education. I attended the Teheran American School and loved every second of it. When I first enrolled, the building was quaint, even by local standards. As the years passed, however, new funding resulted in a new building large enough to house a steadily increasing enrollment. As the name suggested, the school was for American children like us. Just like in the U.S., the boys

439

played football and basketball, and the girls were cheerleaders. Girls were discouraged from participating in sports at school, but while at the Officer's Club or in the Golf District after school each day, we were given free rein. There seemed to be a natural talent for sports among my family. All four of us girls were good swimmers, and could hold our own at softball and tennis. I was especially at home on the softball field, making the city All-Star team every year without fail.

It was in Iran that I first talked my mom in to signing me up for horseback riding lessons. It cost extra, but I knew beyond doubt that it was what I wanted. Later, as a teenager in the States, my love for horses continued to blossom and eventually passed on to my youngest daughter, Janna.

School also taught us the various Iranian holidays. My favorite was a curious custom celebrating growth and the new beginnings which took place during *Nowruz*, the Iranian New Year. *Nowruz* always began on the vernal equinox and lasted for a week, during which the streets became open venues for parties. Our neighbors would keep small fires lit in the streets for the duration of the parties. You would jump over the fires and say, "out with the old year, in with the new."

Not all the holidays were as pleasant as *Nowruz*. One religious festival in particular sent us inside to hide every year. It was the

Day of *Ashura*, a day of mourning for the martyrdom of Muhammad's grandson. There would be a group of Iranian men dressed in black, some holding fire torches. They would march and chant out loud while beating their backs with chains.

We never thought of Iran as a dangerous place. The term "terrorists" was one I'd never been exposed to. To us, Teheran was just "home."

As American youth on foreign soil, we were culturally deprived of such treasures as the Beatles. Our only connections to American pop culture came in the forms of our two favorite magazines, *Tiger Beat* and *Teen Beat*. Nearly every issue featured a centerfold of Donny Osmond, the Jackson Five, or other American pop icons. Without fail, these would go straight onto our bedroom walls.

Dad spent our first five years on Iranian soil as a U.S. government employee, which allowed us access to the Officer's Club, softball fields, and the Teen Club. The last five years, after Dad was recruited in to the Imperial Iranian Air Force (IIAF), we'd have to wait for our friends and enter with them as guests. The clubs had a wide selection of scheduled activities, including dances, to which we were regular attendees.

The only time I ever felt unsafe in the city was during one such dance at the Teen Club. After dancing and enjoying ourselves for the better part of the night, my friend, Jamie, and I decided to take a walk outside for some air and a bit of downtime on the bleachers. I only knew enough Farsi to get around the streets, so I was at a loss for words when two guards approached us. One of the men grabbed my girlfriend's arm, causing us both to panic. I immediately leapt down from the bleachers and ran for help. For whatever reason, they had released my friend and she was close behind me as we sprinted back inside to report what had happened to Carolyn, my oldest sister. The authorities wanted me and Jamie to pick out these guys in a lineup. The night culminated in us being brought before a line-up of Iranian men to identify our harassers. The grown-ups impressed upon us the importance of being absolutely certain before choosing, so as to make sure we weren't condemning an innocent man. Jamie and I were still terrified, and the Iranian men looked so alike to us that we couldn't bring ourselves to choose.

Growing up as a blue-eyed and blonde-headed girl, I was something of a rarity in Iran. People would cross the street to touch my hair. As I matured and my body did the same, some of the local boys began to set their sights on less socially acceptable parts of me than my hair. I learned to fight as a direct result of their unwanted physical attention. This led to a number of instances where our doorbell would announce the presence of an Iranian woman and her son, often still sobbing from the beating I'd given him. Such situations led Mom and Dad to make an arrangement with a local taxi service. They knew and trusted a driver who was always available to take us anywhere in the city. As long as we girls were together, we felt safe.

Mom and Dad used to love to throw parties at the house. My sisters and I would perch on the stairs and appraise the guests as they arrived, to see which woman had the most elegant hairstyle, best-dressed, etc. We considered ourselves the pinnacle of knowledge when it came to fashion.

Having American clothes was a big deal to my sisters and me. Our options were limited, though you could buy some Westernized clothes at the nearby market. Our saving grace was the Sears catalog Grammy would send to us every month. Mom would measure us, and we were allowed to pick out the dresses and accessories we wanted. A month or two later, a giant box would arrive with our new clothes. These arrival days were a huge deal in our household. When we got back to the States, the first place I wanted to see was Sears, and I wasn't disappointed. I'd never seen anything like that store in my life.

Our other fashion vices came from an Iranian merchant, Lolazar, who would come to the house with his big black mat full of jewelry.

Dad bought some beautiful Iranian pieces for Mom which she still has to this day. Each of us kids got a gold crucifix necklace, a silver bracelet with our names on them and a four piece puzzle ring.

Another fond memory for my family is visiting Dave's farm. It was way out in the middle of nowhere. On the journey, we'd pass a little village with mud huts. The rural inhabitants would always be seated outside, weaving thick Persian rugs. The farm was made up of numerous buildings with domed roofs.

My dad wanted us to know how to jump out of a moving jeep. He felt that was an important part of our education. So he and Dave would drive the Jeep slowly around the desert and Dad would yell, "Jump!" We learned fast, that there is a right and a very *wrong* way to exit a moving vehicle. Dad would let us practice driving and then show us how to jump and roll away from the car. Jump out and roll, let your legs buckle as you go out, so they don't break. We were taught how to exit the back of a Jeep, real fast in case a wild animal got in. (Sometimes an animal would jump into the Jeep, so this was a useful trick to know.) You'd have to get out of your seat and jump out the back where there's an open spot. One time I was in the Jeep and an animal did get in. Dad picked up his .357 and casually blew its brains out . That's a powerful weapon; it explodes with great force and makes your arm jerk up. With a .357, you could hit a paint can at 100 yards. A 9mm doesn't have that same knock-down force. Dad used our visits to the farm as a great out-of-the-way place to teach us the nuances of firearms. We were all taught how to shoot using glass bottles as targets. Over time, practice with the bottles evolved into full-blown boar-hunting trips with Dad.

One not-so-pleasant memory from the farm was the time my friend, Susan, and I elected to spend the night outdoors. We slept on the roof and had a great time, until I woke up the following morning. Every inch of my body was covered in mosquito bites. Mom's remedy was to toss me in a bathtub and have me soak in oatmeal. While I washed, she counted bite marks, declaring the final tally to be 101. Being the nurse she was, Mom seldom took us to the doctor; preferring her own advice over that of a local physician. Often as not, her advice was to "wait until tomorrow, things will be better." When I had an earache, she would tell me to, "blow into the pillow, then put your ear on the warm spot." I have used this particular treatment on my own children.

Looking back today, Iran was a different world. We had freedoms I would never give my children today. Mom said she never really feared for us as long as we were together. As a Middle Eastern country known to reward

445

criminals with amputation, Iran boasts a fairly low national crime rate. I don't remember ever being afraid of war, or kidnappings or any of the things one might expect. My mind, my world, was absorbed with school, my friends, and all our recreational activities.

When we arrived in America, I was 13 and in the eighth grade. The next two school years were nothing but review to my sisters and me, so I spent most of my time catching up on other issues; like fashion, the latest movies, and politics. We discovered that the U.S. had just fought, and lost, a war in Vietnam. We had to learn how to handle American money by comparing it to the more-familiar Iranian *rial*.

Everything was different in the States. After Iran, kids in the United States seemed kind of immature. I had never realized how far advanced we were, academically and socially. Possibly the most annoying social aspect of our return was the effect the increased humidity had on our hair. Frizzy-headed children weren't what you'd call "high-ups" on the popularity chain.

We knew we weren't going back to Iran, so we tried to make the best of it. I hated the first year with all the unbridled passion my adolescent mind had to offer. When Mom and Dad finally followed us to the States, it marked yet another change in schools, along with the standard adjustment period. I spent four years in four different schools during this period, changing from junior to senior high school, then starting all over at a different high school in Quakertown once the new house was built. Not the easiest thing I've ever had to do. When I graduated from high school, I went into nursing. I always adored my mom; I wanted to be like her. Years later, when I read Dad's first draft of his story, I realized just how much I hadn't known about him and what was going on in Iran. He had developed a talent for protecting us by keeping certain things hidden.

'Cretie

We moved to Teheran when I was two years old. However, my first memories are of kindergarten. It was held in the old building, the original Teheran American School (TAS). We'd have cookies and lemonade before nap time. I slept under the table with T. a little boy who lived next door to us in Teheran for many years.

I met my best friend, Tracy Brown, in first grade. We're still best friends. I remember one time she was riding on the back of my bike and somebody shot her in the leg with a pellet gun. Iran, our *badji*, was yelling "drink milk!" It was an Iranian kid who shot her. At the top

447

of our street was an Iranian school. We would go on the roof and throw snowballs at them as they walked by. There was some rivalry between the American kids and the Iranian kids. Nothing serious, but it was there.

When I was in second grade, there was an uprising in Afghanistan and the American kids who lived there were just loaded onto planes and sent to Teheran. We were each assigned a kid to buddy with, so they wouldn't feel alone. That was so traumatic to me. I couldn't imagine being taken away from your family at such a young age.

When I was in 3rd grade, the Shah built a huge school for us. This was the middle school and it had seven buildings spread across a large campus. Classes were scheduled with 7 minute breaks in between each one, because you had to walk so far to get to each building. We had a lot of kids in that school. I don't know how many but, I know we had five football teams -- we had enough teams to play each other. Sharon, Shelly and I were cheerleaders. We cheered at all kinds of games, including basketball and football.

In addition to school activities, my sisters and I were on the swim team. Every morning, we got up early and Mom drove us to the Gulf District for swim practice. Mom made us eat Jell-O for breakfast so our stomachs wouldn't be too full. Carolyn was the best swimmer. She'd compete in swim meets all the time and

came home with so many medals. One time
she received a medal from the young Prince
of Iran! We spent a lot of time in the Gulf
District. Dad took us to the Officer's Club on
Sundays after church for breakfast. At home
in Teheran, we spent most of our time on the
walls, and on the roof tops. Every house was
surrounded by an 8 foot wall, wide enough to
walk on. We played digit, now called
manhunt. That was our favorite game.

Our street was called a *kuchi*. We lived
amongst Iranians, but there were a lot of
Americans in our neighborhood. Every street
had a *kuchi* guard, and they carried whistles
around their necks. Every hour, they would
blow the whistle, to signal each other things
were okay. I felt safe because our *kuchi* guard
always stayed right in front of our house.

We kids liked going up to The Circle. The
streets were so hot, the tar would melt under
your feet in certain spots, and it was so gooey.
We knew all the shady spots. One of the
shopkeepers in The Circle sold what they
called Negro kisses, chocolate cookies topped
with marshmallows. They were delicious. Our
favorite gum was called Rooster Adams. My
friend, Tracy, loved that gum. When she
moved back to the States, I would pack up
some gum and ship it to her new home in
Georgia.

My parents hosted a lot of parties. All the
grownups dressed up. The ladies wore

evening gowns and had their hair done. The men wore tuxedos. They had candles floating in the pool and waiters serving at the bar! Sometimes we were sent to the neighbors, but we'd go up on the roof or hang out the windows to watch the party. When we were allowed to stay home, we'd perch on the stairs and peek at the glittering crowds below. We liked to pick out which woman wore the prettiest gown. Carolyn, Sharon, Shelly and I would play games like Miss America. Carolyn was always the judge, and Sharon always won. I didn't think that was fair. I got tired of playing that game real quick!

We always had pet rats. At parties, Dad would have us get our favorite one, Mr. Rat. One of us would put him on our shoulder and let his tail peek out from our hair. We would mingle with the party goers and scare the heck out of the ladies! Sometimes we forgot to feed Mr. Rat, so he'd get out of his cage at night and jump on my parents' bed. He knew to tickle Mom's cheek with his whiskers, so she'd get up and feed him.

"The Dump" was one of our favorite places to play. There was a big creek running through it, and wild dogs lived there. The dogs chose to have their puppies at the dump, so we would bring them food. A lot of our dogs came from there. All kinds of people came to the dump. One lady came down there to bathe and we used to watch her. There

450

were times when it was dangerous to be there
– we heard gunshots one time.

We liked going to the farm with Dave. We'd
spend the whole day there. It was surrounded
by a huge desert. Outside the farm was a mud
village. It looked like an upside-down egg
carton, old conical mounds of mud with but,
no one lived in them. We used to climb on
them. There were pomegranate trees nearby.
We all loved eating ripe pomegranates. There
was a giant hole, really a deep cave in the
ground, where we enjoyed playing. Iran was
such a hot country, but the cave was nice and
cool. People would store meat there because
they had no refrigeration.

Dad took us boar hunting at the farm too.
He would have us wait by a tree. One time a
mother boar came out and Dad yelled, "run!"
When Dad yelled like that, you knew to move,
fast. Whatever he told us, we did. I wasn't
scared, though, because my Dad was there.
When I was very little, he would zip me up in
his leather jacket and take me on his
motorcycle. I thought he was the handsomest
man ever; I was so proud to be with him. He
is still my hero.

Our usual vacation spot was near Chalus, on
the Caspian Sea. The roads we took to get to
the Caspian were steep, narrow and very
winding, a real challenge for our Buick station
wagon. In many places, there would be just
one lane. One time I fell out of the car on one

of those winding roads. I guess I was asleep and the door wasn't closed properly. Anyway, I rolled out and this old guy caught me. I don't know where he came from. The roads were so narrow; how could anyone walk there? I believe he was an angel! I remember swimming in the sea and staying in cabins. The Caspian Sea was so huge; it was just like being at the beach.

There was no advance warning, when it came time for us to leave Iran. One day, in the fall of 1976, Mom and Dad just announced that we would be leaving. The date was set, and everything was arranged. Sharon, Shelly and I were to go back first, and the rest of the family would follow. I remember we three came back by ourselves.

At this time, I was 12, Shelly 13, and Sharon was 14. We had a layover in Germany on our way back to the States. It was a very long flight and we wanted some chocolate. So we left the airport and looked around at the shops to find some. For some reason, we weren't afraid of getting lost. We got back all right and boarded our plane for the final leg of the journey. It was a huge plane. I remember lying across the seats, sleeping. It was strange, leaving Iran, and the rest of our family. Shelly and I went to Georgia and stayed with the Tracy and Jody Brown. We spent all summer with them. Sharon stayed in Whitehall, near Allentown, with our Uncle

Richard. Later, Carolyn and Mom came back with Michael, Mark and Christel.

My mother found us a house in Whitehall. A few months later, Dad came back too. We lived there for one year. I don't remember that school at all. I was so traumatized by being back in The States. I remember thinking how weird it was that everyone could understand what we were saying. We weren't used to that. Not many Iranians spoke English in the 60s.

One thing I loved about being home was the wonderful aromas. I loved the smell of green grass being cut, a smell I'd never known before. Grammy Gladis took us to the Mall; it smelled like bubble gum but the best smell of all was Grammy's house! In Iran, everything stinks. You get used to it, but even the money smelled bad. Unfortunately, the smells were just about the only thing I liked about the States. Everything else was weird. I had left the States as a two-year-old and didn't remember anything. Iran had been my whole world. There didn't seem to be much to do in the States. We used to go to the Lehigh River with our cousins and their friends. We'd swing on a rope there. Often we'd walk to the playground instead of going to church.

Back in Iran, we'd go to the CRC where there were all kinds of activities going on. In Iran we had movies, bowling, parties and lots of games. There was a horse-racing game we liked; we'd each stand in our place and we'd bet on the horses. Sometimes we would win some money. As soon as my parents dropped us off for Sunday school in Iran, we'd head for the CRC!

I think my parents did a good job of keeping things from me, when we lived in Iran. We didn't know about terrorists and kidnappings, at least I didn't. Most military families came and went. The usual assignment was two years, so there were always new kids in every grade. I would see others leave Iran and think, "That's never going to happen to us. We'll never leave here." Iran was my home.

I remember being jealous of the kids in Quakertown and Whitehall who had been friends with each other since kindergarten. Most kids there grew up in a comfortable group of peers, going from one grade to another. They had that security of knowing who they were, where they belonged. I didn't -- my childhood had been left behind in Iran. At least I will always have Tracy.

I remember celebrating *Nowruz*, the Iranian New Year. We'd put greens on the roof of our car and drive around until they blew off, Another *Nowruz* tradition was jumping over a line of little fires in the courtyard. One spring, Mark unexpectedly jumped into the fire with me. He fell and burned his hands pretty badly.

454

We kids developed our own language, gibberish. We all knew it, even our best friends like Tracy and Bev. We'd add the letters "d," and "g," and the word "the," in the beginning, middle and end of words. Our parents didn't understand this, though they pretended to.

American teenage guys formed bands in our high school in Iran. We'd go to the parties at the Gulf District. One night we went for a walk there. Even though it was a military facility, a guard tried to take Shelly. I think they wanted to rape her, but she got away. That was scary. We always thought we were safe, in Iran.

Mrs. Ordebadjian was our teacher. She taught us Iranian Culture Studies. We learned all about Iranian traditions and holidays. We'd celebrate them at home and at school. And, of course, we all knew the Iranian national anthem.

Our swimming pool at the house in Teheran was only knee deep. We spent countless hours at the neighbors' pool next door. It was much bigger than ours. They had a big fence around the pool, with spikes. One time, T., the boy next door, landed on a spike; right on his groin, and had to be rushed to the hospital. That was something I'll never forget. His dad had videos of us kids playing together. I'd love to see them now but, somehow they were lost.

I remember sometimes it was beneficial to be in the middle of a large family. If I wanted to, I could wander off and do as I liked. Once I told my mom, I wanted to be an only child, so she granted my wish. She gave me a weekend alone, just the two of us. It wasn't long before I was crying, I didn't like that after all; I wanted my sisters and brothers back.

I don't remember much about that first year in the States, just that the change was so traumatic. Every time I started in a new grade, it was the same thing; they'd have roll call, go down the list of students until they got to the "R's." Then, they'd stop. I knew they were having trouble pronouncing my name. It was embarrassing to be singled out, every time. Back then, I wished my name was anything but Lucretia.

Carolyn was already a junior in high school when we returned to the States. My dad had bought some land in Quakertown, out in the sticks, and we were busy every weekend, helping him build a house. We put up drywall, nailed shingles on the roof, painted. I fell off the roof one time, and landed right next to a pile of cinder blocks. That was the last time I went up there.

I didn't like Quakertown at first; it was so rural and we'd always lived in the city, in Teheran. We went from this busy, active society in Teheran, to nothing, living in the sticks. "Mom where do all the people live?" I asked her one time. We felt we were in the middle of nowhere. That bothered me until Sharon got her driver's license. Then, we could go somewhere, to parties, football games. Eventually we all got our licenses. My dad got us a Volkswagen bus and we'd all share it. I think by high school I was pretty settled into life in the States. Soon, my older sisters were starting college and the younger ones were involved in soccer.

Two years ago, Carolyn and I went to a TAS reunion in Washington D.C. Many people were older than me, but it felt like we were one big happy family. It was like going back in time and getting back a little bit of your past. There was a sense of belonging. These people understood where we had been; they remembered Iran.

Chapter 22

Michael and Mark

Michael

I remember the mountains of Iran. We were surrounded by mountains. I used to go hunting with my Dad a lot. He took me boar-hunting when I was about five years old. We also hunted jackrabbits at night and bull frogs during the day. I remember going to the Caspian Sea for vacations and going to the farm, climbing on these nomad houses there made of mud. Iran was always so hot.

One time Dad took me duck-hunting and his friend, Dave was with us. I forgot to tell them I'd been playing in the boat with my friends and accidentally burned a hole in the bottom of the boat. That is, I forgot about it until I saw Dave sinking in the river when the boat filled up with water.

One time we went hunting and I found a car that had crashed in the mountains. There was so much blood, everywhere, just piles of blood. Dad said the wolves must have dragged off the bodies. Wolves were all over the country. They do attack and kill people.

I remember the Iranian holidays. There were men and boys who would wear red clothes instead of black. They would parade through the streets, beating themselves with heavy chains. We called it Chain Beater Day. On *Nowruz,* their New Year, we used to jump over fires. I remember the camels in the streets. We got to go on camel rides when they came by the house. Lots of people had mopeds; they would ride them in the streets. You'd buy a goat from a man. They'd hang it from a tree and chop it up right there in the street for you. Then, we'd go by the mosques and hear the man in the tower saying prayers to their god. You could watch people making rugs. That was just ordinary life in Iran.

Back home in Teheran, I remember running across the flat roofs in our neighborhood. Sometimes the people would yell at us. One of our neighbors used to get mad and chase us off when he found us in his yard, stealing cherries from his cherry trees. In winter we'd hear the men with shovels walking through the streets calling *barfparoo, barfparoo!* meaning they will shovel snow off your roof. It piled up high on those flat roofs. We would jump off the roof into deep piles of snow. We used to get into a lot of trouble with the next door neighbor's kids. Sometimes I'd skip school and go down by this creek that was close by the school, just to play. There was another creek, a really big one, at the dump; we played there a lot. Sometimes we had rock fights there, with the Iranian kids from down the block. Grandma Gladis came to visit us one time. She brought me a toy that climbed the walls. It was a cool toy.

Dad's friend, Dave, had a pig farm outside Varamie. It wasn't that far from Teheran. We went there a lot to play. My dad would help Dave put ear tags on the pigs. At the farm there was a big dirt tunnel, just an enormous hole in the ground which led to their water supply. We'd go down there to enjoy the freezing cold.

Mark and I found another tunnel right in Teheran. Another friend was with us. It turned out to be a big sewer pipe that started at the dump and ran right downtown into the heart of the city. At the dump, the opening was about fifteen feet high. It got smaller as we followed it, and it was getting dark, so it was hard to see. We ran all the way to the end of the tunnel. Then we heard a person in the dark. We thought people were chasing us, so we ran like hell, back towards the dump. It seemed like forever 'til we got out of the pipe. What a scare that was! We never went into the pipe again.

We often seemed to be in danger; we'd fight with the Iranians all the time. Snowball fights, rock fights. My sisters were all good looking so I had to defend them. They were all cheerleaders for the school football games, so we'd go to watch teams like the Broncos and Raiders play each other. Life at home in Teheran was comfortable. We had pet rats and a little white dog, Pepi. There were a couple of hours of TV after dinner, so we could watch Tarzan. I remember watching it while we had a steak dinner one time. Another night, we went out to dinner with the family and had roast duck. We went to the Officer's Club all the time. I remember watching mechanical horse races there. My parents would have grown-up parties where everyone got dressed up, had drinks and danced together. We kids were allowed to watch from upstairs. Next morning, we'd go down and look for money in the couches. We usually found some coins; that was fun.

I remember my dad threw a screwdriver through a windshield one time. A driver had run over a kids' bike or something, and Dad got mad at him. He picked up the man and threw him through the windshield too. The man was spitting out glass from the broken windshield. Dad threw him pretty hard.

Our life in Iran was okay at the beginning. I remember celebrating the American Bicentennial in 1976, in an Iranian park. But by then, when we were getting ready to leave, people were unfriendly, saying mean things, picking fights more than usual. I was glad we got out when we did.

Coming to the States wasn't fun. In Iran, we kids used to watch each other's backs, but in the States people were mean to each other. It was so different. I didn't know who the Beatles were, or what music was popular, I didn't really fit in. We kids spoke some Farsi, but I spoke English most of the time, In the States, I had to deal with bullies, something new. We hadn't seen many Negroes in Iran either.

I started listening to American music when I was 16. I had no interest in it before. I don't know if I ever did fully adapt to life back in the States. Here, in the American schools, you're considered a loser if you don't wear the latest styles. When we lived in Iran, nobody cared about that.

One of our next-door neighbor's kids, T., came to the States and lived with us for a while. That helped, because I had a buddy to hang out with, someone who knew what life was like back in Iran. T. smoked reefer and had got in trouble in Germany. The authorities over there were pressing charges on a drug deal.

Unfortunately, T. hadn't learned anything from that experience; he was still doing drugs in the States. He actually shot at my brother and I with a 22 one time, when he was high.

We heard the bullets zip past us, so we hid in a hay bale and shot at him with a bow and arrow. The arrows went right through the hay bale. T. got scared and ran. My dad had taught us how to handle guns, bows and arrows. We used to practice on frogs; we would shish kabob them.

Back in the States, I played a lot of football, but I didn't like school. It was boring. I didn't do well. There was nothing for me. My dad had a big property, eleven acres, but there wasn't much to do. I needed action and adventure all the time; that's what I was used to in Iran. So I joined the military. I stopped using drugs and went into the Air Force. I had a great time there.

Mark

I don't remember much about our life in Iran. I was a little kid, five or six years old when we left Iran. I remember the Iranian women couldn't keep their hands off me. They would touch my hair, pinch my cheeks. We were all blonde; I guess they liked that. I didn't like it that a lot of the women were all covered up. I would say to my friends we should step on their chadors and find out what was underneath.

At one point, Michael and I went out walking around late at night. The moon was so clear in Iran, we tried to follow it. We walked toward it for hours, trying to get under it. I think we got into a more urban area. I must have been five, Michael was 7. Dad was at home when we finally got back, so we got into a lot of trouble.

I remember the desert. There were old mud buildings with rounded tops. One was in a field by itself. We climbed on top of it and broke through the roof. There was a bigger compound nearby.

I remember the Iranian religious people beating themselves with chains. We didn't understand why people were doing this and we would joke about it amongst ourselves. I saw it several times; it may have been an annual festival. We'd taunt the younger guys into chasing us. We'd climb up telephone poles, up to the rooftops, and get away. You could run on the walls around each house, then run across the rooftops.

Since I was born in Iran, I thought our life there was just ordinary. We had a wealthy friend in Iran, the kids had Loony Tunes cartoons, no sound. He had a lot of things we wished we had. We lived in a middle class neighborhood. I remember the next door neighbors had American food from the PX. We liked that. (Mike: We lost PX privileges when I started working for the IIAF, but we bought food from other people, from their umbar, which is what everyone called their storage place.)

The Circle had OK gum and rock candy, and I remember the bakery. We'd watch them sliding the freshly baked flat bread out of the oven. I remember going to the Catholic Church. For some reason, I remember walking with Dad and he said you have to swing your arms when you walk.

I remember being at some kind of camp, singing songs about Jesus. I liked the vendors walking by, selling bitter green fruits. We would walk on the walls around our house. One old neighbor didn't like any of us, except for my baby sister, Christel. He would give her flowers.

I attended first grade at the Teheran American School. I went to a huge building, but it was only first and second grade. We had an inside gym, two floors. They had stations for each subject, science, math, and reading. It seemed you went from one to the other at your own volition. I could learn at my own pace. It was a British-based system, with booklets on each subject at a different level of difficulty.

They had football games; I remember going to some of those. My older sisters were cheerleaders. The stadium at TAS was on a raised mountain. In 1976, there was the big celebration in the school for the United States

Bicentennial. We got on a plane and went back to the States soon afterwards.

The first thing I noticed when we were back in the States was the rooftops. They were pointy, not flat. I was used to our flat roofs in Iran. I went into second grade at Steckel Elementary. There was an Iranian boy in our class and I could speak to him. He didn't know any English. I knew some Farsi, could ask for water, food, basic stuff. I don't remember much of it now.

Chapter 23

Back In The States

Lucretia:

I think all the children had a hard time, coming back, except for Christel. We returned to the States in August 1976. Sharon, Michelle and Lucretia Ann went first, staying with relatives near Allentown. Carolyn and I brought the younger ones a week or so later. Mike would stay for four long months, to finish out his contract.

The older girls attended Whitehall High School, which was a great culture shock to them. They would speak to each other in Farsi. All four older girls, especially, were so displeased with everything back in the States. They were not familiar with American money, not used to paying taxes on items. It took a while for them to adjust to a different lifestyle.

The boys weren't used to the restrictions we put on them now. Life was more dangerous, back in the States, it seemed. They were used to taking off and doing things on their own, but we couldn't let them do that here. In Iran, at the Teheran American School, they'd been able to choose which subject to work on first, but that flexibility wasn't part of the program in their Pennsylvania school.

Only Christel was fine; five years old, she went straight into kindergarten and made lots of friends right away. She excelled at soccer and took up flute. She seemed to fit right in, and liked her school, so that was nice.

When we came back, we stayed in an inn in Allentown and I started looking in the paper for places to rent. I found a place in Fullerton, where my mom lived. I was looking for a year rental while we built our house in Quakertown. An agent found us a big house. The older girls liked it. It had bats in the attic and a large upper floor. It was a mansion, and had belonged to a doctor. We lived on one side of the house; the landlord/realtor had his office downstairs on the other side.

Suddenly, I had to clean the house as well as take care of the kids. I had been used to more freedom in Iran, because I had help. I realized I had been spoiled in Iran. I wasn't happy and the kids picked up on that. They were always complaining how they didn't want to be there.

I saw a notice for Parent Effectiveness Training (PET) at the high school in Whitehall, right after we got there. I figured I needed help. It was very good. I think it was a six or eight week course. We had sessions where families could talk about their situations. I started implementing some of the things I learned from PET. For example, when I'd ask the kids to take the garbage out, I would say "I would be happy if you would-" not putting the blame on the kids, describing rather than blaming. Mike ruled by fear, but I wanted to try a more pleasant approach. I could understand why the children, especially the older ones were confused and disoriented. I knew how I felt, coming back to the States. This PET training did seem to help.

I talked to my mom and a few friends, my sisters and sisters-in-law. I felt I had nobody to talk to, like I did in Iran. There, the people I associated with were more educated, more traveled. I missed the parties in Iran. Compared to what we had there, our social life in Pennsylvania was nil.

We were busy, working on the house. I decided I needed to go to work, but the staffing agencies wouldn't place me anywhere, because I'd been gone too long from nursing. I finally got a job at Easton Hospital. They had an 8 week Intensive Care Unit (ICU) training course and I took that. My mom watched Christel while I attended class from 9-12, and the other children were in school. I passed the course by the skin of my teeth, and then I was able to get a job.

I didn't stay at Easton very long, maybe three months. I went to Allentown Osteopathic Hospital and talked to the nursing director. I told her my situation and she assigned me for 3 months in each section of the hospital, to get me acclimated. After that, they employed me per diem. I worked all different shifts. After a while, I got a job in ICU at Allentown. They sent me to another intensive care training at Lehigh Valley. Once I'd completed the training at Lehigh Valley, they wanted to hire me but I felt I should be loyal to Allentown Osteopathic. Every hospital has its own personality it seems. At Allentown, there was a ghost in the ICU. The room would get chilly, so I always brought a heavy sweater. One day, we opened the window and the ghost left.

I felt going back to work was a life-saver for me. It helped me find a balance in my life between caring for the children and having my own life. I was using my skills and helping people. The children started getting used to school. They figured out how to use American money by estimating the cost of things in *rials* first.

We stayed in the Fullerton house for exactly one year, from September of 1976 until we moved into our Quakertown house in September 1977. The older girls had been attending Whitehall High School while we lived in Fullerton. They all transferred to Quakertown High School. Carolyn was a senior then.

I had earned about 30 college credits by the time we left Iran. I was able to transfer them back to Penn State later. The easiest specialty for me to complete was Nursing Administration, so I went into that. Penn State offered a distance learning degree in Nursing Administration through the University of Ottowa, one weekend a month. So, technically I graduated from Ottowa University in Kansas City. It was 1988 when I finally went back and took the last few classes I needed, to finish my degree through Penn State.

I worked in Quakertown Community Hospital from 1979 to the present. I still work one weekend a month, per diem. I've been there for 30 years. The hospital changed its name to St. Luke's in 1985.

The essence of my life in Iran is still very present. I can't walk into any room in my house without being reminded of something to do with Iran. Over the ten years we collected so many things -- brass, paintings, and copper trays —everywhere I look, something reminds me of Iran. We started sending things back to the States in early 1976 when we realized we were going to have to leave. We shipped carpets and paintings back to the States too. We lost a lot of things on a boat which took on water. Our friends, Jim and Lil, took some of our things back to the States for us in early 1976; they went to

California. We had boxes of pictures stored with them. We did sell most of our beautiful furniture before we left Iran – so many lovely pieces! Frederick Duckloe and Brothers, a family-owned furniture store near Delaware Water Gap, actually in Portland, Pennsylvania, makes custom furniture. We had bought our custom furniture from them in 1969, and shipped it from Pennsylvania to Iran, but we had no way to bring it all back when it came time to leave Iran; we had to sell it.

The kids always want me to make Iranian food. I was visiting Christel, out in Arizona recently and taught her to make *Ghormeh Sabzi*; her husband loves it. Shelly, down in North Carolina, also makes her own Iranian dishes. Her husband, Ed, has a restaurant he manages there. Ed requested a recipe for *Fesenjoon*, so they are continuing our family's love of Iranian food and sharing it with others. So, there are always constant reminders of Iran in every facet of my daily life, whatever I do. Everything we went through is ingrained in our lives.

We did make some friends here in Pennsylvania. We'd throw a party and invite people, to have a social life. Over there, we were in a ready-made community with parties for the adults and lots of activities for the children. There was an openness there and people were nice. Here, we only met people through our children, and through the church.

And, we had our family nearby. Some neighbors, Paul and Kathy, did come by to visit when we were first building our house and we got to know them. Kathy would come over and help babysit my grandchildren sometimes. She and Paul got to be a part of our lives here. Kathy converted to the Catholic Church and joined the choir. Aside from that, I got to know a few people at work, but it wasn't the same. Another neighbor, Maryellen had a daughter Christel's age. She taught soccer and the girls were friends. That's probably how I got to know a few friends here, after we moved to Quakertown. She and her husband are still our friends. The nicest part of my social life now is getting together with my three sisters. We've grown closer since my mom died three years ago. Iran will always be a part of my family, but we've come to think of the States as home, once again.

Afterword

Mike: In 1976, my life changed for the worse, because of rampant corruption throughout Iran. Relations between the United States and Iran also went through a dramatic change. For decades, the United States policy had been to build up the Shah as a stabilizing power in the Middle East. The Shah genuinely loved Iran and wanted to help his people. But the CIA didn't care about the Iranian people; they cared about keeping the US government a powerful entity, so they could control things.

When Jimmy Carter was elected President that November, I was mobbed by many educated Iranians at a party in Teheran. "You stupid Americans, you just signed our death warrants. How could you do that?" I didn't know what they were talking about at the time. In 1977, President Carter abandoned the Shah. Now both sides, the revolutionaries and those loyal to the Shah, hated Americans. Those loyal to the Shah were furious that the Americans would abandon them. How did they know that it was going to happen?

There is no doubt that my name was smeared by many people that it would benefit. The reason for this is rather obvious. It would discredit things that I might say about them and probably saved their lives. The dangerous thing to people who were close to me was that they would share in the outcome of that smear.

Iran provided one challenge after another. It never stopped. I learned to be on my guard at all times. When my family and I moved back to the States, it felt strange to walk out of my house unarmed. Not long after I left Iran, my good friend, General Rabii, sent an emissary to get in contact with me. He was not aware that I had left the country for good. When he found out, he got in contact with me through this person and said that they needed me back. After some thought, I wrote him a letter and stated the terms of my return. My family would not accompany me and the guarantees stated in my contract would be very high and strict. If something happened to me, my family would be taken care of. I almost left for Iran but the political situation changed. In 1979, revolutionaries led by Ayatollah Khomeini got information from the same corrupt individuals who would have caused harm to my friends. Some of my dearest friends were shot or died mysteriously during the Iranian Revolution of 1979. The Revolution was about to happen and it did. My dear friend, along with thousands more, were killed by the revolutionaries. My home from then after would be "The Good Ole USA."

*   *   *

When I began writing *Zehbel,* my intention was to write about my life in Iran for my children and grand-children. My work took me to Iranian air bases and other locations all over Iran; I spent most of my time away from my family in Teheran. My children never knew exactly what I was doing, or the dangers I faced.

My original plan was to write a book as soon as I left Iran in 1976, but I soon realized this would endanger the lives of many dear friends we had left there. Parts of my memoir expose corruption going on at very high levels of Iranian government. So, in *Zehbel: The Clever One,* friends and acquaintances names have been changed. Situations were modified so as to make them unidentifiable, but the events I describe really happened. This is a true story.

Iran is always in the news. How different things are today! The Shah was a benevolent dictator but now it is really an Islamic dictatorship disguised as a sort of democracy. It is, in reality, run by the Head Mullah. Nothing they say can be believed because of their hidden agenda. Strangely enough, things are happening now that happened then and we still can't see the objectives of the Muslim extremists and their strategies.

Forty-five years have passed since our family first arrived in Iran. Our youth, the need for adventure and the need for more money

479

drove us to that land. We saw it as an opportunity to enrich our lives and looked forward to it with great anticipation. Ten years were spent deeply immersed in Iranian society, culture and military life. Our decision changed our lives and how we see things forever.

My mindset has changed since I began writing this story and I find myself shedding tears as I read over it. Faces appear and overwhelming feelings grasp me as I go back to the time when these events actually happened. Youth are so open to adventure, with little thought to the consequences. I do not regret the past; I've learned valuable lessons about who I am and what I'm capable of in life and death situations. It was my youthfulness at the time that kept me alive. Without it, I would not have survived and there would be no story.

Ah, my beloved, fill the cup that clears

Today of past regrets and future fears

Tomorrow? Why tomorrow I may be

Myself with yesterdays sev'n thousand years.

--Omar Khayyam, 11th century poet

Glossary*

Agha Mohandes – honorable engineer

Ambar – storage place

Ashura – a national day of mourning for Husayn ibn Ali, a grandson of Mohammad, killed at the Battle of Karbala in 680 A.D. Celebrated on the 10th of Muharram, the first month in the lunar Islamic calendar.

ASR – Airport Surveillance Radar

Barfparoo – shoveling snow

CEMSET Communications Electronics Meteorology Supervisory Evaluation Team (25 cm Team)

Chelo – Persian rice, mixed with saffron

Chelo Kabab – national dish of Iran. Saffron rice and beef or lamb kabobs, served with butter on top of the rice. Grilled tomatoes, cucumbers, onions, gherkins and yoghurt are served on the side, along with fresh white cheese *(panir)* and a dish of greens *(sabzi)*. A dish of *somagh* (dark red ground sumac) is served on the side, to be sprinkled on the *chelo kabob*.

483

Chi Migui - What did you say?

DCS/CEM – Deputy Chief of Staff/Communications, Electronics and Meteorology

Douk – yogurt or *mast*, mixed with water, to drink

FAA – Federal Aviation Agency (now called Federal Aviation Administration)

Fesenjoon – stew, made with veal, crushed walnuts and pomegranate syrup

Gendeh -- prostitute

Haleh Shoma Chetoreh? – How are you?

Hasir – awnings/window shades

IIAF – Imperial Iranian Air Force

Jahkish – owner of a house of prostitution

Jandarmeri – military police in Iran at the time

Jube – deep, narrow, concrete gutters or drainage ditches (deeper than those in the U.S.) on either side of the street

Jube hopper – a three-wheeled vehicle, sort of like a rickshaw

Kallepache – the head and feet of a sheep, served for breakfast in Esfahan

Khoda Hafez- may God protect you (a farewell greeting)

Khoob - good

Koobideh- barbequed minced beef or lamb

Kosskish – pimp

Kucheh -- alley

Kucheh guards – street guards

Limoo Shirin – native Iranian sweet lemons

MAAG – Military Assistance Advisory Group

Mast - yogurt

Mullah – in Iran, an educated man or religious/secular leader

Naronge – native Iranian (sour) orange. Sweet oranges were grafted with oranges from Portugal, in fact, sweet oranges were simply called Portugual.

Oftabeh – metal can with spout, used to sprinkle water when toileting

Panir – fresh white cheese, like feta

PAR – Precision Approach Radar

Pedar sag – "your father is a dog," considered a serious insult

Peykon – Iranian-manufactured car

Qorbani – sacrificing a sheep, for a blessing on a family

RADADS – Research Aircraft Data Acquisition and Display Systems

RAPCON – Radar Approach Control system

Rial – the currency of Iran. A *rial* was subdivided into 100 *dinar*, but the *rial* was worth very little. In 1967 the exchange rate was approximately $1USD=75 *rial*. A twenty *rial* note was worth about twenty-five cents.

Sabzi – greens served with chelo kabob and other dishes: basil, cilantro, fenugreek greens, tarragon, watercress (*shaahi*)

Salam Alaikom – traditional greeting, wishing someone peace and good health

Salamati - To your health

Salome -- hello

Sarbaz – soldier (pl. *Sarbazie*)

SAVAK – *Sazman-e Ettelaat va Amniyat-e Keshvar*, Iran's national intelligence organization, known as the secret police

Shiite – a follower who claims to be in the lineage of Mohammed Hosayain. His only daughter, Fatimeh's, husband was Shemr Ali.

Sigheh – temporary marriage